cl

D0339989

The Late Talker

The Late Talker

What to Do If Your Child Isn't Talking Yet

Marilyn C. Agin, M.D., Lisa F. Geng,
and Malcolm J. Nicholl

St. Martin's Press ♨ New York

A Note to Readers

This book is for informational purposes only. It is not intended to take the place of individualized medical advice from a trained medical professional. Readers are advised to consult a pediatrician or other qualified health professional regarding their children's speech difficulties or other medical problems before acting on any of the information in this book.

www.stmartins.com

Library of Congress Cataloging-in-Publication Data

Agin, Marilyn C.
    The late talker : what to do if your child isn't talking yet / Marilyn C. Agin, M.D., Lisa F. Geng, and Malcolm J. Nicholl.—1st ed.
      p. cm.
    Includes bibliographical references (page 207) and index (page 223).
    ISBN 0-312-28754-2
    1. Language disorders in children. 2. Speech disorders. 3. Children—Language. 4. Slow learning children. I. Geng, Lisa F. II. Nicholl, Malcolm J. III. Title.
RJ496.S7 A357 2003
618.92'855—dc21

2002035993

First Edition: April 2003

10   9   8   7   6   5   4   3   2   1

Contents

Contents

Acknowledgments

First and foremost, all three authors wish to thank the many parents who allowed us to share their stories and their children's stories with you. A special thanks to Cindy Mustafa for research assistance and to the numerous professionals who took the time to explain how their techniques can be beneficial for any late talker. We are particularly grateful for Dr. Paula Tallal's thoughtful foreword. We are also appreciative of Heather Jackson's skillful, thorough editing, which helped structure a more readable book.

MARILYN C. AGIN

I want to thank my husband, Lennie, for his love and patience, and my children, Gabby and Julian, for becoming so self-sufficient and understanding during the writing of this book. And to all my friends who appreciated that my reclusion was no reflection on them. I also want to acknowledge Sandra Ginsberg, Assistant Commissioner of the New York City Early Intervention (EI) Program, for her support, and thanks to my young patients and their families, who have taught me so much and who have given me the inspiration to write this book.

LISA F. GENG

A special thanks to my husband, Glenn, for his love, encouragement, and support while I was busy writing this book. Thanks to my two boys, Dakota and Tanner. Your communication delays were a motivating wake-up call to do something to help both of you and others. Your success from early intervention is an inspiration, providing hope for all late talkers. Without you there would not have been a CHERAB Foundation and the greater awareness of speech challenges that has helped so many others, and this book would not have been written.

MALCOLM J. NICHOLL

To Sandy—eternal gratitude for understanding the lost weekends, and for support and insight when needed the most.

Foreword

There are many reasons why a child might be a late talker. The most well-understood reasons relate to the fundamental building blocks on which speech and language development depends, including hearing, motor, and cognitive systems. Indeed, because language development depend on so many systems working together efficiently, developmental language impairments are among the most prevalent of all developmental disabilities, affecting an estimated 20% to 30% of all children. Language impairments are well known to accompany hearing loss, oral structural or motor deficits affecting the speech musculature, as well as syndromes where there may be cognitive impairments (including autism, Fragile X, and Down's Syndrome).

However, even when these known causes of language impairments are accounted for, there remains a large number of children who experience difficulty developing speech and language for unknown reasons. A recent epidemiological study funded by the National Institutes of Health demonstrated that over 7% of five-year-old children entering school met the clinical diagnostic criteria for specific developmental language impairment of unknown origin. There are two very surprising things about these findings. First, the number is nearly twice as high as was previously reported in the scientific or clinical literature. Even more striking was the finding that over 70% of these children, who were found on testing to be significantly behind in their language development, had never previously been diagnosed or treated for their language impairment. How could this be?

Some late talkers have quite obvious deficits in speech production, such as the apraxic children who are the focus of this book. For these children their speech and language problems may be clearly recognized because their speech sounds very different from that of typical children their age, and in some severe cases may be virtually unintelligible or even nonverbal. However, other late talkers may have more subtle speech problems that are difficult to differentiate from the typical mispronunciations of young children. In addition, there are considerable individual differences within the normal range of how rapidly speech and language milestones are achieved. For example, a child may say *pada tat* when they mean "pet the cat." If the child is eighteen months old, this would not be a cause for concern, while it would be for a child of four years. But exactly when should such a pattern of mispronunciation raise concern sufficient to lead to a formal speech and language assessment? Most parents, teachers, and even pediatricians have a hard time answering this and other questions pertaining to appropriate timing for reaching specific speech and language milestones.

It is important to understand that not all children with speech production problems have language problems, and conversely not all children with language problems have speech problems. In addition, children who have difficulty producing speech or language may or may not have equal difficulty perceiving (understanding) it. One of the problems that leads to difficulty in recognizing when a child is having significant difficulty with speech and/or language development is that there are several different component parts of language to consider. Language is comprised of phonology (the smallest units of sound that differentiates word meaning), semantics (vocabulary), morphology (word parts, including prefixes and suffixes), syntax (grammatical rules), and pragmatics (conversational rules). There are separate normal developmental milestones for each of these components, both for production and comprehension. To further complicate matters, children can have difficulty with one or more of these components of language while developing others well within normal limits. For example, it is not uncommon for a child to be learning individual vocabulary words normally, while struggling to learn how to string words together to form grammatically correct sentences.

Exactly how many vocabulary words or word combinations should be understood or produced at what age? Which rules of grammar develop at what age? How often are children who are delayed in language onset and/or are slow in progressing through the early language milestones (i.e., late talkers) likely to "catch up" as compared to remaining behind in various aspects of language learning? Are late talkers at risk for subsequent reading and other academic achievement problems? Are late talkers more likely to have behavioral problems such as attention deficit disorder? *The Late Talker* provides a practical guide for parents and professionals to find the answers to these and many other frequently asked questions pertaining to speech and language development.

Scientific research on language development and disorders has led to growing empirical evidence for, and hence increasing awareness of, the critical role that language plays in most other aspects of healthy development—from social interaction with parents and peers, to behavioral development, to academic achievement. Unfortunately, there also is increasing empirical evidence for, and hence awareness of, the multiple negative consequences of unremediated language learning problems, including not only academic failure (especially in the area of literacy), but extending to increased incidence of juvenile delinquency, drug abuse, unemployment, depression, and even suicide.

However, despite the obvious, extreme importance of language learning disorders and an explosion of scientific knowledge pertaining to them, most parents of late talkers continue to experience remarkable difficulty in obtaining correct information, advice, and a sense of shared concern and urgency about their child's speech and language development from pediatricians and other professionals. They are, more often than not, told to "wait and see," and are misled to believe that most late talkers will eventually "catch up," often resulting in many months or years of lost time during the most critical periods for language development.

In *The Late Talker*, Dr. Marilyn C. Agin, a developmental pediatrician, and Lisa F. Geng, the mother of two late talkers, have created a comprehensive handbook for parents concerned about their child's speech or language development. *The Late Talker* is an empowering call to action to parents to trust their own instincts and intuitions (which generally have proven to be correct) about the status of their child's speech and language development. The book provides the detailed knowledge as well as practical advice needed to recognize a late talker, as well as information on how to seek, evaluate, and obtain the early interventions that will afford a child the most positive developmental outcomes.

—Paula Tallal, Ph.D.
Board of Governor's Professor of Neuroscience at Rutgers,
the State University of New Jersey, Newark Campus

The Terms We Use

Every field has its own vocabulary, and speech pathology is no exception. As you read *The Late Talker*, you'll encounter terms to describe children who are lagging behind their peers in the development of communication skills. There is no standardized terminology used by all speech professionals to describe the different types of communication disorders. So to avoid any confusion, we need to provide you with our definitions. Understanding the terminology from this entry point should prepare you for the journey ahead.

Apraxia: A serious neurological speech disorder. In the medical literature, a variety of terms are used to describe this condition, including apraxia of speech, verbal apraxia, and developmental apraxia of speech. Unless directly quoting another source, we use the simple term "apraxia."

Late talker: Term used to describe children who are
- eighteen to twenty months old and have fewer than ten words
- twenty-one to thirty months old with fewer than fifty words and no two-word combinations such as "mommy car"
- age-appropriate (or close to it) in other areas of development, including comprehension, play, motor, and cognitive (problem-solving) skills

Communication: The definition from the American Speech-Language-Hearing Association is a good one: the ability to receive, send, process, and comprehend concepts or verbal, nonverbal, and graphic (written) symbol systems. *Communication* is an umbrella term that includes language, speech, and/or hearing abilities.

Language: A system of symbols (usually spoken or written) that enables us to understand what others say (receptive language) and express ourselves using words or gestures (expressive language).

Speech: The oral production of words.

Delay or **disorder:** What does it mean to have a *delay* in speech, language, or communication versus a *disorder?*

A *delay* is a maturational lag in development, for example, a four-year-old who exhibits the language capabilities of an average three-year-old. Often, with time, the child "catches up" to his or her peers without specific interventions. Some refer to such children as "late bloomers." Unfortunately, it is not always evident at an early age if your child has a delay or disorder.

A *disorder* is a significant (severe) delay with a disruption in the normal sequence of development that's in stark contrast to his or her typically developing peers. The child does not catch up if you adopt a "wait and see" attitude. Neurologic "soft signs" like coordination difficulties, low muscle tone, a history of seizures, or the physical signs of a syndrome (for example, Down syndrome) may be present.

The following table is a simple guideline.

COMMUNICATION, SPEECH, AND/OR LANGUAGE		
	Delay	**Disorder**
• Severity	• Mild lag in development	• Significant delay or abnormality
• Developmental sequence	• Slower development, speaks like a child who is chronologically younger	• Disruption in normal sequence; may have been developing normally and then suffered a regression
• Presence of neurological soft signs	• Not typically	• Usually
• Prognosis	• Usually resolves over time with parent training and relatively short course of treatment	• Frequent and intensive treatment is necessary usually for a period of years—outcome less predictable than for a delay

Introduction

It's one of the most important milestones in an infant's life. Parents eagerly await the moment that their young offspring utters his or her first recognizable word. Often, the waiting is accompanied by friendly spousal competition: Will that word be *mama* or *dada*? It's a scene played out in homes across the world, day in and day out. Not all children, of course, develop at exactly the same pace, but most infants can be expected to say "mama" and "dada" sometime between the ages of twelve and fifteen months. As these dates pass and the magic words fail to come forth, eager anticipation often turns to anxiety, even fear. As months go by and the child continues to remain silent, worried parents consult family, friends, and the pediatrician only to receive automatic reassurances.

"Don't worry; he's just a late talker."

"Aunt Mary didn't speak until she was four."

"Einstein didn't talk until he was three."

"She'll speak when she's ready."

"His older brother is talking for him."

"Just give him time."

All too willing to believe that their son or daughter is "just a late talker" and that sooner or later there will be an explosion of words, parents frequently and happily accept such well-meaning counsel. However, many parents—especially the mother—instinctively suspect *there is something wrong.* Nevertheless, they bow to the experience of older relatives and the wisdom of the medical practitioner, and agree to give the child that time. More often than not the child *is* just a late talker. In all likelihood, he will eventually catch up with his peers. He will become as fluent as the child who delighted his parents by beginning to speak "on time."

But there are a growing number of children who are not just a little behind in speech development. They have a speech disorder such as apraxia, a neurologically based impairment that needs to be identified and treated as early as possible. Although the incidence of apraxia seems to be growing, it is still not well recognized by the medical community. Fortunately, knowledge about apraxia and other neurological communication disorders is evolving, thanks, in part, to the Internet's ability to speed communication among those who know these children best: their parents. Some pioneering researchers are also beginning to conduct studies that should provide answers to puzzling questions about the causes of communication disorders and the most effective treatments for them. One thing we know for sure: Children with these disorders need *early* treatment. Adopting a "wait and see" policy means losing precious months during which these kids could be receiving the intensive therapy they need if they are to have a chance of communicating normally.

We aren't alarmists, and it's worth repeating that most late talkers are exactly that: late talkers. But early intervention is undoubtedly beneficial, even if the child does turn out to have nothing more than a delay. The benefits of one-on-one speech therapy as early as possible are overwhelming, so much so that parents need to be aware of their options and their rights. In comparison, the downside to a late-talking child getting early speech therapy is minimal. In the short term it might increase your concerns and incur extra expense, if you have to pay for treatment out of your own pocket. But the gamble you take by not intervening may have profound implications for later development. A communication disorder can lead to a lifetime of challenges—from learning difficulties and ridicule at school to lost opportunities and communication failure as adults. There's even increased risk of juvenile delinquency, imprisonment, and suicide. Sadly, it's often a hidden handicap with no outward sign of disability—until a child actually tries to talk.

What is it like for a child with a serious communication delay or disorder? Try to imagine not being able to say your own name, or not being able to tell your mother that you're hungry or in pain. Imagine living in a world where you understand perfectly well what people are saying to you. You want to respond to them. You know exactly what you want to say, but you simply don't have the voice to communicate. You are intelligent, maybe very intelligent, yet you may be misdiagnosed as autistic or mentally retarded. You become so frustrated at your inability to communicate that you lash out at the world with temper tantrums or crying fits. It's equally frustrating for the parent. Consider having a child who seems normal, but you've never heard that child say "I love you," or even "mama" or "dada." Raising a nonverbal child can be an enormous emotional burden on the entire family, especially for parents who convinced themselves that their child was just a late talker, only to discover that instead he or she had a severe communication disorder. Many parents often sequence through a kaleidoscope of emotions: denial, guilt, blame, frustration, anger, and despair.

Such emotions are completely understandable. After all, the ability to communicate complex thoughts is a fundamental human attribute and is essential for anyone to get ahead in the world. At its most basic, the gift of speech, often taken for granted, enables us to make our needs and opinions known—from the simple act of ordering a hamburger to debating the merits of a baseball pitcher. Speech can be the soaring rhetoric of a famous orator, the eloquence of a Shakespearean play, or the poetry of Wordsworth. To be without speech is to be deprived of one core element of human existence.

But it's a harsh reality for many. The incidence of communication disorders is a far bigger problem than has been realized, and it seems to be getting worse. Here are some statistics from the American Speech-Language-Hearing Association (ASHA) and the U.S. government's National Institute on Deafness and Other Communication Disorders (NIDCD).

- Speech and language disorders are the number one developmental impairment in children under the age of five.

- Sixteen million Americans have a speech or language disorder. An estimated 15 to 25 percent of young children and approximately forty-six million Americans have some kind of communication disorder (which includes hearing problems).
- Speech and language disorders are the leading cause of academic failure and emotional distress.
- Communication disorders cost the United States $30 billion a year in lost productivity, special education, and medical expenses.

This book is for all parents concerned about a child's difficulty speaking at an age when she's expected to be making those first all-important utterances. The key question: Is she truly just a late talker, or does she have a communication disorder that requires early and intensive therapy?

In *The Late Talker* we review the typical developmental milestones and tell you what to expect and what you can do if expectations are not met. We explain the various speech and language disorders, and discuss when and how to get the right kind of professional evaluation. We explore the appropriate therapy your child should receive from speech-language pathologists (SLPs) and other therapists, and we detail what you can do in support of their efforts. We give you many tips for easing the inevitable frustration experienced by a late-talking child, as well as tips for alleviating your own frustration. We also present details of an intriguing nutritional supplement that has achieved promising results in helping late-talking children. Of great significance, we make you fully aware of your rights and how, if necessary, to navigate the school system and the insurance maze on your child's behalf. And throughout the book we share numerous stories of other parents who have struggled with the "will he, won't he grow out of it?" conundrum.

Together, from the perspectives of a mother and a doctor, we provide comprehensive information empowering parents of late talkers to make educated decisions. Our collaboration dates back to a parent-doctor consultation in August 1999 and the diagnosis by Marilyn, a developmental pediatrician, that Lisa's three-year-old son Tanner had apraxia. At the time we had no idea of the train of events that were about to be set into motion, but ultimately we realized that there were many late-talking children whose speech disorders were going undiagnosed and untreated. As a result, Lisa formed the CHERAB Foundation to raise awareness of early childhood communication disorders in the general public and the medical community. CHERAB stands for "Communication Help, Education, Research, Apraxia Base" and is now the fastest-growing organization of its kind. But before going further, it's useful to give you the individual backgrounds and experience that enable us to speak with some authority on this subject.

A MOTHER'S PERSPECTIVE: LISA F. GENG

The real wake-up call was on Tanner's second birthday when he couldn't blow out the candles on his birthday cake. He couldn't purse his lips, and he just didn't have the ability to extinguish two little candles. My husband, Glenn, and I had been concerned about his speech development for a year or so, but this was the turning point. Up until the age of eleven months, Tanner had seemed such a healthy baby, especially compared with his older brother, Dakota, who had severe respiratory and developmental problems due to a traumatic forceps delivery. Dakota had suffered torn neck muscles, crushed facial nerves, and internal head bleeding—and he was a late talker. From birth he had been under the observation of a neurologist and receiving therapy.

In comparison, Tanner had appeared perfectly normal. He had babbled and smiled and said "ma" and "da," as well as a lot of other sounds. Then, at eleven months, he had two weeks of high fevers and a rash associated with a viral infection, probably roseola. It was pretty scary. He got better, but he continued to be lethargic. He stopped saying "da." He still said "ma," but everything else was "mmm." He also seemed to gain weight. He certainly felt a lot heavier. Our happy Tanner was gone. If he started crying, we couldn't calm him down no matter how hard we tried, and he would scream until he fell asleep, exhausted.

We didn't realize at the time that the changes in Tanner were significant. We were worried only that he had not found his voice. Everyone, including his pediatrician, reassured us that he was just a late talker. Relatives told us that my Aunt Betty hadn't talked until she was three, but once she started they couldn't shut her up, and now she was fluent in two languages. I also got the "Einstein didn't talk until he was three" story. But I suspected there was much more to Tanner's problem. I was concerned about his lack of expression. No matter how hard I tried, I could not get him to smile. Professional photographers could not get him to smile. He almost always had such a sad, serious expression. He would just sit and stare at you. But with his soft, blond curls and big round baby face, he looked adorable, just like the Gerber baby. Strangers commented that he looked like a cherub, so we affectionately nicknamed him "Cherub Boy." But that chubby look, as we later discovered, masked a bundle of problems. Tanner also couldn't lick his lips. He couldn't lift his tongue to remove peanut butter or chocolate from his lips, and he would push food into his mouth with his fingers. He seemed really smart, and developmentally he was ahead of all of the milestones—except speech.

I remember being in a supermarket with Tanner when he was about two years old and he spotted a toy that he just had to have. Trying to tell me what he wanted in the only way that he knew how, he pointed and loudly kept repeating, "Mmm." An older boy who was watching turned to his mother, and asked innocently, "Mommy, what's *wrong* with him?" It killed me because it was the same question that was gnawing away at me. I wanted to wrap my son in a protective bubble and keep him from hearing such things. It made me determined to find out what was wrong with Tanner and what we could do about it.

The family pediatrician, however, who had aggressively pursued early treatment for Dakota, continued to reassure us and suggested that we wait another year, until Tanner's third birthday, for a speech and hearing evaluation. But we just couldn't wait that long. We felt compelled to do *something*. We pushed for a speech and hearing evaluation and we pushed to get him into therapy, even though we hoped he would just start talking. Nobody told us at the time that Tanner qualified for free early intervention services and, as the insurance company refused to cover private therapy, we had to pay for it ourselves. After about four months of thirty-minute, one-on-one sessions two or three times a week, there had been very little progress. Tanner, who was now close to three years old and still nonverbal, could manage to say only simple sounds like *t, ch,* and *sh,* sounds most babies and toddlers make when they babble.

Then the speech-language pathologist dropped a bombshell and told us that she thought Tanner had apraxia. I hadn't a clue what apraxia was. My first question was, "He'll still learn to talk, though, right?" I'll never forget the long pause before the therapist finally answered, "It depends." I immediately began to find out everything I could about this disorder and spent hours on the Internet researching it, all the time telling myself that Tanner didn't really have it, until I found Scott Bilker's "talking page," a Web site featuring the voices of children with apraxia. Scott's son Brandon was saying the ABC's, and the quality of his speech sounded just like Tanner's. That's when I knew for sure that Tanner had apraxia, and I broke down and cried. My poor little baby couldn't smile, and now I wondered, What if he'll never talk? I started to feel guilty. Was it something I had done? Was it because I didn't eat healthy foods? Tanner wasn't just a late talker. It wasn't a speech delay; it was a serious speech disorder.

My husband and I decided to take Tanner to see a developmental pediatrician, Dr. Marilyn Agin. We detailed Tanner's history and Dr. Agin examined him. She talked to him and paid a lot of attention to what he could and couldn't do with his mouth, his tongue, and his jaw. In a matter of a few minutes she shook her head and confirmed the diagnosis. I'll always remember her saying, "He doesn't know where his tongue is in his mouth. I wish I'd seen him a year ago. I could have told you then that he had apraxia." After this appointment, Dr. Agin wrote a critically important report that helped us get the right kind of intensive therapy for Tanner and persuaded the insurance company to cover the cost. In addition, we discovered why Tanner felt heavier to pick up than other kids of the same weight, why his face had no tone, and why he had such a cherubic-looking body. He had hypotonia—decreased muscle tone—a condition that often accompanies apraxia.

This was the beginning of our quest to help Tanner find his voice. We were shocked at how little information was available and how few people, including pediatricians, were even aware of apraxia. Having

seen what early intervention had done for Dakota, I could not understand why late talkers like Tanner were not being given the same opportunity. I became outraged when I realized that some children with
apraxia and other speech disorders were being misdiagnosed as mentally retarded or autistic. I couldn't sit back and do nothing, so I started
a nonprofit foundation to raise awareness about the need for early
evaluation and intervention and to press for more research.

For me, reaching out and helping others is a way of channeling my
energy into positive endeavors. My attitude is that no child is an island,
and raising awareness about communication disorders for all kids helps
my child more than if he had only me working for him. Tanner is now
very happy in a wonderful private school, an out-of-district placement
that we were able to secure. His vocabulary is growing all the time, and
he's overcome most of his sensory problems, thanks to intensive therapy and nutritional supplementation. He's found his voice and he's
found his smile. When I started the CHERAB Foundation, I couldn't
think of a better person to have as my resource for medical guidance
than Dr. Agin. As time goes on, I still can't.

A DOCTOR'S PERSPECTIVE:
MARILYN C. AGIN, M.D.

It was a routine day at a busy pediatrics practice in a small New Jersey
town. I would see twenty-five to thirty kids in the course of a day, often
wishing that I could spend more time with each individual child. I
didn't realize when I saw Lisa and Tanner that I'd made such an impression on her. It was just part of my job. I wasn't aware that my diagnosis
of apraxia had such significance. I didn't know then that the disorder
was something other pediatricians were not identifying and, since it
was not being diagnosed, these children were not getting the intensive
speech therapy they needed.

I'd met Lisa's family before. I'd seen Tanner's older brother Dakota
because of the birth injuries he had suffered in a very difficult delivery.
Now Lisa was concerned about Tanner's lack of speech. The speech
pathologist thought that he had apraxia, and the homework that Lisa

had done on the Internet had led her to agree. Now she wanted my professional opinion. When I looked at Tanner, he had a hypotonic (low tone) tongue which was sitting on the floor of his mouth. He couldn't lift it up and back. In fact, his whole face was low tone and, of course, he couldn't speak. I knew for sure that he had oral apraxia and hypotonia, and quite probably verbal apraxia, although I wasn't a hundred percent sure about that. I remember saying that he really needed oral-motor therapy and referred them to a good therapist. I'm sure I made the diagnosis in no more than fifteen minutes. Quite frankly, when you know what the disorder is, it is not hard to recognize.

With the benefit of hindsight it seems obvious why I was more attuned to these speech disorders than other doctors. Quite unusually for an M.D., I had begun my career as a speech-language pathologist after obtaining my master's degree in speech pathology at the University of Massachusetts. For more than seven years (between 1974 and 1982), I worked as an SLP. Initially, I was responsible for the diagnosis and treatment of speech and language disorders in children with developmental disabilities. I then went on to work in a Veterans Administration medical center where I diagnosed and treated adults suffering communication disorders including aphasia, dysarthria, apraxia, and vocal pathologies. Back then, apraxia was a recognized condition in adults who had lost their ability to speak as a result of a stroke or traumatic brain injury. But apraxia was not commonly diagnosed in very young children.

In 1982, I decided to fulfill my dream of becoming a medical doctor and attended the University of Medicine and Dentistry of New Jersey in Newark. From 1986 to 1991, I pursued my internship and residency at the New York University Medical Center and the Rusk Institute of Rehabilitation Medicine in New York. It was a combined five-year residency in pediatrics and physical medicine and rehabilitation (PM&R), also known as physiatry, preparing me for a career in helping children with developmental disabilities. I became board certified in both pediatrics and PM&R and took a position as a pediatric physiatrist at Children's Specialized Hospital in Mountainside, New Jersey.

Over the years I have carried my knowledge of communication disorders with me, and I am now in private practice in Manhattan as a neurodevelopmental pediatrician certified in neurodevelopmental disabilities by the American Board of Pediatrics. I have also been the medical director of the Early Intervention Program in New York City since 1998. It is a huge program that receives about fourteen hundred new referrals of infants and toddlers each month. In this role, I am consulted on cases of medically complex children and hold staff trainings on normal and atypical development of infants and toddlers and assessment of developmental disabilities. I also discuss topics like prematurity, autistic spectrum disorders, cerebral palsy, and identification of various syndromes. In addition, I lecture at conferences of pediatricians and other professionals about the importance of early identification and referral of young children who need its services to early intervention. This position gives me the ability to reach out to pediatricians across the city, spreading word about the need for developmental surveillance and screening to identify children who may need a comprehensive evaluation. Our slogans are "the earlier the better" and "listen to parents' concerns."

My entire career has given me a unique experience and ability to identify children with speech and language disorders, especially apraxia. The diagnosis of apraxia in childhood is still somewhat controversial and clouded in confusion, partly because there are different names for essentially the same condition, and partly because too few therapists and pediatricians really understand the disorder. This is why parents need to become fully informed and act as a child's primary advocate. *The Late Talker* provides you with essential information about childhood speech disorders, and it's a useful and practical guide even if your child turns out to be just a late talker. The book is also intended to heighten awareness among pediatricians, teachers, and therapists. It's vital that professionals are alert to the warning signs of apraxia so that they can err on the side of early intervention. You, however, know your child better than anyone and may well have to make the first tentative diagnosis yourself and then consult with the appropriate medical and speech professionals to confirm it—as Lisa did.

The Late Talker

1. The Road to Speech

We weren't too concerned when his first birthday arrived and he didn't have any words.—STACEY ABENSTEIN, mother of Evan

- Your eighteen-month-old son is bright and inquisitive but can't say a word, not even *ma*. When he wants your attention, all he can do is grunt "Eh-eh" and reach out to you.
- Your twenty-one-month-old doesn't point, but she moans. She holds you only when she wants something. Sometimes you feel she doesn't care if you are in the room or not.
- Your two-year-old has his own elaborate sign language that only your family understands. He said "mama" and "dada" at twelve months of age, but since then you haven't heard any true words, or even much babbling.
- "Me dih tootie!" exclaims your four-year-old daughter as you walk down the cookie aisle of the supermarket. You understand that she's saying, "I want these cookies," but a stranger wouldn't.

Although most late talkers eventually catch up and speak normally, it's important to be aware of warning signs that may indicate a communication disorder. Before we can explore what is "abnormal," we need a basic understanding of how speech, one of the most complex and remarkable of human acts, usually develops. Although for most of us it is an automatic act, speech is so complex that neural pathways orchestrate a phenomenal fourteen sounds *per second*, according to researchers

Anthony Caruso and Edythe Strand. Simultaneously, precise movements of the lips, tongue, jaws, and palate have to modulate a stream of air passing through the vocal chords. Such a feat is not something to be taken for granted.

We actually absorb the sounds of language from the moment of birth—most probably, even before. As Geoffrey Cowley eloquently expressed it in a special edition of *Newsweek* magazine: "The journey toward language starts not in the nursery but in the womb, where the fetus is continually bathed in the sounds of the mother's voice." Alison Gopnik, Andrew N. Meltzoff, and Patricia K. Kuhl, in *The Scientist in the Crib: Minds, Brains, and How Children Learn*, suggest that most of us looking at a baby in the crib "see a picture of innocence and helplessness, a clean slate." The reality, they say, is quite different: "what we see in the crib is the greatest mind that has ever existed, the most powerful learning machine in the universe. The tiny fingers and mouth are exploration devices that probe the alien world around them with more precision than any Mars rover. The crumpled ears take a buzz of incomprehensible noise and flawlessly turn it into meaningful language."

Babies not only listen and comprehend from the day they are born, but they also communicate, starting with that initial, unforgettable outburst of crying. It doesn't take them long to realize that crying is guaranteed to summon food and comfort, and thus begins three years of remarkable brain development in which the intricacies of speech are formed. Over the first few months, the baby's crying diminishes as he makes reassuring eye contact with the adults in his life. He begins to watch a speaker's mouth and responds to smiles and chatter by making sounds of his own. The way that parents and others instinctively talk to infants—"parentese"—is an entirely different mode of communication from adult conversation. When we use parentese we talk in a higher pitch. We stretch our words and we greatly vary the tone. And it appears to be universal. Whether you speak English, Russian, Zulu, or Mandarin, you employ parentese when talking to a baby. Research by Dr. Patricia Kuhl at the University of Washington shows that infants as young as twelve weeks attempt to mimic the vowel sounds they hear, an indication that parentese may play a specific role in helping them speak.

Dr. Kuhl's extensive work has also revealed that babies, even as young as eighteen weeks, have an amazing understanding of the visual element of speech. In one of her studies, infants were shown identical faces silently articulating different vowel sounds—*ee* and *ah*—while they heard just one of the sounds. The babies stared significantly longer at the facial gesture that matched the sound that they had heard, demonstrating awareness of the link between the sight and sound of speech. Work at Cornell University's Sackler Institute for Developmental Psychobiology suggests that the brain has distinct regions for every aspect of the ability to understand a word. According to Dr. Michael Posner and his team, there is one region for recognizing the sound of a word, for instance, and another region for recognizing the meaning of that sound.

During the first year of life, infants develop important methods of nonverbal communication, a critical element on the way to acquiring verbal language. There is "joint attention" when the baby and his or her caregiver both pay attention to the same item, such as a toy. There is "gestural communication" when the baby lifts his or her arms, asking to be picked up. And there is turn-taking during social interaction, such as engaging in a game of peekaboo. These prelinguistic skills and certain cognitive abilities must be in place for communication to develop.

What actual sounds do babies make on the road to speech? During the first six months, quiet, pleasant cooing sounds are produced, followed by prolonged vowels with changes in tone. In the second half of the first year, a baby babbles and progresses to the use of repetitive syllables such as *baba, dada, kaka, papa,* and *wawa.* Throughout the world, all babies make the same babbling sounds up until about eight months of age, when they narrow their range to the sounds of their native tongue, the language that surrounds them every day. The babbling turns into a kind of nonsense speech. It may appear that the baby is talking, but the speech does not contain real words. At eight months there is some true imitation of sounds, and between nine and twelve months there are various vocalizations in which the baby calls for attention.

Dr. Kuhl found that even before their first birthdays children begin to categorize sounds, another crucial step toward learning a language. In one study, she compared the ability of thirty American and Japanese babies to distinguish between the *r* and *l* sounds. Japanese adults cannot hear the difference between the two sounds but, at the age of six months, the Japanese babies were able to distinguish between them just as well as their American counterparts—about 64 percent of the time. Between ten and twelve months, the American babies' scores rose to 84 percent while the Japanese babies' dropped to 59 percent. Therefore, by the time they are one year old, says Dr. Kuhl, the Japanese babies are already developing a code for their language that does not require two categories for *r* and *l*.

Usually, the first real words—quite commonly *mama, dada, up,* and *more*—emerge between twelve and fifteen months. At the age of eighteen months, vocabulary explodes, and some toddlers start learning as many as twelve words a day. Parents, to their dismay, often discover that their offspring is particularly fond of the word *no*. At this stage, the child's comprehension far exceeds his ability to express himself. By twenty months, two-word phrases such as "Wha dat?" or "Aw gone" come into use. Two-year-olds *understand* hundreds of words and thousands of sentences and they begin to be able to communicate their needs more effectively. They start to stick two words together in "sentences," which hold meaning beyond the two-word combination itself. They may well say, "Mommy ju," meaning, "Mommy, I want juice." They might say, "Daddy car," which could mean, "Daddy, I want to ride in the car" or "Daddy left in the car." You might hear them ask, "Go dore?" which could represent either, "May I go to the store with you?" or "Did mommy go to the store?"

Between twenty and thirty months, to the relief of parents, most young children are more able to express their frustrations with words, rather than temper tantrums and crying fits. And then, at about thirty months of age, there is another great burst in the acquisition of vocabulary, proportionately greater than at any other period in life, when the child's verbal ability may jump from two hundred to twelve hundred words. By three years of age, most children pick up some of the rules of grammar and use regular plurals—being able to say and understand *books* and *toys*—and regular verb tenses—understanding the difference between *walk* and *walked, jump* and *jumped.* Sentence structure becomes more adultlike, within the limitations of the child's environment. During three to five years of age, children are usually able to engage in conversation, using increasingly complex elements of language and forming sentences that may be eight or more words long. These preschoolers can tell stories and anticipate future events, saying things such as "Tomorrow, we're going to the zoo." They can respond to *wh* questions, like *"who?" "what?"* and *"where?"* but may have difficulty responding to *"why?"* This does not prevent them from frequently asking *"why?"*

THE MAKEUP OF WORDS

Words are comprised of individual sounds known as phonemes. The act of speech involves the ability to orally produce and articulate them. As the sounds become more difficult to pronounce, increased coordination of the muscles in the lips, tongue, jaw, and soft palate (the articulators) is required. The ability to master ever more complex combinations of sounds usually occurs naturally as the child matures. In general:

- By age three, most children (about 90 percent) can say *p, m, h, n,* and *w* in words. They may say "wabbit" for *rabbit* and "nana" for *banana.*
- By age four, most children are able to say *b, k, g, d, f,* and *y* in words. They may say "danwit" for *sandwich.*
- By age six, most children can say the sounds *t, ng, r,* and *l* in words but may say "ticken" for *chicken.*
- By age seven, most children can say *ch, sh, j, v,* and *th* (as in *thin*) in words but may say "thiziz" for *scissors.*
- By age eight, *s, z, v,* and *th* (as in *the*) are mastered, and the average child is correctly pronouncing all of the sounds in conversational speech.

THE "RULE OF FOURTHS"

The overall clarity of a child's speech—speech pathologists call it "intelligibility"—also improves with age. A framework for the development of phonology, the rules for combining speech sounds to form words and phrases, is set forth in the commonly accepted principle of the "Rule of Fourths."

- By one and a half years of age, the average toddler's speech is understandable to strangers one-fourth (25 percent) of the time but is clear to her mother 95 percent of the time. For example, a child, with tears running down her face as her mother leaves the house, may ask the new baby-sitter, "Mama hoe me?" for "Mama come home to me?"
- By two years of age, Great-Aunt Clara, who doesn't get to see her nephew very often, probably understands him two-fourths (half) of the time while 98 percent of his speech is intelligible to both parents. The child may say, "Dop white deer!" for "Stop right there!"
- By three years of age, the average child's speech is expected to be comprehensible to strangers three-fourths (75 percent) of the time while being 100 percent clear to close family members. At this age, she may say, "Mommy, pwease gib me a wowipop!"
- By the time the average child is four years old, his speech is completely understandable all of the time to all listeners. However, he may say, "I got a new toy, but I breaked it."

ASSESSING PROGRESS

It's important to note that children vary in the rate at which they acquire language skills. However, as you have seen, there are commonly accepted milestones that a child is expected to reach. Perhaps from the examples above you have already identified some areas in which your child is lagging. The following tables set out the milestones in greater detail. They are not provided for you to make a diagnosis but to let you know when your child should be assessed by a medical professional, an SLP, or an early intervention specialist. If your child is not meeting the "Normal Language Milestones," check the "Clinical Clues." If your infant or toddler falls into an area of concern, make an appointment with your pediatrician to discuss the situation.

NORMAL LANGUAGE MILESTONES AND CLINICAL CLUES FOR A POSSIBLE COMMUNICATION DISORDER	
NORMAL LANGUAGE MILESTONES	CLINICAL CLUES OF A POSSIBLE PROBLEM
Typically seen during the first 3 months	Cause for concern during the first 3 months
• looks at caregivers/others • becomes quiet in response to sound (especially speech) • smiles or coos in response to another person's smile or voice • cries differently when tired, hungry, or in pain	• lack of responsiveness • lack of awareness of sound • lack of awareness of environment • cry is no different if tired, hungry, or in pain • problems sucking/swallowing
Typically first seen from 3 to 6 months	Cause for concern at 6 months
• fixes gaze on face • responds to name by looking for voice • regularly identifies location of sound (turns toward the source of a sound/speaker) • cooing, gurgling, chuckling, laughing	• cannot focus; easily overstimulated • lack of awareness of sound; does not look toward the source of a sound/speaker • lack of awareness of people and objects
Typically first seen from 6 to 9 months	Cause for concern at 9 months
• imitates vocalizing • enjoys social interaction games structured by adults (peekaboo, pat-a-cake) • has different vocalizations for different emotional states • recognizes familiar people	• does not appear to understand or enjoy the social rewards of interaction • lack of connection with adults (lack of eye contact, reciprocal eye gaze, vocal turn-taking, reciprocal social games)

NORMAL LANGUAGE MILESTONES	CLINICAL CLUES OF A POSSIBLE PROBLEM
Typically first seen from 6 to 9 months	**Cause for concern at 9 months**
• imitates familiar sounds and actions • reduplicative babbling ("bababa," "mamama"), vocal play with variations in tone, lots of sounds that sound like words • cries when parent leaves room (9 months) • responds consistently to soft speech and environmental sounds • reaches to request object	• no babbling, or babbling with few or no consonants
Typically first seen from 9 to 12 months	**Cause for concern at 12 months**
• attracts attention (vocalizing, coughing) • shakes head no, pushes away undesired objects • waves "bye" • indicates requests clearly, directs others' behavior (shows objects; gives objects to adults; pats, pulls, tugs on adults; points to object of desire) • coordinates actions between objects and adults (looks back and forth between adult and desired object) • imitates new sounds/actions • shows consistent patterns of reduplicative babbling, produces vocalizations that sound like first words ("ma-ma," "da-da")	• easily upset by sounds that do not upset others • may look at a desired object but does not clearly indicate that he or she wants it • does not coordinate action between objects and adults (does not look back and forth between adult and object of desire) • lack of consistent patterns of reduplicative babbling ("bababa," "mamama") • lack of responses indicating comprehension of words or communicative gestures (does not respond to your words or gestures, for example, ignores hand motion to "come here") • does not understand language unless it is in context (for example, needs to see the cup when asked "want juice?")
Typically first seen from 12 to 18 months	**Cause for concern at 18 months**
• single-word speech begins • requests objects: points, vocalizes, may use word approximations	• lack of communicative gestures • does not attempt to imitate or spontaneously produce single words to convey meaning

NORMAL LANGUAGE MILESTONES	CLINICAL CLUES OF A POSSIBLE PROBLEM
Typically first seen from 12 to 18 months	**Cause for concern at 18 months**
• gets attention: vocally, physically, maybe by using word ("mommy") • knows that an adult can do things for him or her (such as activate a wind-up toy) • uses ritual words ("bye," "hi," "thank you," "please") • protests: says "no," shakes head, moves away, pushes objects away • comments: points to object, vocalizes, or uses word approximations • acknowledges: eye contact, vocal response, repetition of word	• does not persist in communication (for example, may hand object to adult for help but then gives up if adult does not immediately respond) • limited comprehension vocabulary (understands fewer than 50 words or phrases without gesture or context clues) • limited expressive vocabulary (speaks fewer than 10 words) • lack of growth in production vocabulary over 6-month period from 12 to 18 months
Typically first seen from 18 to 24 months	**Cause for concern at 24 months**
• uses mostly words to communicate • begins to use two-word combinations: first combinations are usually memorized forms and used in one or two contexts (for example, says "daddy car" each morning when daddy leaves the house) • later combinations (by 24 months) include greater variety and meaning (such as "more cookie," "daddy shoe") • by 24 months has at least 50 words, can be approximations of adult form	• reliance on gestures without verbalization • limited expressive vocabulary (speaks fewer than 50 words) • does not use any two-word combinations • limited consonant production • largely unintelligible speech • compulsive labeling of objects in place of commenting or requesting • regression in language development, stops talking, or begins echoing phrases, often inappropriately
Typically first seen from 24 to 36 months	**Cause for concern at 36 months**
• engages in short dialogues • carries on purposeful conversation • talks when playing alone • expresses emotion • begins using language in imaginative ways • begins providing descriptive details to assist listener's comprehension	• words limited to single syllables with no final consonants • few or no multiword utterances • does not demand a response from listeners • asks no questions • poor speech intelligibility • frequent tantrums when not understood

NORMAL LANGUAGE MILESTONES	CLINICAL CLUES OF A POSSIBLE PROBLEM
Typically first seen from 24 to 36 months	**Cause for concern at 36 months**
• uses attention-getting devices ("hey") • begins to include the articles (a, the) and word endings (ing added to verbs; regular plural s [cats]; is + adjective [ball is red]; and regular past tense ed) • understands simple two-step commands (go to your room and get your shoes)	• echoing or "parroting of speech" without communicative intent • unable to comprehend language unless it is spoken simply and slowly and includes gestures
Typically seen from 36 to 48 months	**Cause for concern at 48 months**
• improvement in listening skills and begins to learn from listening • can carry on conversations using adultlike grammar • asks questions and answers who? how? how many? • uses pronouns I, me, you, and he properly • uses language to create pretend situations with others	• frequently says "huh?" or needs directions repeated • speaks in "telegraphic" style using immature grammar ("mommy, doggie run!") • limited vocabulary • frequent expressions of frustration in communicative situations • substitutes me/I, him/he, her/she • little language heard during pretend play
Typically seen from 48 to 60 months	**Cause for concern at 60 months**
• can explain how an object is used • can talk about past, future, and imaginary events • participates in long, detailed conversations • people outside the family understand most of what he or she says	• difficulty with word finding when asked to explain how objects are used • unable to retell stories or relate recent events clearly • sentences seem unorganized with difficulty getting to the point • only family members understand him or her

Primary source for tables adapted from the *Clinical Practice Guideline: The Guideline Technical Report, Communication Disorders, Assessment and Intervention for Young Children (Age 0–3 Years)*, 1999, with permission of the New York State Department of Health. Additional references for 36 to 60 months include the Communication Checklist developed for the Toronto Preschool Speech and Language Services through www.hanen.org; D. Kelly and J. Sally, "Disorders of Speech and Language," in M. Levine, W. Carey, and A. Crocker, eds., *Developmental-Behavioral Pediatrics*, 3rd ed. (Philadelphia: W. B. Saunders, 1999), 623; L. Nicolosi and J. Collins, "Developmental Sequences of Language Behavior: Overview," in L. Nicolosi, E. Harryman, and J. Kresheck, *Terminology of Communication Disorders*, 4th ed. (Baltimore: Williams and Wilkins, 1996), 315.

GETTING HELP

What does it mean if your child fits the profile under "Clinical Clues of a Possible Problem"? Does it mean he or she has a communication disorder? And what should you do next? If any of these clinical clues exist, you should consult your primary health care provider. Your insight will provide a useful and valid starting point for his or her evaluation. Your doctor will want to explore other risk factors, which we cover later. If you seriously feel there's a problem, there's a good chance that you're right. Studies have shown that parental concerns about a child's development are generally accurate indicators. After all, you spend more time with your kid than any health professional. Don't feel intimidated, or think that you might be worrying unnecessarily, or that you might be wasting the physician's time. Your child's well-being is at stake. In fact, the American Speech-Language-Hearing Association, the nonprofit organization that represents more than 100,000 speech-language professionals, urges, "When you become concerned, don't delay. You and your family members know more about your child than anyone. No child is too young to be helped. If there is a problem, early attention is important. If there is no problem, you will be relieved of worry."

Quite often a child with clinical clues ultimately develops normally. The child, it is subsequently discovered, had a delay in maturation, not a disorder. At this stage of life it's not easy to distinguish between a delay and a disorder, but a child who is not meeting the accepted milestones should be monitored more closely and have a formal assessment conducted. In the next chapter we explain why it is dangerous to delay having an assessment with qualified professionals. We present warning signs that there may be an underlying disorder rather than a maturational delay, and we recommend when early intervention should be considered.

2. The Danger of Delay

The earlier the diagnosis, the better the prognosis.
—MARVIN I. GOTTLIEB, M.D., Ph.D., Department of Pediatrics,
Hackensack University Hospital

What are the chances that your child is not just a late bloomer but has a speech disorder? How can you tell? Does it really make any difference? Why not let nature take its course rather than have your child undergo speech therapy? What's the hurry? These are some of the questions that may be racing through your mind after reviewing the clinical clues in the previous chapter, especially if you've already been on the receiving end of the "wait and see" advice from family, friends, and the doctor. So what are the odds? How many children are late talkers? How many have speech disorders?

At the age of twenty-four months, 15 percent of children in low-income families and 7 percent in middle-class homes have an expressive language delay. Studies show that 50 percent are likely to catch up by the age of three, even without early intervention, and another 25 percent will have normal speech by the time they start school. This leaves a staggering 25 percent of late-talking children who do not grow out of their problem before starting school. Waiting and seeing is no great comfort if your child is one of the unfortunate 25 percent. Research shows a grave downside in delaying a speech evaluation and appropriate treatment *when necessary*. The children who do not get early treatment are at increased risk of:

- language-based learning disabilities, including dyslexia
- academic failure

- social rejection
- behavioral and self-esteem problems
- anxiety disorders
- juvenile delinquency, possibly imprisonment
- suicide

It may he hard to envision consequences of this magnitude for your young child, but evidence is mounting that early intervention can prevent a host of academic and social ills, a subject we explore further in this chapter. It's obvious to parents when their child is unable to express himself or herself using words. As a result, it's one of the most common and most serious questions raised with pediatricians. It also becomes one of the most frustrating because of the inclination to wait and see, and because there is no simple diagnostic tool. Identifying the child who will not outgrow his or her speech difficulties and who may face a lifetime of ordeals is not an exact science. It's a real challenge for the professional as well as for the parent, especially for doctors not acquainted with disorders such as apraxia. There are no blood tests or brain-imaging techniques that can identify a speech disorder. While ongoing research and the development of sophisticated technology hold the promise of more definitive tests, at present a diagnosis is dependent on a thorough examination by a *knowledgeable* professional. We emphasize the word *knowledgeable,* as speech disorders such as apraxia require a level of expertise that the average pediatrician may not have acquired.

Warning signs of speech disorders show up in the first years of life and, if left untreated, they can cause persistent problems. Unfortunately, medical and speech professionals don't always know them. One major review of all of the relevant research paints a profile for us of those toddlers at risk of language impairment and who should receive early intervention. The following predictors and risk factors are taken from the study led by Lesley B. Olswang at the University of Washington. The more of these warning signs your child exhibits (especially the closer he or she gets to three years of age), the greater the need for speech-language therapy.

PREDICTORS

Patterns of Sound Production

Toddlers who have little sound-play as infants, who produce a limited number of consonants (many of which are inaccurate), and who make vowel errors are at increased risk of continued delay in speaking. The greater the variety and accuracy of toddlers' sound production, the better their outcome for learning speech.

Verbal Variety

A "particular red flag," say the researchers, is children who have "less diverse verb repertoires." They rely on general "all purpose" verbs in their conversation, compared with typically developing kids. They frequently use simple words such as *want, go, get, do, put, look, make,* and *got* instead of more "sophisticated" words or longer word combinations. As an example, compare two thirty-three-month-olds playing in a sandbox. One child, who can use only general all-purpose verbs (GAPs), says, "Me make water down." The other child, who can use sophisticated verbs, comments, "I pour water like this."

Phonology

Babbling babies who don't use many consonants in their prelinguistic efforts at communication fall behind their peers in the acquisition of speech. At the age of twenty-four months, a child who uses only four or five consonants and a limited number of vowels is at risk for future delay. At age thirty-six months, there's cause for concern if your child makes numerous vowel errors (saying "beg" instead of "big"), frequently omits the beginning and ending consonants in words ("ive" for "give" and "mi" for "milk"), and substitutes back consonants for front consonants ("koe" for "toe" and "gun" for "done").

Imitation

Children usually imitate word combinations, particularly when prompted, before they spontaneously make the sounds for themselves. Toddlers who don't imitate are appropriate candidates for treatment.

The Way They Play

The way young children play, and its complexity, is an early indicator of how well they will develop language. There are three stages of play: (1) exploratory—shaking and banging toys; (2) combinatorial—using toys together in a meaningful way, such as putting a doll to bed; and (3) symbolic or pretend play—make-believe cooking or serving dinner, for instance. A toddler who sits and spins the wheels of a car, or simply lines up his or her cars and trucks (manipulating and grouping) is exhibiting immature play behaviors and would be an appropriate candidate for intervention. A toddler who begins to engage in more elaborate play is more likely to have a surge in word production.

The Significance of Gestures

One study has shown that late bloomers (toddlers who caught up with their peers within a year) used significantly more communication gestures than those with a persistent delay. Other research has homed in on the different kinds of symbolic gestures: complementary and supplementary. Complementary gestures match the word being used; shaking one's head from side to side while saying "no," for example. Supplementary gestures provide added meaning; shaking one's head while saying "juice" to mean "no juice." Children who don't produce any gestures at all and those who don't use supplementary gestures are more likely to need intervention. Other research has shown that a child is likely to outgrow his lack of speech if he uses "recognitory gestures"—pretending to drink out of an empty cup, for example. Note: Apraxics are an exception to the rule! Apraxic children tend to create elaborate gesture language to help them communicate their wants and needs. This, in part, reflects their typically developing receptive language and problem-solving skills.

Social Skills

Several studies have shown that preschool children who prefer to initiate conversations with adults rather than their peers, and those who have behavior problems, are less likely to outgrow their disorder.

RISK FACTORS

All in the Family

Research has consistently demonstrated a strong heritability factor. There's a higher risk of continued delay if one of a toddler's parents or siblings had long-term language and learning difficulties.

Otitis Media

Otitis media is an acute ear infection typically associated with an upper respiratory infection (cold), sometimes with pain and fever. Many children with these infections have residual fluid behind the eardrums (called an effusion), causing a temporary hearing loss. Recurrent otitis media with effusion may place children at risk of language delay and later articulation problems.

Parental Characteristics

A family's socioeconomic status can have an influence. Young children growing up in poverty are not usually exposed to good speech models. In general, mothers are less educated and less available to interact and stimulate their children with language and through play. There is also more exposure to crime, substandard housing, poor nutrition, and illiteracy in their communities. Therefore, low-income families are more likely to have a child with a negative outcome.

The way that parents interact with their child is also an issue. Parents need to follow a child's lead and provide a language model using simplified speech. Some parents of children with delays tend to do the opposite. Excessive parental concern can also impede the child's language development, and counseling may be needed for the parents.

Other Factors

Recent research has identified several other clues in the late preschool years that might serve as clinical markers of a true impairment. They involve the "explosion" of speech, the use of grammar, and the ability to handle nonsense words.

The Explosion Clue

Most children experience a spurt in vocabulary around the age of eighteen months, but late talkers don't. Some late talkers have an "explosion" of speech later—between twenty-four and thirty months. If your child has not had a vocabulary spurt by thirty months, he or she is more likely to remain at considerable risk of continued language delays, says Leslie Rescorla, chairman of the department of psychology at Bryn Mawr College.

The Grammar Clue

Another clue that your child may have an impairment and not just a delay is the use of grammar—understanding and correctly using tenses and forms such as "he walks" and "he walk*ed*" and *is, are,* and *am.* In children who have specific language impairments, experts say that the ability to use this grammar is extraordinarily weak. An example is a three-year-old who says, "Me doe too," or a four-year-old who says, "Her goed to the store."

The Nonsense Clue

The ability to repeat multisyllabic nonsense words is another giveaway sign. Children with a language disorder perform badly on this test, suggesting that they have difficulty with auditory recall, an important facility for language processing. It's hard for their brain's short-term language storage center to hold the syllables in correct sequence.

WHY IT'S TIME FOR THERAPY

In spite of these early warning signs, there is debate about the need for children under the age of three to get speech therapy. Many pediatric practitioners and even some speech-language experts prefer "watchful waiting." Quite understandably, many parents are happy to accept the well-intentioned reassurances from these professionals. It's human nature to hope for the best, to want to believe that a lack of speech is a problem that will resolve itself in time. Many parents don't want to think of all of the ramifications for a child who can't speak. Others postpone a medical specialist's assessment out of fear that the outcome might be the "stigma" of a special needs label attached to their child that may never go away. But dismissing the warning signs of a possible speech disorder is taking a gamble with your child's future development, and the stakes are too high when it's your child who's at risk. *Any kind of delay during these all-important formative years can have disproportionately negative consequences.*

Many experts believe that beginning therapy by twenty-four months is essential for children who have more serious delays. We feel it's important for any child exhibiting speech delays to receive the right kind of therapy, as early as possible. The age of twenty-four months is not too soon! As Dr. Judy Flax, senior research speech pathologist at Rutgers University's Infancy Studies Laboratory, so aptly puts it, "Six months for a two-year-old is equivalent to a quarter of their lifetime developmentally. Early intervention services are benign in their delivery but can be extremely beneficial. So, don't wait."

A panel of experts in communication disorders also emphasized the potentially dire outcome of delay, no matter how short-lived, in a report for New York State's Early Intervention Program. Even a temporary communication delay at a young age can hinder your child's ability to form relationships with peers and adults and, therefore, may affect his or her overall development. Impaired communication, they say, may injure not only injure the development of a child's social, emotional, and cognitive skills but also later academic success: "A child who demonstrates communication delays as a toddler and during preschool is at greater risk for later language-based learning disabilities, including reading disabilities."

What's the evidence? In one study, Professor H. W. Catts of the University of Kansas gave kindergarten children with speech and language impairment a battery of tests. These included assessments of phonological awareness (the ability to segment words into sounds and identify similarities in sound patterns) and the ability to perform a rapid naming task: Name as many animals as you can in one minute. When retested in second grade, the language-impaired students performed less well on reading tests than a group of children without speech problems.

In a long-term study, Dr. Leslie Rescorla reported on a group of thirty-four nine-year-olds whom she had been following since they were late-talking toddlers, and a control group of twenty-five typically developing children. Nearly all of the children were from two-parent, middle- to upper-middle-class families. The late talkers' language ability had caught up by the age of five. And at the ages of six and seven, when they were all in the early stages of learning to read, there was no difference in reading skills. But notably, by the time they reached nine, the late talkers had significantly poorer language skills and were slightly less skilled in reading. Preliminary unpublished data, analyzing twenty-two of the late talkers, shows that at the age of thirteen they were still lagging behind their peers in grammar, vocabulary, verbal memory, reading, and, to some extent, spelling. During the years of the study, one third of the late talkers received some therapy, but Dr. Rescorla did not take that into account, as therapy was at the discretion of their parents. So we don't know if therapy made any difference. In another study—a fourteen-year follow-up of children who were language impaired at the age of five—73 percent continued to be the same level behind their peers when they were nineteen years old. Early speech problems can dog children academically throughout their school years.

Social Stigma

Scholastic performance is one thing, but communication problems can damage your child's social life and relationships, even from a young age. Because many children with speech disorders don't know the unspoken rules of conversation and social interaction, their behavior can become inappropriate (hitting another child, for instance, to let him know she wants to play) and hurt their chances of making and maintaining friends. Social failure on top of academic failure can lead to lowered self-esteem.

As bad as these children feel about themselves, the way they are regarded by others can be worse—and these others include professionals who should know better. Mabel L. Rice, Ph.D., and colleagues at the University of Kansas found that children with communication impairments were frequently ignored by other kids and were not as popular as their "normal" classmates. The bias was shared by adults, including teachers and speech-language pathologists. In another study, the Rice team discovered that adults consistently rate children with communication impairments as less intelligent and less socially competent. Other researchers have reported that people generally form quick, negative impressions of individuals with articulation disorders, even minor ones. Those with distorted speech are considered to be intellectually slow and handicapped, even though, to the contrary, most children with speech disorders have average or above-average intelligence.

Psychiatric

The stress of coping with a speech and language disorder evolves into more serious challenges. In a fourteen-year study, Dr. Joseph Beitchman and colleagues at the University of Toronto followed 240 youngsters with speech and/or language impairment. At the age of nineteen, all had anxiety and antisocial personality disorders. Unsurprisingly, the most common anxiety disorder was social phobia: problems speaking to others, with public speaking, and in social interaction. The antisocial personality disorders were highlighted by a lack of emotional connection with others and a lack of guilt for wrongdoing. Such attitudes can translate into criminal activity. In fact, there is a high level of speech, language, and hearing impairments among juvenile detention and state prison inmates, says the American Speech-Language-Hearing Association. According to one study, language and communication problems among female juvenile delinquents are three times more common than in the rest of the community.

Meanwhile, Harvard researcher Claudio O. Toppelberg, author of a major review of ten years of studies, says that psychiatric disorders affect a high percentage of children seen in speech-language clinics. In total, 50 to 60 percent are at high risk of a psychiatric disorder—ranging from those with a speech disorder (30 percent) to those with *receptive* language disorder (81 percent). But the psychiatric problems often go undiagnosed. The review concluded that early detection of language problems may be crucial in preventing later psychiatric problems.

How crucial? Suicide is the third leading cause of adolescent death in the United States and has increased at an alarming rate. The rate of suicide among fifteen- to twenty-four-year-olds nearly tripled between

1952 and 1995, and in 1999 the under-twenty-fives accounted for 14 percent of all suicides. The most recent government survey painted an even bleaker picture: Close to three million children age twelve to seventeen considered suicide in 2000, and more than a third of those tried to kill themselves. Studies have shown that youngsters with learning disabilities make up a "disproportionately large" percentage of suicides—as high as 50 percent in one report. A study of twenty-seven adolescent suicides found that twenty-four had significant language problems and difficulties in handwriting and spelling.

The Earlier the Better

All of these facts have led organizations and experts to call for early therapy. The Early Intervention experts who wrote the review quoted earlier commented, "Early detection of language problems may be crucial in psychiatric prevention." Beitchman and colleagues concluded that their findings emphasize "the importance of effective and early interventions," while Dr. Diane Paul-Brown, director of clinical issues in speech-language pathology for ASHA, asserts, "We now know the earlier the intervention, the better the brain can reorganize." The National Academy of Sciences book, *From Neurons to Neighborhoods: The Science of Early Childhood Development*, says that early intervention may be important "because with it, doors swing open that might otherwise have been inaccessible."

The U.S. Department of Education (DOE) agrees, saying that early intervention (EI) increases the developmental and educational gains for the child, improves the functioning of the family, and reaps long-term benefits for society. Early intervention results in children needing fewer special education and other services later in life and being held back in school less often. According to the DOE's annual report to Congress in 2000, 11 percent of school-age children receive special education services in contrast with 4.9 percent of preschoolers and a mere 1.6 percent of infants and toddlers. These statistics clearly tell us that not enough children with learning problems are being identified early enough.

Financially there is also a benefit to early intervention, according to the National Early Childhood Technical Assistance System. In one long-term study, three-and four-year-olds from poor families were followed up shortly after their expected date of high school graduation. It turned out that the kids who had received early intervention had required less special education, were more likely to graduate, and were less likely to get into trouble with the law. Based on projected lifetime earnings and other assumptions, the bean counters assessed that early intervention returned $3 for every $1 invested.

The Einstein Factor

So why is there some complacency and even downright resistance to early assessment and therapy? Hoover Institution economist Thomas Sowell, the father of a late talker, is one high-profile figure who feels that most late-talking children make progress without speech therapy. In his book *The Einstein Syndrome: Bright Children Who Talk Late*, he writes about 285 "exceptionally bright" children who were exceptionally slow to develop speech. The great majority, says Sowell, have close relatives with highly analytical occupations, such as engineers, scientists, and mathematicians, as well as others who play a musical instrument, some professionally. Apart from their inability to speak, the children have precocious mental abilities. Sowell expresses concern that children who undergo early evaluation get stuck with "indelible labels that may follow the child around for years," adding, without substantiation, "There can be negative consequence to endless evaluations and unneeded treatment."

Sowell admits that children with the Einstein characteristics in his book are probably a minority among those who talk late, but his writing has not only given false hope to many, it has also encouraged the "wait and see" approach, even though he himself acknowledges that for most late talkers, ". . . early intervention may be the way to go."

Albert Einstein reportedly didn't talk until he was three years old. Does this mean that children who talk late are potential Einsteins? The comment of *New York Times* writer Randi Hutter Epstein is totally on target: "No one should assume that a silent two-year-old is a budding genius; silence may be a sign of a hearing loss or a neurological disorder."

Many children who are late talkers are extraordinarily bright, but it is unwise to foster the belief that their brains might be so busy developing other remarkable talents that speech has to temporarily take a back seat. We don't see any negative consequences from early intervention. On the contrary, as we have shown, there is growing proof that early treatment at the time when a young child's brain connections are most malleable may even help "rewire" any defects.

What Parents Say

Anecdotally, we hear all the time from parents delighted that they were able to get early intervention therapy for their children. Sadly, we also hear from those who wished they had not taken the advice to wait and see. Ellen Goldstein, a mother who became an EI services coordinator, has an interesting perspective. She knew nothing about EI until her son, Mark, was evaluated at the age of twenty months, when he could speak only five words and did not respond to his name or the commands "no" and "stop." It was discovered that Mark has oral and verbal apraxia and low tone in his mouth and upper trunk area. Thanks to EI, he's doing "fantastically well," says Ellen, who answers the suggestion that some kids get thrown into EI when they don't need it by saying, "The states have very strict guidelines for funding providers to do therapy. Unless they can show cause that a child really needs therapy, he won't get it."

Another mother, Brenda Hunt, is just as enthusiastic about EI. Her son has been receiving speech therapy since he was twelve months old, when he wasn't making any sounds and had poor oral-motor skills. At the age of two years and eight months, says Brenda, he performed at his age level expressively and above age level receptively: "He would be so far behind if we hadn't done it."

Angie Wright concurs. At the age of twenty-four months, her daughter, Mary, was completely nonverbal. Says Angie, "Now she is almost three and we are likely to end speech therapy soon. Every single sound and word she said during the first months of therapy was something that was directly taught to her and reinforced at home. She did not spontaneously just 'start talking.'"

Stacey Abenstein, mother of four-year-old Evan, notes that some parents say they don't want their children to be "put through all that." But she urges, "If you really feel in your gut that there's a problem, call your early intervention program—now." The Abensteins called at twenty months. Their son was evaluated at twenty-one months and started speech therapy at twenty-two months. When the early intervention SLP suspected apraxia at twenty-four months, therapy was increased to twice a week. Adds Stacey, "Parents have the clearest view of what is best for their child. If you think she should be evaluated, then she should be. What is the worst thing? They evaluate her, give her some fun, home-based therapy only to find she is 'just a late talker' and catches up quickly?"

Stacey puts it in a nutshell. There is nothing to be lost and everything to be gained from early therapy. Perhaps your child is a late bloomer and will catch up with his peers. On the other hand, he may not have a speech delay but a speech disorder, and by obtaining therapy you will have gained a vital time advantage. You need to be prepared if this is the situation. In the next chapter, therefore, we outline the specific speech disorders. We tell you what is known about their origins and how to identify them. As a parent you are more familiar with your child than anyone and need to be armed with this information so that, if necessary, *you* can take appropriate action.

3. My Mouth Won't Work

You know what you want to say, but you can't say it. You look socially inept.
You aren't stupid, but people might think you are.
—MABEL RICE, Ph.D., professor of speech-language-hearing,
University of Kansas

"God, help me talk," said one little boy as he knelt to say his bedtime prayers, although what he actually managed to say, according to his heartbroken mother, was "Dod el ee taw." Another toddler, comparing himself to a friend at preschool, asked his mom, "Why I talk different?" We've heard youngsters, well aware of their speech deficiency, proclaim, "Me no talk right" and "My mouth won't work." Acquiring the ability to talk is something most of us take for granted. And why not, when for most of us—unlike these kids—it's just a natural part of growing up? It's something no one really thinks much about—until it doesn't happen. But what if your child is not just a late talker? What could be the problem? How serious is it? What can you do about it?

LANGUAGE DISORDERS

Language disorders can be categorized as either involving *receptive* or *expressive* abilities, or a combination of both. Receptive ability, put simply, is understanding *what* is said. It's retrieving and processing sounds in your brain's storage center and involves hearing the difference between, for instance, *cat* and *pat*. Expressive ability, by and large, is how we verbally put words together to make ourselves understood by others.

Specific Language Impairment

A child with receptive and/or expressive language disorder, and no other developmental disability, has specific language impairment (SLI), a condition sometimes called language-learning impairment, developmental language disorder, developmental dysphasia, or developmental aphasia. In a recent study funded by the National Institutes of Health, the incidence of SLI in five-year-olds was estimated to be 7.6 percent. Children with SLI are usually late talkers, and most—67 to 84 percent—are boys. At the age of three or four they have a limited vocabulary and speak in short phrases rather than sentences. If left untreated, SLI can have a long-term impact on school performance and career choices.

The cause of SLI is still unknown, but it is a disorder that appears to run in families. If a child has SLI, there's a 25 percent chance that another family member is similarly affected. As with all communication impairments, early diagnosis and treatment are critical for future success. Therapy helps, but SLI is a complex problem, and more research into effective treatments is underway, pioneered by Paula Tallal, professor of neuroscience at Rutgers University.

SPEECH DISORDERS

Speech disorders include disorders of articulation and phonology (dysarthria, apraxia, and phonological disorder), fluency disorders (stuttering), and voice disorders (deviations in pitch, intensity, or voice quality). Our focus is on the disorders of articulation and phonology (especially apraxia). Along with specific language impairment, they are the crux of why a child may be a late talker. So what are they exactly?

Articulation refers to individual speech sounds and how they are pronounced. *All* children, not just those with a disorder, misarticulate sounds in the course of normal speech development. They may use sound substitutions, such as "wady" for "lady." They may omit sounds, saying "baw" instead of "ball." Or they may distort a sound, so that "spaghetti" comes out as "psketti." Concern arises when these errors continue beyond the time when a child normally outgrows them.

Phonological development is the gradual process of acquiring adult speech. Most children pick up most of the phonological rules by the age of five. One example is the deletion of the final consonant in words, where the child might say "boo" instead of "book." Most children lose this tendency between the ages of two and three. Another example is a five-year-old saying, "Mommy, tan you div me one?" for "Mommy, can you give me one?" This child uses *velar fronting*, replacing consonants made with the tongue moving toward the back of the mouth, like *k* and *g,* with consonants produced at the front of the mouth, such as *t* and *d.* Children usually outgrow this practice by thirty-nine months of age.

Children with a phonological disorder consistently make the same sound substitutions and, when given auditory and visual cues, are able to imitate correct sounds or words. Usually, they have normal oral muscle tone. Children with apraxia and dysarthria are quite different. It is common, however, to confuse apraxia and dysarthria, says Dr. Andrew Morgan, chief of child development at the Chicago College of Medicine. While experts are able to differentiate between these two neurological disorders, he says, they are poorly understood by physicians and many speech therapists as well. A further complication is the possibility of phonological disorders, apraxia, and dysarthria occurring together in the same child. Language disorders may also be present. And the severity of each may vary.

Dysarthria

The dysarthrias are a group of motor speech disorders that result from damage to the nervous system. The symptoms can be quite apparent to parents as well as professionals, as they include a lack of strength and control of the muscles used for both speech and non-speech functions, such as smiling and chewing. (Many children with cerebral palsy exhibit a dysarthric speech pattern, slurring their words, distorting vowels, and often producing slow, labored, nasal speech.)

Dysarthria can also accompany other neurological disorders such as muscular dystrophy, myopathies (muscle diseases), facial palsy (weakness), or a head injury. Children with dysarthria have difficulty in the actual *production* of speech sounds. In particular, they are more likely to distort consonant sounds. This differs from apraxia in that a symptom of its presence is the omission of consonants.

Apraxia

What's it like to live with apraxia? To give you an idea, the following text presents a word picture of a little boy with the disorder.

To try to make himself understood, Ryan points, grunts, and becomes increasingly angry at his inability to communicate. Sometimes he says the same word four different ways. The more this three-and-a-half-year-old tries to talk, the harder he is to understand. He adds vowel sounds to the ends of words that finish with a consonant. *Up*, for example, becomes *up-pa*. He may drop the final consonant in single-syllable words: *Cat come home* becomes *Ca co hoe*. Within a word, he'll jumble consonants and sounds. Instead of saying "elephant," he'll say "efelant." One day he will say a difficult word perfectly, and then he'll lose it for weeks. He also makes unusual movements of his jaw, lips, and tongue, as if groping to find words, and when the words do come out, it sounds as if he's talking through his nose. It's obvious that he understands most of what is said to him, but he cannot respond.

Of course, not all children who display some of the same symptoms as Ryan have apraxia, and conversely, some children with apraxia may exhibit only some of these symptoms. Apraxia can be as individual as each individual child. There is not a simple checklist of symptoms that can be applied to every child. However, the presence of a large "cluster" of symptoms (see checklist on page 37) is usually a fair indicator that apraxia will eventually be diagnosed.

What is apraxia? Apraxia is a neurological motor speech impairment—a breakdown in the transmission of messages from the brain to the muscles in the jaw, cheeks, lips, tongue, and palate. There is no obvious weakness in these muscles, and the child may well be able to move them when not trying to speak. With apraxia, a child knows what he or she wants to say, but there is a roadblock obstructing the signal from the brain to the mouth. The brain says, "Speak." But the muscles of the mouth either don't "hear" it or choose to ignore it.

"It is much like having a 'bug' in a computer program that does not allow the program to run the way it is supposed to run," says Penelope K. Hall, associate professor at the University of Iowa's Department of Speech Pathology and Audiology. "Just as the program 'bug' frustrates computer users, problems in correctly producing intended speech sounds are often very frustrating to children with developmental apraxia of speech—and to their speech-language pathologists and parents as well." In contrast to dysarthria, children with apraxia are unlikely to have significant feeding problems or obvious neuromuscular deficits, like paralysis of the arms and legs. Children with apraxia, however, may not do well at tasks requiring the brain to plan motor activities. For instance, they may have difficulty imitating gestures or learning how to pedal a tricycle.

Apraxia in children is a speech disorder suffering an identity crisis. In the medical literature it is referred to as apraxia, verbal apraxia, developmental apraxia of speech, developmental verbal apraxia, developmental dyspraxia of speech, developmental verbal dyspraxia, articulatory apraxia, childhood verbal apraxia, developmental articulatory dyspraxia, and motor planning disorder of speech. Confused? Part of the confusion arises from the name *apraxia* being borrowed from the adult medical literature. In adults, apraxia is an acquired condition in which someone *loses* the ability to speak, often as the result of a stroke or head injury. Evidence of damage to the speech center on the left side of the brain (Broca's area) is usually revealed by a CAT scan or an MRI. Apraxia in a child *yet to develop speech* makes this a distinctly different disorder and this has created some controversy about what to call the childhood version. Yet another complication is that the terms *apraxia* and *dyspraxia* are more or less used interchangeably in the United States. In other countries (the United Kingdom, for example), dyspraxia is more commonly employed to describe a motor planning disorder of the body, popularized as "clumsy child syndrome."

Some researchers have suggested that apraxia affects 6 to 10 percent of children and, based on our own observation, that appears to be a realistic estimate, especially when you consider that apraxia is "hidden" in other disorders, a topic we will cover shortly. The best information tells us that apraxia is a neurological disorder that can run in families, although some experts dispute the neurological origin, pointing to a lack of evidence of brain dysfunction in young children with speech disorders, while there is such evidence in adults. In adults who have *lost* the ability to speak, through a stroke or other injury to the brain, scientists have pinpointed the damaged area as the left hemisphere, which is where the language center of the brain usually resides. However, in children who have not *acquired* the ability to speak, we do not yet have the same kind of evidence. Why not?

First, the brains of very young children have not localized a speech center. Babies respond to language with their entire brains until they are about a year old. Then language gradually shifts to the left hemisphere, *driven by the acquisition of language itself.* Second, the most sophisticated brain-imaging technology has not yet been used in children to map the speech areas in most communication disorders.

Furthermore, children with apraxia often have "neurologic soft signs," which we will discuss shortly, including hypotonia, sensory integration disorder, and gross- and fine-motor incoordination. How can it be claimed that apraxia is not neurologic when there is a constellation of associated neurologic signs? Finally, the unlocking of the human genome has led to the discovery of genetic links to apraxia, language impairments, autism, and dyslexia. The first formal evidence of a genetic cause for apraxia was uncovered recently through a long-term study of one family in London, England. Researchers found that fifteen of thirty-seven members of the family, spread over four generations, had severe orofacial and verbal apraxia. The affected family members are virtually unintelligible to strangers, and, in addition to the characteristics of apraxia, have difficulty understanding and using correct English grammar. They confuse verb tenses, plurals, and word order, and, while their comprehension of language is nearly normal, their verbal intelligence quotients are a little below average. The cause of their apraxia, according to a study published in *Nature,* was a single mutation in the gene FOXP2, found on chromosome 7.

It's an exciting age on which we have embarked, one that may lead to the unlocking of communication for all late talkers. Scientists believe that other genes will be identified as being important for speech and language development and they may help us to better understand why certain children may be predisposed to speech and language disorders. It is, however, too simplistic to think that the discovery of the FOXP2 gene is the sole answer to the question of what causes such a complex motor speech disorder as apraxia. As with most developmental disabilities, there are many causes. In some cases, hereditary factors coupled with exposure to environmental influences, like toxins during or after pregnancy, may predispose the child to speech and language impairments. In most cases, the cause of the developmental problems remains a mystery.

Associated Conditions

Identifying apraxia is difficult enough as the symptoms vary from child to child, but a further obstacle is the number of other conditions that can be associated with it, including oral apraxia, hypotonia, and sensory integration dysfunction. We need to explore these conditions if we are to fully comprehend the scope of apraxia. What's the difference between apraxia and oral apraxia? Simply stated, apraxia (*verbal* apraxia) is difficulty producing and sequencing the sounds and syllables necessary for speech on command. Oral apraxia is difficulty executing and sequencing oral movements, such as smiling or licking your lips, in the absence of paralysis. What's it like to have oral apraxia? Let's look at a typical case.

Oral Apraxia

Two-year-old Michael has oral apraxia. With the exception of speech, the youngster passed all of the developmental milestones on time. He hardly talks at all and, because he is so quiet, his family often describes him as a good baby. But he can't lick food from his lips and he uses his fingers to push food into his mouth. He isn't able to blow bubbles or pucker for a kiss, and he doesn't laugh or cry as often as other babies. Most of the time he stares into space, or looks blankly at anyone trying to engage his attention. At times, he grabs his mother's face and brings it close to his own, which may be a sign that he's trying to talk or that something hurts, or that he's happy or sad. But nothing comes out, so nobody knows.

Other signs of oral apraxia include difficulty blowing a horn and problems coordinating air flow with mouth movements (for example, you tell your daughter to say "ma" and she imitates your mouth position, but no sound comes out). These children also have a hard time getting the tongue, lips, and jaw to move independently of each other. Picture a child whose jaw automatically moves forward when he sticks his tongue out. With oral apraxia, a child has trouble performing oral movements—even though there is no weakness in his facial muscles. He may not be able to stick out his tongue, try to touch his tongue to his nose, bite his lower lip, or make "raspberries." Oral apraxia is one key early warning sign of apraxia and can be noted even before the time a child is expected to talk. It's often only in retrospect, when parents give a physician or therapist a history of their child's development, that the red flags are realized. Experts agree that most children with *oral* apraxia will also have apraxia.

A condition that can coexist with oral apraxia is oral-motor hypotonia with weakness of the facial muscles. A classic case is a child who had trouble nursing and now sits with an open mouth and protruding tongue. She drools more than expected and stuffs her mouth when eating. She may not get the normal sensory feedback of how her tongue feels as she moves it inside her mouth. Oral hypotonia may be diagnosed in infancy, whereas the signs of oral apraxia become more evident by eighteen months of age. As stated previously, mild neurologic disorders, also known as neurologic soft signs, are often associated with apraxia. These include hypotonia and sensory integration dysfunction.

Hypotonia

Normal muscle tone allows us to keep our bodies erect when sitting or standing. In children with hypotonia, the muscles feel doughy and soft. They don't have the control over their bodies that most of us take for granted. Severe cases show up in early infancy; more subtle cases become apparent between six and twelve months. The baby with hypotonia usually learns to hold his head straight but may be delayed in the ability to sit on his own, crawl, stand, walk, and develop a sense of balance.

Typically, a child with apraxia has benign congenital hypotonia (BCH) in the truncal region, exhibiting a soft, rounded, cherub-type body. He may feel like a handful of wet noodles when you pick him up, like he is going to slide out of your hands. He may feel heavier than another child of the same weight. (Imagine picking up a sleeping child compared with one who is awake.) The child with hypotonia has a hard time resisting gravity's pull and, when sitting for an extended period, ends up in a slumped-over position, which interferes with his breath control and speech. Because of laxity in his hip joints, the hypotonic child often finds it comfortable to sit on the floor in the "W" position, where the knees are turned inward, almost touching, and the lower legs are splayed out, looking like the letter "W." In some children, the low muscle tone extends to the cheeks, tongue, and jaw. They may have cherubic cheeks beyond infancy. Their mouths may stick open and their tongues protrude. They have to work harder at sucking and chewing, and they fatigue more easily when eating. Some have constipation and gastroesophageal reflux disease.

The cause of BCH is unknown, and although the condition improves with time and intervention, complete recovery may not occur until adulthood. There are more serious hypotonias that lead to muscle wasting, acute breathing problems, and even death, and there are dozens of disorders and syndromes that include hypotonia as a component. Some of the most serious are spinal muscular atrophy, muscular dystrophy, cerebral palsy, and Down syndrome.

Sensory Integration Dysfunction

Children with sensory integration dysfunction (DSI; experts now use the initials DSI instead of SID to avoid confusion with sudden infant death syndrome) have nervous systems that do not properly process the senses of touch, vision, hearing, smell, and taste. Although many children sometimes respond negatively to different kinds of sensory stimulation, children with DSI exhibit extreme reactions like these three apraxic children who also have DSI.

Simon does not cry when he gets a shot at the doctor's office, and he picks mosquito bites until he bleeds. But pat him lightly on the head or tickle him gently and he'll say "Ow." He doesn't like to be cuddled. In fact, he doesn't like to be touched at all. He becomes fixated on keeping something in his grasp; a small car, for instance. If he drops it, or if you try to take it away from him, he throws a fit. If he wants a cup, it has to be the blue one. Nothing will make him drink out of a different colored cup. He hates getting his hair cut and has to be held down at the barber.

Megan isn't bothered by the blare of the TV or other loud noises, but she screams "Hurt, hurt" at the sound of the garage door closing. She can hear things her mother can't hear—the humming of a lightbulb, or construction work that's miles away. She covers her ears when people clap. She's particularly offended by organ music. She hates the wind. Says her mom, "If the wind's blowing, I have to carry her, covering her head with my hands and arms. It freaks her out that the wind makes her hair move."

Tommy has unpredictable and uncontrollable "meltdowns." Usually, to his parents' embarrassment, they're in public. Once, at the supermarket, for no obvious reason, says his mother, "he was screaming this horrible high-pitched noise as if someone was sticking pins in him. His eyes were bulging and his face was turning red." But, just as quickly, the meltdown stopped and he fell asleep.

DSI may result in "sensory-seeking" or "sensory-avoiding" behavior and may also be associated with dyspraxia, the motor planning disorder. Dyspraxic children are clumsy and trip easily, have poor balance, and don't seem to notice obstacles or people in their path. They may have trouble writing or cutting, and may have oral and verbal apraxia.

The **sensory-seeking** child is underresponsive to sensation, so he craves more intense or more prolonged sensory experiences. He may be hyperactive, disorganized, and constantly moving from one activity to another. He may express interest in a toy, only to toss it aside once he gets it and move to something else. At the playground, he crashes into other children or equipment. He loves touching and being touched, and embarrasses you with inappropriate social behavior. He may throw himself on the floor and bang his head repeatedly. Some sensory-seeking children spin for long periods and don't seem to get dizzy; others turn up the volume so the TV is blaring (although, of course, not all kids who do this have DSI!).

The **sensory-avoiding** child is overly sensitive to sensory stimuli. She reacts to normal situations the way most of us would respond if forced to put our hand in a pail of worms. She has "tactile defensiveness," that is, she may withdraw when touched, shy away from messy play, and throw a fit because a label inside her shirt irritates her so much. She stands on the sidelines when there are large groups of children, is overly sensitive to food smells, and covers her ears when she hears loud sounds. She may become aggressive and intolerant of daily routines: combing or shampooing hair, or brushing teeth.

Some children with DSI also have "regulatory" dysfunction; they find it hard to calm and console themselves, and have difficulty establishing normal eating and sleeping patterns. For instance, they may be very picky eaters, and they may have extreme difficulty settling down to sleep, or they make wake up in the middle of the night and end up in their parents' bed. They may also have a complete meltdown when expected to switch from one activity to another. While these behaviors may sound like those of a typical toddler, taken in conjunction with sensory-seeking or sensory-avoiding behaviors, they provide clues about a child with DSI.

Apraxia can be associated with other disorders or syndromes and is often overlooked because it is not so well known. Through our Web site's group list, we have heard of children diagnosed with other disorders, whose apraxia went unrecognized by the doctor until raised by the parent. Such disorders include Angelman's, Fragile X, Kabuki, Klinefelter's, Down, Prader-Willi, Joubert's, and Smith-Magenis syndromes. The fact that a child with another syndrome is nonverbal does not, of course, necessarily mean that he or she is also apraxic, although there have been more than enough anecdotal reports to raise the possibility. We hope that increased awareness of apraxia will enable families to get appropriate diagnoses.

It is generally acknowledged, however, that some children with autistic spectrum disorder (ASD) also have apraxia, although little research is available. Most autistic children have deficits in language development. Sometimes they develop normally until eighteen to twenty-one months of age and then lose their language skills. Evaluators miss identifying apraxia in these children because they are not familiar with the signs. They may not be aware that the child's lack of speech may be due to an apraxic component and not the autism alone. Conversely, apraxic children have been misdiagnosed as having an autistic spectrum disorder *because* they are nonverbal and may have social deficits. Apraxic children have even been misclassified as mentally retarded because of their poor performance on standardized IQ tests, which are heavily weighted on measuring verbal intelligence. On the contrary, apraxic children have normal cognitive abilities.

It is obvious that apraxia has many faces. In children it's a complex, poorly understood, and underdiagnosed condition. There are many associated symptoms and conditions, and even experts are confused and can't agree. So what chance does the average parent have of making sense of it all? The framework for identifying apraxia presented in this chapter gives you a solid grounding in the subject. The following checklist pulls it all together and simplifies the warning signs.

SPEECH SIGNS OF APRAXIA

There is no definitive blood test or brain scan that can lead to a clinical diagnosis of apraxia. We have to rely, therefore, on a list of signs and symptoms to help us zero in on the disorder. It is difficult to assign an age range to a list such as this as the total child and a constellation of signs need to be considered. For instance, taken alone, it is not unusual for a toddler to say "tuck" for "truck" and "wah" for "water." However, if your child fits the criteria of a late talker and has many of the following signs, he or she should be evaluated, as there is a good possibility that he or she has apraxia.

Does your child

—favor the use of one syllable for all words (for example, "da" may be generic for "daddy," "brother," "dog," and "book")?

—often omit a sound or syllable, perhaps saying "wah" instead of "water," distorting vowels, and saying "tuck" for "truck"?

—reverse sounds or syllables, saying "shif" for "fish" or "miskate" for "mistake"?

—add extra sounds or syllables in words?

—find it difficult to produce words with a number of syllables?

—make more errors when trying to craft longer statements?

—find speech easy one day and hard the next?

—correctly say a difficult word but be unable to repeat it?

—speak too slowly or too fast, or place inappropriate stress on certain syllables and words?

—exhibit "groping" behaviors trying to find the proper mouth position, silent posturing, or dysfluencies (stuttering)?

—display expressive language disturbances: limited vocabulary, grammatical errors, or disordered syntax?

—only use restricted combinations of consonants, only saying *b, p, m, t, d,* and *h*?

—comprehend language much better than he or she is able to express himself or herself?

—have signs of hypotonia (low muscle tone), especially in the trunk, and/or oral hypotonia, little facial expression (low muscle tone in oral cavity, cheeks)?

—display gross- and fine-motor incoordination (generalized dyspraxia, "clumsy child" syndrome)?

—have sensory integration dysfunction and self-regulatory issues (difficulty calming himself or herself, for example)?

—use both of his hands (most children exhibit a preference for one hand—"hand dominance"—by age two)?

—come from a family with a history of speech, language, and learning problems?

In this chapter we have given you a crash course on the various speech and language disorders. You are now armed with sufficient information to begin to appreciate whether your child might have a speech disorder instead of a speech delay. In the following chapter we cover the next critical step: how to obtain a professional diagnosis for your child. We explain the roles of the different kinds of specialists you will meet and the kinds of tests they should perform.

4. Meet the Experts: Doctors and Therapists

The secret of the care of the patient is in caring for the patient.
—FRANCIS PEABODY, M.D.

It's time to get an expert opinion. Where do you go to get the answers that you desperately need? What kind of doctor or therapist is best suited for your child? What qualifications should a professional have in order to speak authoritatively about your child's speech problem?

Your first port of call should be your usual "frontline" health contact—your child's primary care professional, normally the pediatrician or pediatric nurse practitioner most familiar with his or her overall health. This practitioner regularly monitors your child even when there are no special concerns, sees the big picture in his or her development, and is generally best positioned to spot any problems and ensure suitable follow-up. Unfortunately, this is not as easy as it sounds, especially in this age of managed care when physicians are rewarded for seeing large numbers of patients and not overreferring to specialists. Quite often, the pediatric practitioner has no more than a fifteen-minute well visit in which to perform a physical exam while offering guidance about eating, sleeping, and safety issues, asking about recent illnesses, administering vaccines, and listening to *your* concerns. It's a daunting task.

Often, unless they have "squeaky wheel" parents, the 25 percent of youngsters who visit primary care practices with developmental issues get short shrift. Even when developmental delays are apparent, some pediatricians don't refer infants and toddlers to a specialist or to the early intervention program. They dismiss parental concerns and make a judgment that given time the child will probably catch up. Sometimes these calls are made by well-meaning physicians who simply do not have enough experience or knowledge about developmental issues to make authoritative judgments. On the other hand, there are frontline pediatricians whose radar goes off when they see a child with communication or other developmental delays. (One thing is for sure: The incidence of communication disorders is on the rise. According to the U.S. Department of Education, during the 1997–1998 school year, 5.4 million children in public schools received services under Part B of the Individuals with Disabilities Education Act. Of these, 1.1 million had treatment for speech and language disorders, a 10.5 percent increase over the previous decade.)

At most well visits, children should receive the benefit of "developmental surveillance and screening" thanks to greater awareness of developmental disabilities as well as research showing how early intervention can change the course of a child's life. Be sure to check that these assessments are done for your child. Medical organizations, including the American Academy of Pediatrics (AAP), have written policy statements emphasizing the need to screen for communication disorders. These expert groups agree that parental concerns are usually well founded and that pediatric practitioners should pay attention to those concerns. Therefore, it's up to you to be proactive in obtaining the right treatment for your child. Mother and father know best! If you have specific concerns, be sure to back them up by taking information to your child's appointments. Ahead of time, write down your observations so that you don't forget anything and so that you can make every minute of your limited time count.

What should you expect when you take your child to the pediatric professional? At every well visit the doctor should ask probing questions to check if your child has age-appropriate developmental skills. He or she should also observe and assess your child's capabilities. Of course, this consumes time that may be in short supply for the busy doctor. That's why parent questionnaires, filled out beforehand either at home or in the waiting room, can be extremely valuable. These questionnaires are a standardized method of assessing your child by comparing him or her to a large group of children of the same age. They are a valuable adjunct to your doctor's experience and clinical judgment, and make the process more objective.

The Ages and Stages Questionnaire (ASQ) screens for developmental delay in youngsters from the ages of four months to five years. Designed to be used at every well visit, it is a series of questions covering each of five developmental areas: communication, gross motor, fine motor, problem solving, and personal-social. There is an additional section where parents can address their concerns. For example, typical communication questions for eighteen-month-olds include, "When your child wants something, does she tell you by pointing to it?" and "Does your child say eight or more words in addition to 'mama' and 'dada'?" The Parents' Evaluation of Developmental Status (PEDS) specifically focuses on the parents' appraisal of the different areas of development. There are other screening tools that a pediatric practitioner can use (like the Denver II), but they need to be administered by a physician or trained assistant.

If your child "fails" a screening by his primary health provider, especially if he has delays in speech, the next important step is to visit an audiologist for a hearing evaluation. Although a hearing impairment at birth is often picked up through newborn screening programs, it's possible that a hearing problem has since developed, which could be the root cause of your child's speech problem. Also, if your child has chronic ear infections with fluid behind the eardrums (otitis media with effusion), he may have a fluctuating hearing loss that could at times affect his ability to hear the differences between sounds. If this is the case, he may need ventilation tubes inserted in his eardrums to drain the fluid.

But let's assume that your child's hearing is fine and is not the reason for the speech delay. What's your next move? If she's developmentally normal in all other areas, you should be referred to a speech-language pathologist for an evaluation. If you or your doctor suspects that your child has other issues besides communication, you should ask for a referral to a neurodevelopmental specialist or a pediatric neurologist. If your child is an infant or toddler, your pediatrician should simultaneously refer her to your local early intervention program where she will receive a multidisciplinary evaluation to see if she is eligible for educational and/or therapeutic services. If she's over the age of three, she should be referred to your school district for a developmental evaluation to see if she requires special services. Also, there is no reason why you cannot approach EI or the school district yourself. We discuss these options in some detail in Chapter 6, "Getting the Help You Need." But first, let's look at the role of the speech pathologist and other therapists who may become an important part of your child's life.

MEET THE THERAPISTS

Your child's principal therapist will probably be a speech-language pathologist, but if your child has associated sensory and motor coordination problems, he may also spend considerable time with an occupational therapist and a physical therapist. These three specialists have the power to make an immense difference in your child's development. It's vital that you understand their different roles and how to evaluate them to ensure they are best suited for your child.

The Speech-Language Pathologist (SLP)

In addition to providing individual therapy for the child, the SLP works closely with your family, the pediatrician, teachers, and other therapists to enhance the benefits of therapy. SLPs who have a graduate degree (a master's or doctorate) and have completed coursework and clinical practice hours from an accredited graduate program can earn a Certificate of Clinical Competence from their national organization, the American Speech-Language-Hearing Association. To do so they must pass a national exam and go through a supervised fellowship year. SLPs are not required to have the certificate, but it is an indication that they have achieved a higher level of qualification. In addition to this national qualification, each state has its own licensing procedure for SLPs.

When you take your child to an SLP for the first time, she asks all about his development to date and tests his receptive and expressive language and speech (articulation) abilities. She listens to voice quality, checking for nasality, resonance, or hoarseness, and evaluates breath support and fluency, including the rate and flow of speech. She also assesses social and play skills. The SLP goes on to perform a physical exam of the lips, tongue, and palate, evaluating how your child is able to move his tongue when asked to lift it, stick it out, move it from side to side, and lick his lips. She gets your child to try to pucker and smile so she can assess lip movements, and she asks him to produce the *aaah* sound to see how well his palate elevates. As part of this process she may observe your child eating. The SLP checks "oral posture"—the ability to keep the lips closed—and she pays attention to the child's ability to control secretions (better known as drooling). There are other tests, too. Will your child allow her to touch his face, lips, tongue, and gums? (Some children with sensory issues are sensitive about being touched on the face and around the oral area. This information helps the therapist plan a program to reduce the child's "oral sensory defensiveness.") The SLP wants to find out what kind of oral muscle tone he has—low (hypotonic), normal, or increased (which is commonly seen in children who have spastic-type cerebral palsy). The SLP also evaluates chewing and swallowing capabilities.

Usually, the SLP uses a "standardized" speech-language test, one with "norms" based on a large sample of typically developing children. This allows the SLP to assess where your child stands compared to other children of his age. Since young children are not always cooperative in sitting through standardized tests, a more informal evaluation through play may be done. You are then given an estimate of your child's standing, based on the SLP's training, knowledge, and experience—her "informed clinical opinion."

Here are the more popular language tests or scales that your SLP may use:

- Rossetti Infant Toddler Language Scale (birth to three years)
- Preschool Language Scale-3 (PLS-3) (birth to six years)

- Clinical Evaluation of Language Functions (CELF)—
  Preschool (three through six years) and CELF-3 (six through
  twenty-one years)
- Receptive One-Word Picture Vocabulary Test (ROWPVT)
  (two through eighteen years)
- Expressive One-Word Picture Vocabulary Test—Revised
  (EOWPVT) (two through twelve years)
- Test of Early Language Development-3 (TELD-3) (two
  through seven years)

Articulation tests use pictures to assess your child's ability to produce consonant sounds. The most common speech-articulation tests
are

- Goldman-Fristoe Test of Articulation (GFTA)
- Photo Articulation Test (PAT)

Two tests designed more specifically to evaluate children with motor
planning disorders are the Kaufman Speech Praxis Test for Children
(KSPT) and the Verbal Motor Production Assessment for Children
(VMPAC). The KSPT is an assessment tool for kids age twenty-four to
seventy-one months. It measures the child's imitative responses, identifying where the child breaks down in her ability to speak, and ranges
from simple sounds to polysyllabic words to spontaneous connected
speech. The VMPAC targets an older age group, three- to twelve-year-
olds, measuring motor speech abilities by first looking at basic processes, like breath support and muscle tone, and then moving to
complex sequencing of syllables.

At your child's examination, the SLP may record or videotape his
level of speech so that she can later take more time to analyze his
expressive language and speech sound errors and more effectively diagnose his condition. Some SLPs may be restricted from making a diagnosis by their employer—a school district, for example—or by law. In
Canada, only pediatric neurologists or developmental pediatricians
are permitted to make the diagnosis of apraxia. But apraxia may be a
difficult diagnosis to obtain no matter where you live. While SLPs are

qualified to diagnose apraxia as part of their "scope of practice," not all of them have the appropriate education, training, and experience to do so, and the criteria for diagnosis are inconsistently applied across the country. If you suspect that your child has apraxia, seek out a speech pathologist with specific training and experience in this disorder. No matter what the reason for your child's speech delay, try to find a local support group and ask other parents to recommend a good SLP.

Physical and Occupational Therapists

Physical therapists (PTs) and occupational therapists (OTs) often become part of the team because many children with severe speech disorders have coexisting coordination and/or sensory motor difficulties. Sometimes the SLP or physician suggests that the services of a PT or an OT would help; sometimes parents themselves initiate the contact. Traditionally, physical therapists are concerned with the child's gross-motor abilities. They use tests of motor function to determine the relative motor developmental skill level of the child. They also look at muscle tone, muscle strength, the persistence of any of the baby reflexes, as well as equilibrium (balance) reactions and mobility—how your child gets from place to place and the quality of her movements.

Your child should be evaluated by an OT if you feel she has any of the sensory processing disturbances discussed earlier. Find someone who has had specialized training in DSI. OTs also play an important role in evaluating and treating children with fine-motor difficulties (including copying shapes, writing, dressing, handling utensils, and so forth) and visual-perceptual (puzzles, mazes, etc.) delays and deficits. The SLP and, quite possibly, the PT and OT may become an integral part of your life—people you see every week and who become friends with your child. Just as vital, although someone your child will see far less frequently, is the medical specialist to whom he or she will be referred if neurological "soft signs" are present, such as hypotonia and motor delays, questionable seizures, or a possible syndrome.

MEET THE DOCTORS

Let's look at the role of the different medical experts and what you can expect of them: the pediatric neurologist, developmental pediatrician, and pediatric physiatrist. A **pediatric neurologist** typically spends two years in a general pediatrics residency and then completes three years of a specialized residency in an accredited child neurology program. A **developmental pediatrician** usually completes a pediatric residency and a fellowship (postgraduate training) in developmental-behavioral pediatrics. Another specialist who diagnoses and treats children with developmental disabilities is the **pediatric physiatrist**, a doctor who is usually board certified in pediatrics and physical medicine and rehabilitation (physiatry). Pediatric physiatrists work closely with physical therapists, occupational therapists, and speech pathologists. Most of them specialize in motor disabilities and also understand feeding and oral-motor difficulties.

VISITING THE DOCTOR

What can you expect when you take your child to one of these specialists? Each begins by obtaining a birth and medical history, looking for clues to a possible neurological cause for your child's developmental disorder. Some physicians may ask you to fill out a questionnaire; others may obtain an oral history. Commonly, there are questions about your pregnancy: Was it full-term? Did you take any medications or drugs? Did you consume alcohol? The doctor will want to know if your child has had frequent ear infections or a serious illness such as meningitis, or if there have been delays or "abnormalities" in sitting, crawling, walking, speech, social, or self-help skills. Have there been any regressions? As speech and language disorders may run in families, the doctor will ask if other relatives have had speech and language delays, dyslexia, or other learning disabilities.

More clues toward a diagnosis come from the physical and neurologic examination. Your doctor should measure your child's height, weight, and head circumference. A small head (microcephaly) or a large head (macrocephaly) compared to other children of the same age can be significant. Microcephaly may be correlated with brain dysfunction. Macrocephaly usually warrants an MRI or CAT scan to rule out anything serious. With macrocephaly, the doctor needs to check the parents to see if big heads run in the family. If they do, this would be an inherited trait and not a cause for concern. There are many syndromes in which head size, certain facial features, and certain skin markings anywhere on the body (neurocutaneous stigmata) are elements. While many children have moles or birthmarks that are of no significance, the pattern, size, and number of markings may alert the specialist to a problem. The neurodevelopmental specialist examines overall muscle tone because benign congenital hypotonia (BCH) may occur in children with apraxia. Muscle strength and coordination are best evaluated dynamically, that is, by watching the child performing activities like lifting his or her arms, throwing a ball, walking on heels and toes, running, and walking up and down stairs.

To be complete, the doctor also checks deep tendon reflexes (DTRs), such as the knee jerk (most children with BCH have essentially normal DTRs). Abnormal DTRs can be seen in a child with high muscle tone (hypertonia), such as in cerebral palsy where the limbs keep beating even after the reflex hammer is removed. At the other extreme, with muscle or nerve disorders, no muscular response will be elicited. The doctor evaluates fine-motor development by watching how your child holds a crayon or pencil and noting how many blocks he or she can stack to build a tower. The doctor observes which hand your child favors when writing or scribbling and throwing a ball. Typically, "hand dominance" is acquired by two years of age. The pediatrician also looks at how your child copies lines and shapes, and whether his or her skills are age-appropriate. For example, three-year-olds are expected to be able to draw a circle.

Information about your child's sensory profile is obtained through questionnaires and observation. Some children are "tactilely defensive," meaning that they don't like to be touched on certain parts of their bodies or exposed to certain textures, while others push their bodies against yours. Others are hyporesponsive and need to be bounced or have deep pressure applied, preferably through the joints ("proprioceptive" input) to get them to respond. Meanwhile, their hyperresponsive counterparts are in constant motion, "bouncing off the walls."

It's not difficult to assess your child's social skills and "pragmatics." Does he make eye contact or "look through you"? Does he play with you or ignore you? While everyone else is excited about a puppy and pointing to it, does he seem uninterested? Some children are shy but warm up over time. The child who raises concerns is the one who just won't let you into his world. It's important that doctors allow parents to observe their child during the evaluation so that they can check if the behavior is typical, or if their son is "just not himself today." All children have off days, especially if they are coming down with a cold or developing an ear infection. In instances like this, to enable the physician to make an adequate assessment, it's useful for him or her to see a videotape of the child in a natural environment, such as the home or the playground.

NONVERBAL CLUES

Actions can sometimes speak just as loudly as words. In evaluating a child with a possible speech disorder, the neurodevelopmental specialist assesses what she *does* as well as what she *says*—or doesn't say. Parents often provide valuable clues by describing how their child seems to have a strong desire to communicate: She uses gestures, eye contact, facial expression, and body language, but no words come forth. Your child may stare and point at the cookie jar to tell you what she wants, perhaps patting her chest, just in case you were not sure who she wanted the cookies for. Or maybe she'll get a book and point to a picture of what she wants.

Most doctors do not conduct as extensive a battery of speech and language tests as a speech pathologist does. Instead, they use pictures, toys, and crayons and paper to assess the child's pretend play and hand grasp. Sometimes, they utilize developmental scales to judge the level at which your child is functioning compared to other children his or her age. These include the Gesell Developmental Schedules—Revised, the Early Language Milestones Scale-2 (ELMS), the Cognitive Adaptive Test/Clinical Linguistic and Auditory Milestone Scale (CAT/CLAMS), and the Lexington Developmental Scale.

The doctor also evaluates *receptive* language, judging how well your child can follow directions, and if he can identify common objects by name and by function: "Show me which of these you use to fix your hair." *Expressive* language is assessed by how well your child can name objects, state his name and age, and express himself in words and phrases. Most doctors gauge your child's intellectual abilities by watching how he plays with toys. Does he have pretend play with purposeful actions, perhaps acting out real-life scenarios? Or does he instead bang his toys, put them in his mouth, or line them up? Such consistent immature play in a toddler or preschooler may be a sign of cognitive delays. Some children on the autistic spectrum, along with a communication delay, may display this type of play behavior as well as inadequate social interactions and stereotypical behaviors such as hand flapping.

Formal cognitive testing is typically performed by a licensed psychologist or neuropsychologist. Make sure that you are referred to one who is familiar with testing nonverbal or unintelligible children and that he or she uses age-appropriate *nonverbal* intelligence tests, such as the Leiter for children two years old and up, the Kaufman Assessment Battery for Children (KABC) for children four years old and older, or the Comprehensive Test of Nonverbal Intelligence (CTONI) for those six and above.

The doctor also documents a sample of your child's functional speech. If she has difficulty imitating words on command, is unable to imitate tongue and/or facial movements, otherwise known as "making funny faces," and has age-appropriate (or close to age-appropriate) receptive language and cognitive abilities, she may be diagnosed as having apraxia.

Some neurologists and developmental pediatricians order laboratory tests to rule out metabolic diseases that can occur in children with a speech delay or hypotonia. Among these are a chromosome analysis for Fragile X (an inherited disorder seen in boys with mental retardation and possible autistic features) and CPK (muscle enzyme). CPK is elevated in some muscle diseases such as muscular dystrophy. Almost certainly, your pediatric practitioner will perform a lead screening because increased lead levels may cause behaviors that resemble developmental delay, autism, or emotional disturbance.

PROBING THE BRAIN

On occasion, a neurologist suggests brain-imaging studies such as MRI. These tests are not routinely conducted unless your child has "focal" neurologic findings, like weakness on one side of the body, or a rapidly enlarging head circumference that could indicate a brain abnormality. Your doctor might order an electroencephalogram (EEG) if your child has had seizures or staring episodes, or if there has been a regression of language skills and/or displays of autisticlike features.

WHICH SPECIALIST?

What kind of specialist is best suited to evaluate *your* late-talking child—a pediatric neurologist or a developmental pediatrician? Take him to a pediatric neurologist if he has a serious neurological history including a seizure disorder, hydrocephalus (abnormal accumulation of fluid in the ventricles of the brain), or progressive muscle weakness causing difficulty climbing and complaints that his legs are tired. This is because the pediatric neurologist's training includes the workup of children who may need brain imaging studies, EEGs to identify a seizure disorder, or electromyography (EMG) to identify a muscle disease. Obviously, such an important decision should be made in consultation with your regular pediatrician.

If your child does not require the know-how of a pediatric neurologist, the choice of medical expert is less critical. You should, however, certainly try to find a developmental pediatrician, pediatric neurologist, or a pediatric physiatrist with expertise in communication disorders. A physiatrist is appropriate if the late talker also has significant motor disability, as with cerebral palsy, or may need orthotics (foot braces).

Take into account your pediatrician's recommendation, those specialists available through your medical plan, and those you have heard about through the grapevine. You may need to talk with the special needs case coordinator at your insurance carrier to get the names of in-network developmental pediatricians or pediatric neurologists, as they may not be clearly listed in your member handbook. Children's hospitals should also be able to recommend good neurodevelopmental pediatricians. Developmental pediatricians tend to look at the "whole child" in the context of the family and discuss all of the developmental domains, feeding and sleep patterns, and behavioral issues. They are able to evaluate children with attention deficit hyperactivity disorder (ADHD) and learning disabilities, and may help you interface with school personnel with regard to your child's special needs in the classroom.

Developmental pediatricians, pediatric physiatrists, and pediatric neurologists vary in training and background. It's important to find the right specialist to get an appropriate diagnosis and investigate the possibility of associated medical or neurological problems.

Getting a neurologic diagnosis with appropriate insurance codes may help you secure private speech therapy, occupational therapy, or physical therapy through your health insurance plan. You may need to ask the specialist to write a "letter of medical necessity" using the correct neurologic codes to get these services. The neurodevelopmental evaluation report may give your child the diagnosis needed to obtain additional early intervention services, or have more "appropriate" education and related services written into your preschooler's services. (How to get these services is covered in Chapter 6, "Getting the Help You Need.") To have the best chance of acquiring services, the report needs to be a comprehensive assessment with diagnoses of apraxia, proximal hypotonia, and sensory integration dysfunction (when present). It should contain a detailed plan and specific recommendations for educational and therapeutic services. An excerpt (the assessment and plan) from a neurodevelopmental evaluation of a child with oral and verbal apraxia can be found in Appendix C. It is an example of the kind of report most likely to secure the type and intensity of services your child needs.

As we have noted, once an official diagnosis has been made, it's essential for your child to get the right kind of therapy from the right kind of therapist. There are many different approaches, and it's important to know that the needs of children with serious speech and language disorders such as apraxia are quite different from those with other speech problems. In the next chapter we review the various treatment approaches that we have found to be most effective for both those children with simple delays in speech and those with speech-language disorders.

5. Unlocking Her Voice: Getting the Right Kind of Therapy

We found an angel who changed our lives forever. That angel was our speech-language pathologist.
—NICOLE CARNELL, mother of four-year-old Justin

It's a lot of hard work for some late-talking children to find their voice. And, for those children with a serious speech disorder, it can be a long, frustrating search that requires patience and persistence. Your child's principal guide will probably be a speech-language pathologist. If your child has a simple speech disorder, the SLP will probably spend just a few half-hour sessions with him or her. If your child has a serious disorder, the SLP may eventually spend hundreds of hours prompting, coaxing, and praising every little word out of him or her. There are many different techniques used by speech pathologists, each with its own legion of advocates. To better understand your options, let's first look at the basic, global approaches used to enhance overall language development. Then we will discuss more specific speech techniques that we have found successful for children with apraxia but that also may be used with a child whose speech is compromised and who cannot make himself or herself understood.

The basic aim of speech therapy, of course, is to improve the acquisition of speech—in other words, to boost speech for the late-talking child instead of "letting nature take its course." The first basic step in speech therapy is to get your child to focus and pay attention. Step two is to create opportunities for speaking by manipulating the environment, so that toys and equipment are engaging and conducive to encouraging a verbal response. For example, a model farm is ideal for working on bilabial (lip) sounds *m* for *moo* and *a* and *b* for *baa*. Third, the child should be rewarded for his or her efforts. Some therapists use food treats such as lollipops, gummy bears, and pretzels; others use stickers, small toys, and stamps; and others add stars to a success chart to acknowledge continued improvement. All use praise, which is probably the most important reward of all.

The two key strategies commonly employed by SLPs are the "directive" and "naturalistic" intervention techniques. **Directive** interventions demand frequent practice sessions targeting specific approximations of individual words and combinations of words at varying degrees of difficulty. In a directive approach, the therapist directs the treatment using modeling and prompting. For instance, the SLP names an object and then prompts the child to repeat the name of the object: "ball, say 'ball.'" **Naturalistic** approaches are usually more fun, as the SLP uses items the child enjoys, such as bubbles or puppets, to encourage specific sounds or words. While this can look like play, the therapist sets goals for the child to achieve. An example of the naturalistic approach is the clinician getting the child to blow bubbles by repeatedly saying "pop" and urging him to imitate her. This gamelike activity not only provides the right setting to work on the lip sound *p*, it also builds air pressure in the oral cavity and the breath support for blowing.

One popular naturalistic model, the Hanen approach, teaches parents how to use daily routines and natural environments, like the home, playground, or day care center, as vehicles for eliciting verbal responses. When you think about how many hours a day you spend with your child, it makes perfect sense for you to become the primary facilitator of your child's speech. This family-centered program gets grandparents and siblings involved as well. Rather than talk to your two-year-old in sentences, you learn to observe, wait, and listen for communication signals. Researchers monitoring a group of children from two to three years found that this approach was successful in increasing vocabulary size, sentence length, and social interactions. The Hanen strategy is most beneficial for children who are language-delayed and don't have other delays, although it also offers a program for parents of children with an autistic spectrum disorder.

A therapy program needs to be individualized for each child. There isn't a one-size-fits-all master plan. The SLP structures the treatment with input from the rest of the team, possibly the OT, PT, special educator, developmental pediatrician, or pediatric neurologist. For a child with a motor speech disorder such as apraxia, or apraxia combined with dysarthria, the following techniques are particularly appropriate. But they may be applied to *any* child who needs some assistance to "use his or her words" (low verbal output), or who has trouble making himself or herself understood (reduced intelligibility). The traditional articulation approaches that just require a child to "look and listen" to a speech model, typically the SLP, are not always successful for the child with a complex motor speech disorder.

The speech therapies fall into three broad categories: touch-cue (tactile-kinesthetic), rhythm and melody, and oral-motor. Children diagnosed with apraxia benefit from a multisensory approach. Therapy that focuses on encouraging sounds only through auditory and visual cues is probably good enough for children with phonological or simple "articulation" delays, but it is certainly not sufficient for those with severe speech disorders. If children can see, hear, *and feel* sounds, they progress faster. So let's look at these important methods.

SPEECH THERAPY METHODS

Touch- and Gestural-Cueing Approach

One key technique is known as PROMPT, an acronym for "Prompts for Restructuring Oral Muscular Phonetic Targets." In this method, the SLP applies pressure at specific places on the face, lips, and chin, and in doing so forms the child's features into the shapes that are made to create different sounds. By physically guiding the child through the necessary muscle movements for speech, he or she receives sensory motor feedback and develops "memory" about how the sound is produced. Tactile information is extremely important for learning speech, and this gives children with apraxia the feeling of how the sound is produced and a sense of the timing of speech. PROMPT also makes sure that the learning is interactive (including turn-taking) and is gamelike or activity based. When a child is not making progress with a "look at me and say what I say" technique, PROMPT is the way to go. The problem is finding a speech therapist trained and certified in the PROMPT system, as they are in demand and often have long waiting lists.

Other SLPs have adapted gestural cueing techniques, using hand signals near their mouths to give additional cues to the child. The hand motions are usually borrowed from the manual signs used by the hearing impaired, or the hand shapes may reflect how that sound is made. For example, the SLP may run her finger across her lips for the *m* sound, which is made with the lips pressed together, thereby cueing the child to press his or her lips together. Therapists use a variety of cueing systems that do not require special training and that you can learn with your child. *Easy Does It for Apraxia—Preschool*, part of the Easy Does It series of therapy books for voice, apraxia, articulation, and fluency, promotes hand signals as part of its recommended system. It is a step-by-step workbook program with structured lessons and activities that provide a predictable routine for the child. Hand signals parallel the sound productions. For example, the *t* sound is made by tapping the index finger on the top lip as you say "t." Whatever method you choose for your child, it's important that everyone who works with him or her uses the same gestures, to avoid confusion.

Rhythmic and Melodic Intonation Approach

What child doesn't like to sing and clap hands? The enjoyment of moving to the beat is inherently human. Melodic methods are employed to slow down or speed up the rate of speech, aid the child's ability to sequence syllables by combining clapping or marching with each syllable, or teach where to place the stress in a word. Young children are more tuned in and cooperative when movement is incorporated into their speech programs. Some examples are

- clapping while saying a sequence of sounds or singing a rhyme or song
- bouncing a ball in rhythm with syllables or words
- touching pictures or words as you say them
- walking on footprints, one step for each word

Combining rhythm and movement is a natural activity for young children, and no special training is required for the SLP. One particular technique that uses singing to foster speech—melodic intonation therapy (MIT)—was first used with adult stroke patients. Adapted for apraxic children, it is part of a total communication approach that incorporates sign language.

Oral-Motor Therapy

Many children with serious speech disorders have an oral-muscle weakness, which probably first came to light as a feeding problem, accompanied by a protruding tongue, open mouth, or drooling. Children with an oral-motor disorder such as oral apraxia have trouble imitating and initiating nonspeech movements like licking lips, smiling, making funny faces, and blowing kisses. For these kids, a program of oral-motor therapy strengthens the muscles of the tongue, lips, and jaw to improve eating, drinking, and clarity of speech. Oral-motor therapy also aids the child who has sensory motor feedback deficits—one who stuffs his mouth. In therapy he learns to feel small amounts of food placed in his mouth, increasing his oral sensory awareness. Exercises to improve oral-motor skills include blowing bubbles, whistles, and toy horns; using a lollipop or lip gloss to stimulate awareness of licking and lip closure; and offering textured foods like gummy bears, dried fruit, or taffy to improve the child's chewing pattern. We provide many suggestions for exercises that parents can do with their kids in the next chapter, "What Parents Can Do to Help."

BUILDING A VOCABULARY

One of the SLP's first tasks is to develop a core vocabulary for your child. This is an integral part of the Kaufman Speech Praxis Treatment Approach, an excellent method that promotes the early establishment of a core vocabulary, consisting of a few functional words like *mama, up, more*, and *me* that are practiced until they become part of your child's "motor memory." Your therapist should provide you and your child with a speech book with exercises, drills, and games as part of your home program. Core words are put into this notebook. By teaching your child that it is okay to use approximations like *wawa* for *water, ba* for *ball*, or *nana* for *banana*, she comes to understand how to say words that she may have been avoiding because she did not know how to simplify them. There are kits with picture cards explaining the Kaufman method that can be used by professionals or by parents at home. Repetition, repetition, repetition is essential for a child with a speech disorder so that the learning of new speech sounds becomes a habit. Once your child has built a core vocabulary of single words, she can move on to word pairs. The goal is to expand the length of the word strings and the word order to produce "kernel sentences"—basic root sentences covering everyday essentials that your child can readily employ at home, at school, or at the playground.

Some therapists believe in getting a late talker to learn sounds in the same order as his typically developing verbal peers—starting with vowels, lip sounds (*p, b, m*), tongue tip sounds (*t, d, n*), up to the more difficult sibilants (*s, z*). This is known as an executive program, building from the bottom up, starting with individual consonant sounds and then combining them with vowels. Therapists call these combinations consonant-vowel (CV), like *ma,* and work their way to vowel-consonant (VC), as in *am,* CVC as in *mom,* and CVCV as in *mama.* An experienced therapist does not necessarily follow this hierarchy of sound development but uses the sounds your child can already produce as a jumping-off point. As your child develops more vocabulary and more precision in the production of sounds, the therapist may move toward more of a planning focus, a language approach to expand on the syllables and

words that have been learned. Phrases like *I want* _____ and *Give me*
_____ are used over and over to increase the use of phrases and sentences while working on particular sounds and syllables. As your child develops more word approximations, the clinician can teach word combinations and early grammatical forms: for example, *eat* _____ (e.g., *apple*), *mommy* _____ (e.g., *kiss*), and *daddy* _____ (e.g., *car*). As your child learns to use a greater variety of early grammatical structures, including the use of pronouns, prepositions, and question forms, the therapist can work on short dialogues with him, like saying, "Hi, I'm Tommy. What's your name?" and "What's that?"

The expertise of the speech therapist can make all the difference in the world, but there are also some very effective tools that can facilitate speech development, generally known as augmentative and alternative communication approaches (AAC). Many people think of AAC as high-tech electronic devices or speech synthesizers, but the field also encompasses low-tech approaches such as sign language and picture exchange communication.

AAC APPROACHES

The Case for Sign Language

There has been considerable debate over the merits of teaching sign language to nonverbal children. Some parents believe that it takes away from the primary goal of getting their child to become vocal. Their fear is that the child will become dependent on sign language and unmotivated to acquire speech. Most speech experts are totally in favor of the introduction of signing as early as possible because it helps build vocabulary, reduces frustration, and expands expressive language. Research indicates that signing is a stepping-stone—and a very important one—on the way to speech. As the child's ability to vocalize increases, signing falls by the wayside. The signs are not an alternative to speech, but a method of helping the child *discover* speech.

Sign language can be simple or complex. Most late-talking children develop their own sign language, which is understood by their immediate family and should be encouraged so they develop enough key signs to make their basic needs known. Nicole Carnell told us that when her son, Justin, was two and a half years old and still saying only one or two words, he and his parents learned how to sign. "He picked it up very fast and his demeanor quickly changed. Now that he had a way to communicate, he was becoming a happy, carefree child," she remembers. "I cried the night I walked into his room and saw him signing in his sleep." Beyond late talkers there is even a growing movement to teach sign language or "symbolic gesturing" to all babies, so they can communicate at an earlier age than has been considered the norm.

Picture Exchange Communication System (PECS)

Another nonverbal mode of communication is picture exchange, in which illustrations are used instead of words. All your child has to do is point at a picture icon to make herself understood. At its most simple, you put together a book of picture symbols for your child to carry with her. You let her decide the contents. One page can be for breakfast items, another page for lunch, one for dinner, one for drinks and desserts, and so forth. You can have pages of faces showing different feelings and pages for activities such as reading a book, going to the park or the library, visiting relatives, friends, or the doctor, and going to the bathroom!

There are many places to find pictures. On-line grocery stores like www.netgrocer.com are ideal for food items, as are the Sunday newspaper's coupon section and magazines. You can take photos, or purchase picture cards from a number of sources. If you wish, laminate the pictures to protect and strengthen them; glue food and drink choices onto self-adhesive magnets and attach them to your refrigerator. But there's more to PECS than having a picture for a glass of orange juice. It begins with the basic lesson that to get a favorite item, your child needs to hand over a picture of it. Your child is then taught to create simple "sentences," such as "I want cookie." From there, he learns to add clarity by using attributes that describe size, shape, position, and color. He also discovers how to respond to simple questions, such as "What do you want?" before learning how to use the pictures to comment about things around him: "I see a train!" "I hear a bird!" Many parents (and some professionals) share the same concern expressed about sign language, namely, that using a picture system inhibits speech development. But there is no evidence of a negative outcome and there is compelling support for the proposition that PECS encourages speech.

High-Tech AAC

For children with extremely serious speech disorders, you may need to step into the high-tech world. High-tech AAC is a specialized field and, as each child has his own abilities and needs, each requires an evaluation by an SLP with appropriate expertise. If your child's SLP feels that a high-tech device is appropriate, she can put you in touch with an AAC technology expert. Cost, however, can be a barrier. Models such as the Dynavox and Liberator cost more than seven thousand dollars, although schools, insurance, and even Medicaid will sometimes pay. High-tech devices have digitized speech capability, allowing the nonverbal child to state his needs by pushing a button. They enable the user to give a simple one-word message or engage in full discourse.

Mauri Blefeld shared her AAC experience with us. She started her son, Arie, with signs and gestures before moving on to the picture exchange system. Then they used small voice-output devices that were too limiting, until they turned to a high-tech Dynamyte that they've had for almost five years. Says Mauri, "All these tools and strategies have really helped Arie along. They have enabled him to communicate and participate academically in school. In fact, now that he is more verbal, he is more reluctant to use the Dynamyte because, let's face it, speech is more natural." Adds Mauri, "AAC will only enhance your child's life and yours. He will be less frustrated and you will get to know your child better. It gives him more control over life's experience."

SCIENTIFICALLY VALIDATED INTERVENTION

There are two programs that have been carefully validated through controlled research trials for use with language learning impairments (LLI). Both incorporate intensive intervention and in the long run are cost-effective compared with traditional one-on-one therapy.

The first program is Fast ForWord Language, developed as a short-term intervention that builds foundational language processing skills. It is based on over thirty years of research into the neural basis of developmental language disorders and neuroplasticity, the capacity of the human brain to remodel itself for improved processing efficiency.

Controlled studies have been conducted in over two thousand labs, schools, and clinics across the United States. They have demonstrated that after training two hours a day for six to eight weeks, children with specific language impairment and auditory processing disorders show one-and-a-half- to two-year gains in both language and processing skills.

Dr. Paula Tallal, professor of neuroscience at Rutgers University, explains that the program uses computers that individually adapt, trial-by-trial, to the specific needs of each child based on a child's ongoing performance on each training exercise. In this way, the child can get precisely the stimulation he or she needs to make rapid advances. Recently, a Stanford University study using functional brain imaging revealed that the program rewires brain regions that are inactive in children and adults with reading difficulties. Most researchers agree that these brain regions are critical to phonological awareness.

The other program backed up by brain research is the Lindamood Phoneme Sequencing Program (LiPS), developed by the Lindamood-Bell organization. This program trains the child to *feel* the sound while saying it. For example, "p" is a "lip popper" because the lips start together and then come apart. The child is trained to recognize the sensory feedback of how sounds are produced, so that as well as seeing and hearing them he has an additional way of recognizing the letter sounds.

MULTISENSORY TECHNIQUES

Many parents of children with communication disorders look beyond "conventional" therapies and embrace a variety of alternative multisensory techniques. Their rationale is that stimulating different areas of the brain can compensate for a malfunctioning area. It may be worthwhile to explore some of them as a supplement to traditional therapy.

One of these treatments is Auditory Integration Training (AIT), which involves testing a child's hearing and noting the frequencies where it's found to be more sensitive. Another treatment, the Tomatis method, primarily uses the music of Mozart and Gregorian chants. These sound-based therapies are gaining popularity with claims of improved auditory processing of speech and language and improved learning abilities. More research is needed to back up these claims.

GETTING THE RIGHT THERAPY

From academic, social, psychological, and financial standpoints, getting early therapy makes sense. Getting *the right kind* of early therapy is of paramount importance, especially for children who are diagnosed with apraxia, because they do not respond to the traditional speech therapy methods. They do not benefit from group therapy. They need more intensive and more frequent therapy than children with other speech problems. They need intensive one-on-one sessions at least three times a week. Generally, the more frequent the better, and they need it consistently, week after week. If they take a break, they are likely to regress. Children with apraxia do not "grow out of it." Some school districts try to save money by delivering speech therapy in a group setting, but this is not sufficient for a nonverbal or severely apraxic child. You need to agitate to get more therapy provided and also be prepared to fill in the gaps with either private therapy sessions or by consistently working the drills with your child. To make consistent progress there is no substitute for daily practice. Frequent short sessions are more useful than longer less frequent sessions.

Penelope Hall of the University of Iowa says, "Experience has shown that children with developmental apraxia of speech progress slowly in the treatment process. Because of this, these children need treatment sessions that provide intense training several times a week. Even so, you can probably expect your child to need a great deal of therapy, extended over a number of years." And Professor William H. Perkins of the University of Southern California urges that the condition receive "all-out attention." Perkins makes an analogy that we particularly like. He points out that when children begin going to school, they do not attend two or three times a week for just a half hour at a time, even in kindergarten. Similarly, special education for children with developmental apraxia of speech needs to be intensive and frequent, for it may be the most important part of their entire education.

And it's an education that may continue for a long time. Therapy is not a quick fix. Children with apraxia need many years of treatment, according to most experts. Penelope Hall, based on her experience following children with apraxia into their mid-twenties, says that the disorder needs to be thought of as a "lifelong communication problem" and that the hope of "attainment of totally 'normal' speech skills may be unrealistic." Perhaps the best evidence, however, comes from Thomas F. Campbell, Ph.D., director of communication disorders at the University of Pittsburgh. In a study comparing the intensity of speech treatment for children with a phonological deficit and those with apraxia, the apraxic children required 81 percent more individual treatment sessions in order to achieve the same results. In the study of sixty children, average age four years, parents were asked to rate how much of their child's speech an unfamiliar listener could understand. To get the phonologically disordered children understood three quarters of the time required an average of twenty-nine individual forty-five-minute sessions. To get the apraxic children to the same level necessitated an average of 151 individual sessions.

FINDING THE RIGHT THERAPIST

Finding the right therapy for any late talker can be a challenge. Finding the appropriate therapy for a child who may have apraxia can be a *major* challenge. Sometimes the biggest hurdle is locating a qualified SLP capable of recognizing apraxia and who knows the techniques and intensive program to implement. If you are dependent on your child receiving therapy through the public school system, you need to closely monitor the situation and follow the advice that we give in the next chapter, "Getting the Help You Need."

Typically, school speech therapists have too many children to handle. In spite of ASHA's recommendations that the maximum caseload should not exceed forty students, many SLPs find themselves working with sixty or more kids. One former therapist in the Florida school system complained on an Internet list that she had had a caseload of 180 kids! (Which explains why she was a *former* school therapist.) In addition to state-funded or school-based therapy, you should really endeavor to obtain private one-on-one therapy for your child, and try to have your insurance carrier pay for it. Another option is to investigate universities that have a speech and hearing department. They often offer supervised speech therapy sessions with graduate students for a nominal charge.

What are the hallmarks of a good, "on the ball" therapist? You want someone who has a genuine interest in your child and has a rapport with her, someone who sets measurable goals for her to achieve and is enthusiastic about her progress. The therapist should listen to your input and value it. You don't want an SLP with a know-it-all attitude because, when it comes to your child, there's plenty that you know. You do want an SLP who communicates with you and is happy to give you "homework" to do with your child to supplement her therapy. As one parent put it, "If you find a great therapist, you will know it. You will actually look forward to the sessions along with your child." It's important for you, your SLP, and any other therapists on your child's team to reassess goals and techniques if progress comes to a halt. Sometimes it pays to bite the bullet and switch to another SLP, who may have success with a different approach.

Make sure your SLP realizes that speech treatment involves the whole child and is not restricted to the mouth alone. Speech begins below the neck! You have to breathe right to speak right, and upright positioning is necessary for the respiratory support of speech. The SLP should be able to recognize if your child has underlying hypotonia in his or her trunk. Children with motor planning difficulties benefit from gross-motor activities prior to their speech sessions. You also want the SLP to collaborate with the other professionals in your child's life, especially his or her physical and occupational therapists.

THE ROLE OF THE PHYSICAL THERAPIST AND OCCUPATIONAL THERAPIST

Children with severe speech disorders frequently have coexisting coordination and/or sensory motor difficulties. Coordination is impacted by gross-motor (large muscle) and fine-motor (small muscle) development, and by muscle tone. As we have noted, speech does not begin at the mouth but is affected by our posture, which affects the breath stream used for speaking. This is where the physical therapists and occupational therapists become part of the team.

Traditionally, physical therapists are concerned with gross-motor abilities. They use tests of motor function to determine the relative motor developmental skill level of your child and identify skills that are not completely developed. We are not going to cover specific therapeutic interventions in any detail, but the goals related to speech production include improving truncal muscle tone using a therapy ball or trampoline, and muscle strengthening. All enhance postural stability. When it comes to muscle tone and posture, there is some overlap between the function of the physical therapist and the occupational therapist. Whereas the PT focuses on gross motor, the OT plays an important role in evaluating and treating children with fine-motor difficulties (including copying shapes, writing, dressing, handling utensils, and so forth) and visual-perceptual (puzzles, mazes, etc.) delays and deficits. If your child has any of the sensory processing disturbances discussed earlier, find an OT who has had specialized training in this field. Treatment is fun and usually takes place in a sensory-enriched gym with swings, balls, and mats. Most OTs also develop a home program that can become part of your daily activities.

When an OT talks about a *sensory diet* for your child, he or she is referring to a combination of alerting, organizing, and calming activities. *Alerting* activities benefit the underresponsive, sensory-seeking child who needs to be aroused, and may include eating crunchy foods (like popcorn or pretzels), bouncing on a therapy ball, or jumping in a ball pit or on a trampoline. *Organizing* activities help regulate the child's responses. Examples are hanging from a chin-up bar and pushing or pulling a heavy load. *Calming* activities help the oversensitive, sensory-avoiding child reduce the hypersensitivity to sensory stimuli. This may take the form of slowly rocking the child, brushing over the skin, or wrapping him or her in a blanket and giving firm hugs. A growing number of OTs (and other professionals) are also incorporating therapeutic listening programs, using electronically altered CDs to help children improve attention, self-regulation, and behavior.

So what is the ideal speech program? In considering therapy, the following general principles should be borne in mind for all late talkers.

- Speech therapy should be individualized for each child's specific needs.
- There is not one single type of intervention that is best for all children.
- Frequency of therapy depends on the severity of the communication delay.
- Specific short-term and long-term goals need to be developed and measurable, with outcomes that are drawn up consistent with the parents' concerns. (For instance, the long-term goal might be: Johnny will speak in three-word sentences 80 percent of the time. The short-term goal might be: Johnny will use *I want* _____ as a carrier phrase to express his wants and needs 80 percent of the time.)
- There must be ongoing monitoring and modification of therapy depending upon whether the child is progressing.
- Parents need to be taught specific techniques for how to speak to their child and how to elicit responses.

For a child two years or older with a severe disorder such as apraxia, our recommendations include

- therapy that is intensive and frequent
- individual, not group, therapy
- repetitive practice to make motor learning of speech more automatic
- a progressive systematic approach from word approximations to target words and phrases, such as the Kaufman Method
- a multisensory therapy method, incorporating auditory, visual, tactile, and movement cues
- use of rhythms, rhymes, and melodies combined with movement
- use of a total communication approach
- emphasis on postural control
- oral-motor therapy techniques when there is muscle weakness, sensory or motor planning dysfunction of the lips, tongue, jaw, or palate
- a multidisciplinary team approach for children who have associated hypotonia, sensory integration dysfunction, global dyspraxia (motor planning disorder), and other neurologic problems

We're often asked what a typical week of therapy is for a child with apraxia—and the answer is that there is no such thing. Each individual has to deal with a unique set of circumstances. But we can give you a general idea by peeking inside an average week for Lisa and her son, Tanner, when he was three years old. You'll find this in Appendix A.

GOING FORWARD

Finding the right therapists and the right therapy is of prime importance. If your child has a serious speech problem, the therapists will become a fixture in your world for many years, so you need to be sure that they are ideal for your child. Free therapy is available under federal legislation and private therapy may also be covered by your insurance carrier. However, they're not automatically provided, and you may have to fight to get the quality and frequency of therapy that your child deserves. All of the information provided in this book so far, including details about speech disorders, warning signs to consider, visiting specialists, and the right kind of therapy, has given you a firm knowledge base. Now you have information on which to act and which, if necessary, will help you fight the system on your child's behalf. The mechanics of putting that to work and taking on the school and the insurance company is the subject of the next chapter.

6. Getting the Help You Need

As a parent of a nonspeaking child it is up to you to be his voice.
—KAREN D. ROTHWEILER, mother of three-year-old Justin

Know your rights. Know your child's rights. One of the greatest challenges faced by parents of children with speech delays is making sure that their kids get the assistance they deserve. Parents often find they have to fight their way through a bureaucratic maze on at least two fronts. On the one hand, you may encounter an educational system that's not geared to meet the needs of a nonverbal child. On the other hand, you may find that your health insurance company refuses to pay for the intensive therapy your child must have. You may have to be tenacious. You may have to fight tooth and nail. You may have to learn more than you care to know about the minutiae of the law. But it's your child, and if you're not going to be his or her number one advocate, who will?

In this chapter, we give you an essential step-by-step guide: how to acquire early intervention, how to handle the school system, and how to overcome insurance company roadblocks. While much of this information is useful for parents of children with speech delays, it is essential reading for parents of children with apraxia and other moderate to severe speech disorders. Let's start with education. Under the law, your child is entitled to a "free and appropriate public education" (FAPE). The Individuals with Disabilities Education Act (IDEA) guarantees a public education to every child, age three through twenty-one, in need of special education services. Public schools must provide services in the "least restrictive environment," and must create and implement an Individualized Education Program (IEP) specifically designed to meet each child's needs. This program is usually called a "preschool disabled program."

In addition to the educational component, the IEP must include "related services" such as speech, physical, and occupational therapies. It also covers the provision of transportation, augmentative communication devices, and counseling services. As the U.S. Department of Education's Office of Special Education and Rehabilitative Services puts it: "Each IEP must be designed for one student and must be a truly individualized document. . . . The IEP is the cornerstone of a quality education for each child with a disability." Amendments to IDEA, passed in 1986, extended the legislation to provide early intervention services for children from birth through the age of three.

EARLY INTERVENTION

If your child is under the age of three and you're concerned about his development, obtain an evaluation through your local early intervention program. *Any* child suspected of having a delay in *any* aspect of development is entitled to an evaluation to see if he is entitled to special education services. To be eligible for services, children must have a disability or established delay in physical, cognitive, communication, social-emotional, or self-help development. For the purposes of EI, a developmental delay is documented as a 33 percent delay in one area of development or a 25 percent delay in each of two areas of development. For example, a twenty-four-month-old month toddler would qualify for services if he was functioning at the sixteen-month level in communication ability or at an eighteen-month level in both communication and physical (motor) areas. EI, also known as the Birth to Three program, is family centered. Parental consent is required for an evaluation, and parents are part of the process of establishing goals and monitoring outcomes of treatment. In some states, the program is free; in other states there may be a sliding scale of costs depending on your income.

Unfortunately, many children with speech disorders never have the opportunity to benefit from early intervention because their parents listen to the standard advice to "wait until he's a little older." Our advice: Contact EI as soon as you're seriously concerned about your child's ability to communicate. There is no age that's too young for referral to EI. The Clinical Clues table on pages 7–10 gives guidance on appropriate warning signs. (Quite often, preschool teachers or day care personnel alert parents if they suspect a problem.) Ask your pediatrician for a referral, or call EI yourself. You can find your state's EI coordinator through the National Early Childhood Technical Assistance System, www.nectas.unc.edu/contact/ptccoord.asp, or your local Department of Health.

Early Intervention services are usually provided in natural environment, which may be the child's home, the day care center, or the playground. Services vary from state to state, but no matter where you live the initial evaluation will probably be conducted in your own home. Although your entire focus might be on your child's speech delay, EI programs perform a full multidisciplinary evaluation. The professionals test your child's ability to communicate and perform gross- and fine-motor tasks, as well as evaluate cognitive, self-help, and social, behavioral, and emotional skills.

If your child does not qualify for services, ask how the speech and language assessment tests were scored. Make sure that the evaluator did not average the receptive and expressive language scores. It's possible that your child has age-appropriate auditory comprehension (receptive language) but significant speech and expressive language delays. Averaging the scores artificially inflates the overall communication score and could disqualify your nonverbal child from EI services. For example, if your thirty-six-month-old's receptive language is typical for his age, but he has a twelve-month delay in expressive language, the average of the two scores (thirty-six and twenty-four) brings him to thirty months, which may disqualify him from services. If services are declined, you have the option of getting a second opinion from a private therapist. If you cannot obtain free EI services and you feel that your child needs therapy, you will have to obtain this through medical insurance or pay yourself. If cost is an issue, approach subsidized programs such as Easter Seals or Scottish Rite, or check out clinics at teaching hospitals or universities, as they may offer services at reduced fees.

After the EI evaluation, the multidisciplinary team writes a report about your child's developmental status. If your child is found eligible for services, your service coordinator, a member of the evaluation team, an EI representative (early intervention official designee—EIOD), and you meet to develop an Individual Family Service Plan (IFSP), which describes your concerns, priorities, resources, and desired outcomes for your child. States vary with regard to the extent of delay that warrants EI services and the amount of therapy they provide. Typically, you can expect to get two hours of therapy a week, which is not enough for a child later diagnosed as apraxic. If that's all you can obtain, ask for it to be divided over four days, as more frequent, shorter sessions are best for apraxics.

Because it has been designed by experts, is based on solid research, and fully involves families, EI stands a good chance of enhancing your child's development and improving his or her chances of educational success. If you disagree with the findings of your child's evaluation team or the IFSP, in most states you can request a second evaluation or exercise your right to mediation or an impartial hearing.

PLAN AHEAD

When your child is three years old, whether she was in early intervention through the state or not, she may qualify to enter the school system's Individualized Education Program, in which you and a team of experts agree on the quantity and quality of service she will receive. This is an essential right and key to ensuring that she receives at no cost the kind of education that she specifically needs. But don't wait until her third birthday to request services. When she's two and a half, call your school district and request an evaluation. This way you won't miss a day of services. If she's been receiving therapy through EI, they can help with the transition. As with the IFSP, special education laws vary from state to state. The U.S. Department of Education has a fifty-page "Guide to the Individualized Education Program" that emphasizes that the creation of an effective and unique IEP requires parents, teachers, school administrators, and specialists working together as a team. It can be downloaded from www.ed.gov/offices/OSERS/ OSEP/Products/IEP_Guide/.

IDENTIFYING THE CHILD

The state is responsible for finding and evaluating all children with disabilities who need special education. Referrals to this Child Find system can come from the school or from the parents. When a school initiates the process, it has to give you written notice and a detailed explanation of the procedural safeguards available to you. If you feel that the educational needs of your child are not being met, you can begin the process by asking the school for a testing referral. The school district is given "reasonable time" to review all relevant records and agree or disagree that the student is a candidate for evaluation. The time period varies from state to state but is generally around twenty days.

GETTING CONSENT

The school must obtain parental consent before conducting an initial evaluation and placing your child in special education services. You can always withdraw your consent. On the other hand, the school, once it provides services, cannot stop providing all services because you don't approve of one specific component. The last uncontested IEP remains in place.

EVALUATING THE CHILD

Your child will be evaluated by each member of a team of professionals—the Child Study Team (CST). Usually, there is a psychologist, educational specialist, social worker, SLP, and PT and/or OT if needed.

When your child is going to be evaluated, investigate the whole procedure. Ask to speak with the person who will do the evaluation. Ask exactly what it will involve, what kind of testing and evaluation tools will be used, and how long it will last. Also find out who will be there, what their roles will be, and what their qualifications are. Tell them politely yet firmly that you do not want your child evaluated without being present. Assure them that you will be as helpful as they want and participate only as much as they want—otherwise you will be an unobtrusive presence. You are the person most familiar with your child's abilities and best able to advise if the skills, attitude, and behavior he or she is exhibiting are typical or otherwise. You are also best able to make your child feel safe and secure.

If you disagree with the outcome of the evaluation, you can insist on an Independent Educational Evaluation (IEE) to be paid for by the school system. A group of qualified professionals and you review the evaluation results. If it's decided that your child does not meet IDEA's "child with a disability" requirements, you have the right to appeal.

PREPARING FOR THE IEP MEETING

Seek Outside Evaluations

Regardless of whether you ask the school to test your child's ability or the school initiates the process, it's a good idea to seek private evaluations from respected and knowledgeable medical, speech, and educational professionals. Obtain written statements from them outlining your child's diagnosis as well as his or her educational and therapeutic needs. These professionals can not only help you advocate for appropriate therapy, they can also help oversee and track your child's ongoing progress. Sometimes the school agrees to accept these private evaluations rather than conduct its own.

1. Speech evaluation: If it's financially feasible, get the opinions of an expert SLP separate from the early intervention SLP and the school's SLP. An evaluation from someone respected for working with children with severe language disorders will

prove to be a worthwhile investment. You need the SLP to write a report that states the severity of your child's condition, recommendations for one-on-one therapy, and how many sessions are required each week. It should also be pointed out that children with severe delays in speech, such as apraxia, do not respond to typical speech therapy and require an SLP skilled in oral-motor therapy, PROMPT, or other touch-cue, multisensory methods.

2. Medical evaluation: You may want to find a developmental pediatrician and/or child neurologist who recognizes and understands the nature of the various communication disorders and the neurological soft signs that may accompany them. Have the doctor write a report recommending the type and frequency of therapy required for your child. This is the most powerful ammunition that you can muster, especially if your child has a neurological disorder and not a delay. Combined with a speech therapist's opinion, a letter from your developmental pediatrician or neurologist stating that your child has x condition, requiring y sessions of individual therapy per week is hard to ignore. Even more persuasive is a statement from the experts (in their own words, of course, and if it is accurate in your child's case) that his or her prognosis is bleak if he or she does not receive the therapy they recommend.

3. Other evaluations: If appropriate, obtain evaluations from a private occupational or physical therapist and a pediatric neuropsychologist.

Matrix Matters

An excellent guide to the amount of therapy appropriate for each child—depending on the severity of his or her condition—is the Illinois State Board of Education's Severity Intervention Matrix. Even though this was created to help school-based SLPs, it is useful to show this to your private professionals *before* their evaluations are written. You'll find the matrix in Appendix D.

Getting Services

Once it is agreed that your child is eligible for services, the Individualized Education Program team must meet within thirty days to write their plan. The school staff has to set up the meeting at a time and place agreeable to the parents. Parents need to be told who else will be present as well as given an opportunity to have their own experts attend.

Equal Footing

You're a valuable member of the IEP team and have equal input. Ask for copies of the child study team evaluation reports at least a week before the meeting. Ask any outside professionals you've recruited to interpret test scores or any language you don't understand. Some schools prepare a draft IEP ahead of the meeting to use as a "working" document. Ask for a copy in advance so that you have time to study it and prepare any counterproposals.

E-Help

Don't underestimate the power of the Internet when getting ready for an IEP meeting. There are on-line groups on Yahoo whose sole topic of conversation is the vagaries of the IEP system, and there are many Web sites offering guidance. If you have an official diagnosis for your child's speech impairment, find reliable Web sites (such as those listed in the Resources section of this book) and download relevant information about it to present to the IEP meeting.

Legal Help

If you have serious concerns about the school's desire or ability to provide necessary services, take legal advice from a special education attorney. If nothing else, this will give you added knowledge and confidence. Sometimes you can get a free or low-cost consultation, or even have a simple question answered by phone or E-mail.

AT THE IEP MEETING

Strength in Numbers

The school team and parents meet to work out the contents of the IEP, which establishes annual goals describing what your child can reasonably be expected to achieve within a year. Don't go to the meeting alone. You may face a lineup of school personnel including a teacher, speech-language therapist, occupational therapist, case manager, and others, which can be quite intimidating. It's always better if husbands and wives can attend together to present a united front and to show how important you regard the meeting and your child's well-being. You can also find an advocate, ask your private therapist to attend, or get a friend to tag along for moral support (and to take notes).

Tape-Record

An "official" record of the meeting will be important if you find yourself in a dispute with the school. Don't be afraid to tell them that you'd like to tape-record the meeting. After all, you will want to be able to accurately remember what was said, and you may need the recording for someone who could not be present.

Understanding It All

Make sure you fully understand the school's position. If something is not completely clear, keep asking questions until you understand it. Disagreements are often based on simple misunderstandings. If you still don't understand, even after school personnel try to clarify, ask them to put the statement in writing so you can look into it after the meeting.

Keeping Your Cool

If the school resists providing the services you feel your child needs, it may be hard not to become emotional, but one of the worst things you can do is become angry or tearful. Behave in a serious, professional, and forthright manner. Don't get defensive or personal. It's a good approach to assume that the other participants are also working in your child's best interests. Remember that you will need to keep working with this group of people, so it's better not to get heated. As the Learning Disabilities Association says, "Be sincere, honest, positive, and assertive, but not aggressive."

What Ifs

What if the school officials make observations that make you uncomfortable or that you believe are inaccurate? (Perhaps, for instance, they say there's no way they can supply therapy more than two or three times a week.) Your response should be, "That's interesting. Can you please explain all of that in writing for me?"

Signing on the Dotted Line

At the end of the IEP meeting you'll probably be presented with the IEP and asked to sign it, "so that your child can receive services." You don't have to sign it there and then, unless you're one hundred percent thrilled with the outcome. You can take it home to discuss with family, friends, and experts before agreeing to anything.

WHAT TO ASK FOR

Each child is a unique individual and you should tailor your requests to the Child Study Team based on your child's personal challenges and needs. If you have a good private therapist and developmental pediatrician, they will be able to guide you. From wide experience, these are some guidelines that will appropriately serve the requirements of most children with speech and language delays and impairments.

A Qualified Therapist

Ask to see the credentials of the professionals who will be working with your child. Not all SLPs are conversant with every type of speech and language impairment and some may not have treated other children with the same condition as your child. If your child needs someone with particular expertise, you have the right to insist that the school bring in a specialist to work with and train the school's SLP—at the school's expense.

Intensity and Frequency

Whether or not your child is in private therapy should have no influence on the amount of therapy he or she receives through the school. There are various types of service delivery options. A child with a simple delay in speech may be fine getting group therapy in a preschool disabled program. However, children with more serious speech disorders such as apraxia do not improve in such groups and may require intensive, one-on-one "pull out" therapy sessions at least three times a week. Group therapy is generally successful for children with mild to moderate delays in speech, but it may be detrimental for those with severe to profound delays.

Individualized Means Individualized

The Individualized Education Plan is exactly what it means. The key word is *individualized*. Your child's IEP must be designed to meet his or her specific needs, not to fit into preexisting programs or services because of convenience for the school. Lack of availability or funding is not a reason for denying services that your child requires. If your town's school cannot provide appropriate therapy, it has various choices. It can bring in consultants or other experts to work with your child and to oversee and train the school's SLP, it can pay for your child's private therapy, or it can pay to send your child "out of district" to a private school. Appropriate services have to be provided free of charge to you.

Good Ol' Summertime

Many children with severe speech impairments regress without continued therapy, so make sure your child gets enrolled in the extended school year (ESY) program, especially for the long summer break. ESY services must be considered at the annual IEP meeting and documented in the IEP. The ESY also has to be the same as what your child receives during the regular school year. For example, if he or she normally has a ten-hour-a-week schedule, his or her ESY should also be for ten hours a week.

AFTER THE IEP MEETING

Providing Services

Your child should start receiving services as soon as possible after the meeting. The school has to make sure that each of your child's teachers and service providers delivers his or her specific responsibilities. The IEP must specify how many hours a day will be spent in a special education setting and in the regular classroom, and it must detail the type and amount of therapy. Your child's progress toward the annual goal as stated in the IEP is monitored, and you have to be kept abreast of his or her development and chances of achieving that goal.

Reviewing the IEP

The IEP team is required to review the Individualized Educational Program at least once a year—more often if requested by the parents or the school. You must be invited to attend and can disagree with the IEP and placement, and suggest changes. If it becomes necessary, you can ask for additional testing, an independent evaluation, mediation, and a due process hearing. You can even file a complaint with the state education agency.

More Frequent Evaluation

Many people assume that the IEP meeting is an annual event. Not so. You can insist on a much more frequent review (even as often as every three months) and have it written into the IEP. The only caveat is that specific school personnel who need to be present may not be able to attend so many meetings. The IEP, in effect, is a contract among you, the school, and your child. And, just like any contract, it's negotiable.

Put It in Writing

If the IEP team won't agree to the services that you want, or if the school subsequently does not provide agreed services, always back up your verbal concerns with something in writing. Before doing so, obtain a copy of the Special Education Administrative Code from your school's special services department. It may not be bedtime reading, but it's worth wading through. It should provide you with the deadlines that the school must honor. If there isn't a fixed deadline within which it has to respond, create one by requesting a reply within ten days of receipt.

Create a Paper Trail

In case you need to take your complaint to a higher level, keep a record of what transpires at lower levels. After a meeting, always memorialize the proceedings in a letter. Write an outline of what happened and state that if they disagree they should reply in writing. You can fax the letter, but also send it by certified mail, return receipt requested.

Here's an example of a brief follow-up letter.

Dear Mr. X,

I'm writing to thank you for meeting with me yesterday in connection with my son's IEP. I would like to memorialize the meeting to make sure that we agree on the issues at hand.

My understanding is as follows:

- *Bobby is approved to begin the preschool disabled program on January 7, 2004, which is two weeks before his third birthday.*
- *Bobby will receive one-on-one "pull out" speech therapy three times a week for thirty-minute sessions with RuthElyn, the school SLP.*
- *Bobby will receive two sessions a week of occupational therapy "in group" with Linda, the school OT.*
- *Bobby will attend the summer program and will continue with the same amounts of therapy for both speech and OT.*
- *We will review Bobby's progress at the next IEP meeting in April to see if the goals we agreed upon are close to being met.*

If you disagree with my recollection of our meeting, please contact me, in writing, with your comments. If you find this to be accurate, there is no need to respond. Thank you for your time in this matter.

Yours sincerely,
Mrs. A. Parent

Whether or not you receive a reply, you have secured in writing an account of the meeting, which eliminates any he said–she said conflict.

Solving Disputes

If you just cannot reach agreement with the school, there are various ways to proceed. First, ask the person in your district responsible for special education services if the school will agree to mediation. Some states cover the cost of mediation. You can also file a complaint with the state department of education if you believe that the school is violating state or federal special education statutes. Your ultimate recourse is to request an impartial due process hearing and/or to seek the counsel of a special ed attorney. As one parent put it, "It sounds like an uphill battle, and it can be extremely exhausting. But if we don't fight for our kids, who will?" Or, as Karen Rothweiler, mother of a three-year-old boy with apraxia, says, "No one knows or loves your child like you do, and it is up to you to be his advocate."

There are, of course, excellent school districts where caring teachers and therapists go to extraordinary lengths to accommodate the needs of children with learning disadvantages. Gretchen Weggenmann of St. Charles, Missouri, has nothing but praise for the help given to her six-year-old son, Kevin. Says Gretchen, "I guess I am really blessed. The school district has been intervening in Kevin's care since he was two and I have not had to pay one penny for anything. I was even reimbursed for mileage because I chose to transport him to and from school." Kevin attended preschool three times a week, and received speech therapy three times a week and OT twice a week. He now attends kindergarten in a regular classroom and is pulled out four times a week for speech therapy and twice a week for OT.

Karen Rothweiler, however, had more of a struggle. All of the reports she had heard about her school district were "negative and scary, to say the least," she says. She thoroughly prepared for her three-year-old son Justin's IEP, putting together a presentation outlining why the district's program was not suitable for his needs. It included observations of the proposed in-district classroom both by Karen and their developmental pediatrician. Karen also included a statement that the

SLP had acknowledged that she had no experience with apraxia but had expressed a willingness to learn. Says Karen, "I appreciated her attitude, but my son's clock was ticking and we couldn't afford to wait while she learned. Justin was already three and completely nonverbal."

When Karen walked into the IEP meeting, she says, "I was actually shaking because I felt so strongly about what I wanted and knew that I was going to have to fight tooth and nail for it." Finally, they agreed to have Justin out-districted to a school experienced in working with apraxic kids. "There are a lot of awful towns out there that will give you as hard a time as they can," says Karen. "But in spite of what I'd heard, my town was willing to admit that it wasn't an appropriate placement for him." The key, she says, is to be prepared and to have all of your paperwork in order. To this end she created a three-ring binder with tabs, topic by topic, and made extra copies to hand out. "I know they were impressed that I'd done my homework and was so organized," she says.

Not all professionals, unfortunately, are as impressed, and all too often parents have to fight pitched battles to get the right kind of schooling. Like Karen, Stacey Abenstein put together a comprehensive presentation including information about the need for frequent one-on-one therapy, proven methods of therapy, statistics supporting the danger of future learning disabilities, and the standards for receiving ESY services. She added a table of contents, put it all in a binder, and made copies for everyone attending the meeting. One member of the team did not react favorably. "She actually told me I had too much time on my hands," says Stacey. "I told her that she would be surprised what you can accomplish at three in the morning when you are trying to advocate for a tiny child whom you love more than life itself." Nevertheless, in spite of her experience, Stacey still believes in doing your homework. She says, "The most important advice I can give is be prepared. Make sure that you have all pertinent information to back up everything that you want. Stay positive and strong. And remember, you are 50 percent of the IEP team."

Kathleen Gottshall, mother of an apraxic child *and* herself a teacher for seventeen years, provides an interesting perspective: "I have sat on both sides of the table. Parents do not know what is available and are intimidated, for the most part, by the teachers and professionals who are supposed to know what is wrong with their child. When a mother or father feels that something is wrong, then they need to go with their gut."

Obtaining services through the school system is just one challenge that confronts most parents of children with speech disorders. Now let's turn our attention to another that's just as vital and often even more challenging: getting the insurance company to pay for appropriate therapy.

INSURANCE: GETTING WHAT YOU NEED

The insurance industry is a paper-ridden bureaucracy that often places an overwhelming burden on families struggling to have medical bills paid. The result is extra stress when families are already stressed out. For parents of children with speech problems, there is a minefield of terminology and codes to cross. Make a wrong move and you can ruin your chances of obtaining coverage. The difficulty cannot be underestimated. In a survey conducted by Patricia Lohman of New Mexico State University, parents of late talkers reported that it was their number one challenge. So what can you do to successfully navigate the minefield?

First, be sure that your doctor is an ally in your negotiations with the insurance carrier. A seasoned medical or speech professional may well be wise to the pitfalls of using incorrect language when dealing with insurance companies which, after all, make a profit by paying for only what they believe your policy covers. However, you may need to coach your doctor and speech pathologist in the way they describe your child's condition and the insurance codes they select. Don't be reluctant to raise these issues. *Preventing* an altercation with the insurance company in the first place is easier than later getting them to remedy a rejected claim.

Don't Say "Developmental"

Your doctor will probably write a "letter of medical necessity" or a "letter of predetermination" for the insurance firm. It's vital to state the "correct" code number for your child's condition. Various communication disorders are neurological in origin and not developmental. One of the biggest mistakes in a professional's report is using the word *developmental*. Although "developmental apraxia of speech" (DAS) and "developmental verbal dyspraxia" (DVD) are often medical descriptions of the condition, in the insurance realm they are frequently used as grounds for disqualifying your claim. As soon as claims evaluators see the word *developmental*, they automatically think "developmental delay." This leads them to conclude that the problem will correct itself *with or without* therapy.

The key to obtaining coverage is to research your child's condition and what your insurance company covers, and make sure the appropriate codes are used.

Avoid Saying "Therapy"

You can't be too careful. Suggest that your doctor or therapist recommend treatment for your child's condition, rather than therapy. The word *treatment* is more indicative of medical necessity than *therapy* and in some cases makes it more likely that your claim will be approved. It's also a good idea to stress that the treatment is "medically necessary."

Experience Counts

Your doctor's report should state that intensive treatment by qualified and experienced speech and occupational therapists is required. It may be necessary to explain the specialized type of therapy your child needs (PROMPT, oromotor, or sensory integration, for instance) and justify why *your* therapist is more qualified than the one who is "in network" for the insurance provider.

Prognosis

Make sure it is emphasized that without treatment the prognosis for improvement is poor, and that without intensive, appropriate help children do not outgrow severe speech impairments.

Cracking the Code

Your pediatrician or therapist will need to use diagnostic codes for your submission for insurance coverage. Make sure you know what code he or she intends to use, as that too can make all the difference in the world.

- CODES TO AVOID: 315.3, 315.31, 315.39, and 315.9 are codes for developmental speech and language disorders. Use them at your peril, as you may not be reimbursed.
- CODES TO USE: Good ICD (international classification of diseases) codes for apraxia of speech are 784.69, 315.40 (most 315 codes are developmental, but not this one), or 718.3. The latter code is also used for hypotonia, sensory motor integration disorder, and coordination disorder, all of which may be associated with the apraxic condition. The code to use for dysarthria or slurred speech due to a neurologic impairment is 784.5. If there is an associated expressive language disorder with the apraxia, which is commonly the case, use code 784.6 ("other symbolic dysfunction"). More generic codes include 783.4, which may be used for neurodevelopmental dysfunction, and 742.9 for static encephalopathy (neurologic impairment). Other useful codes are 343.0 cerebral palsy, 314.0 ADHD without hyperactivity, 314.01 ADHD with hyperactivity, 299.0 autism, 299.8 PDD—NOS, 381.1 chronic serous otitis media (persistent fluid behind the eardrums), 388.4 central auditory processing disorder, 783.3 feeding disorder, 765.0 prematurity. Sometimes you need to "rotate" these codes. If one is not successful, resubmit with another. (An example of a good "letter of medical necessity" is provided in Appendix C).

Try Again

In spite of your best efforts and those of the health professionals, your provider may agree to only a limited period of therapy. Take what you are given and later reapply with a new set of goals presented by your speech pathologist. Your policy may specify that therapy is a short-term benefit. If so, your speech therapist will need to submit and resubmit his or her objectives and goals, perhaps a couple of months at a time.

Don't Give Up

Don't be discouraged by a rejection. Don't let them wear you down. Be prepared to do battle and back up your justifiable claim with solid evidence. Some insurers are better than others, and it's sad but true that some will never pay for speech services unless your child has had a stroke or an accident. If you have a choice of insurers, choose wisely. Scrutinize the benefits *before* you sign up.

IF YOU GET DENIED

In spite of your best efforts, an insurance company may still deny coverage. Typically, you might get a response that says, "Speech therapy is covered under your plan if the service is to restore a speech function that has been lost due to an illness or injury. The speech therapy requested was reviewed and it was determined that your child's speech delay is not a result of an illness or injury." One mother who got this reply told us, "We were requesting an evaluation, not therapy. But they must be psychic because neither my daughter's pediatrician nor her neurologist has been able to determine her lack of speech."

If you are denied services, get it in writing and carefully plan your appeal. Most people give up, which is what the insurance companies expect. Find out the insurance company's appeals process and follow it to the letter. Don't give them an opportunity to delay further. Keep meticulous notes every time you contact them. Write down the full name of the person with whom you speak, time of call, and what you are told. As a last resort you might be able to appeal to your state's insurance commission, so you will need to compile a complete file.

Ask to see the Master Policy. All insurance companies have one. If they quibble, insist that it is your legal right. This policy contains all of the small print and enables you to check if coverage should be granted. Perseverance is the key. One mother who didn't give up after coverage for her son, Matthew, was initially denied on the basis that his speech disorder was "developmental," told us, "They denied. I appealed. They denied again. I filed a second-level appeal. They denied again. I wrote two fantastic letters regarding my son's need for therapy that included information I found on the apraxia Web site. My son's speech therapist, early intervention people, and primary care physician all commented on the strength of the letters, but to no avail. Insurance was still denied."

It wasn't until Matthew saw a pediatric neurologist that she was able to get the insurance company to pay. She took the neurological evaluation to a second-level hearing and took Matthew with her to put a small human face to the claim. Later the same day a representative called to say that therapy was approved because of the documentation that apraxia was neurologically based. This mom's advice: "Make an appointment as soon as possible and fight for your insurance coverage rights. Don't back down. I'm glad I didn't. Matthew is now receiving private one-on-one therapy and I hope I will hear his first words soon."

GETTING HELP

Don't be disheartened. Getting appropriate therapy for your child and getting your insurance carrier to meet its obligations can be tough battles, but they are winnable. And they are battles definitely worth winning for your child's overall development. But regardless of how much therapy you can obtain from the professionals, they are not the only ones who can mold your child's future. It's largely up to you. As we've said, you spend more time with him or her than anyone, and how you spend that time is all-important. You can make a difference. Late talkers, especially those with apraxia, need constant speech practice. In the next chapter we tell you all about the therapy that you can do at home.

7. What Parents Can Do to Help

Christopher called me "Mama." I am overjoyed, elated, flying high, and touching the stars.—SUSAN SELIGMAN, mother of a young boy with apraxia

Parents are a child's first teachers. They usually spend more time with their child and know their child better than anyone. As we have discussed, quite often parents are the first to recognize that their son or daughter has a problem that may require a specialist's attention. And, while it is essential that children with complex speech disorders receive intensive therapy from a speech-language pathologist, there is also an important role for parents or other caretakers. Parents can provide activities to stimulate speech as part of the daily routine, even if the late talker is not getting professional therapy. For the child who is receiving expert help, home exercises can complement these sessions. (While the oral-motor therapy exercises that follow are only for children with oral-motor problems, most of the others can be used to help all late-talking children regardless of whether or not a speech disorder has been officially diagnosed.)

If your child is getting speech or occupational therapy, you should ask to observe the therapy sessions, especially if your child is a preschooler. Most SLPs and OTs will agree to your presence. Alternatively, some therapists have two-way mirrors in their offices so that you can unobtrusively see what happens. By watching the expert at work you not only obtain firsthand intelligence about your child's progress, you're also able to assess the techniques that work best. Ask the therapists to recommend appropriate activities for you to conduct at home and to establish goals for your child to attain, as it's vital that you and your child's therapists are in sync. In this chapter, based on our combined personal and professional experiences, we put forward some home therapy techniques that we have found particularly useful. (You must consult a professional for appropriate exercises for children who are gagging, choking, or have other severe feeding problems).

First, let's look at the younger child. It's a mistake to overlook any type of feeding problems since the same movements that are used for eating are used for speaking. Children with sensory, feeding, swallowing, and oral-motor problems need help to get their lips, tongue, and jaw ready for speech. It's essential to "wake up" their mouths. For all exercises that you introduce, develop self-confidence by making the challenge just hard enough for your child to accomplish it.

THE WAKE-UP CALL: INCREASING SENSORY AWARENESS IN THE MOUTH

Food, glorious food! Strong flavors put your nervous system in a state of instant alert. For children with oral-motor issues it's not just a question of taste; they need this extra stimulation to help them become aware of their mouth's capabilities. Children who have reduced sensory awareness in their mouths may stuff their mouths with food or avoid certain foods. They can benefit from a variety of eating experiences: foods with stronger or unusual tastes, varied temperatures, or assorted shapes and textures. This is all designed to stimulate the mouth receptors so your child has a better awareness of the position of his or her tongue in relation to the gums, teeth, and jaw. Oral-motor planning like this helps improve chewing and oral-motor skills, and motor planning for speech. Here are some examples.

SWEET OR SOUR: Heighten the taste of foods with flavorings. Experiment with spices not commonly chosen by children, such as pepper, Tabasco, mint, or garlic. Have your child suck on fresh lemon or lime slices, or Altoid mints. Sour candies such as War Heads can also wake up the mouth. For the really bold, try the Harry Potter All Flavor beans by Jelly Belly.

HOT OR COLD: Vary the temperature of food and drink. For cold snacks, serve chilled peas or chilled grapes cut into smaller pieces. Serve warm (not hot) drinks through a straw. Prepare different kinds of frozen fruit drinks and ask your child to identify flavor combinations.

SOFT AND HARD: Make food more interesting by changing its texture. Mix harder foods with softer foods to increase the tactile sensation. For instance, add sliced fruit to yogurt or applesauce. Keep your child's favorite cereals crunchy by adding a minimal amount of milk. Spread peanut butter on celery, or ranch dip on raw vegetables. Crisp foods provide auditory, tactile, and kinesthetic feedback to help biting and chewing. The kinesthetic input is the increased sense of movement and positioning of the tongue. Textured foods obviously demand more chewing effort than softer foods.

LOLLIPOP HOLDERS: Any vibration that the child tolerates in the mouth area helps develop sensory acceptance and stimulates muscle tone. What better for a child than vibrating lollipop holders, found in toy, drug, and gift stores? A particularly good one is Sound Bites, a battery-operated lollipop holder from Tiger Electronics that plays FM radio stations or silly sounds that can be heard only by the person sucking on the candy. The holder sends vibrations through the lollipop and the sound travels through the child's teeth and directly into the inner ear.

TOOTHBRUSHING: Brushing your child's teeth is an ideal way to provide sensory input to the tongue, gums, lips, jaw, and cheeks, and stimulate muscle tone. Brushing the sides of the tongue encourages the sideways movement of the tongue for chewing. Motivate your child to go along with this activity by letting him choose the toothbrush. Electric toothbrushes, especially those designed in the shape of a race car or other novelty item, are appealing to kids. Starting without toothpaste, brush the inside of the cheeks, the tongue, the gums, and the roof of the mouth, but away from the throat. If he's resistant, dip the toothbrush into something tasty that he likes to eat. Introduce toothpaste after the child has accepted the oral stimulation. Increase the "spice" of the toothpaste as tolerated; try mint or Tom's cinnamon.

ORAL AEROBICS AND MUSCLE BUILDING

Those children with weakness and/or motor planning difficulties of the tongue muscles cannot move the tongue to the precise location in the mouth where it should go to produce different speech sounds. The lips, jaw, and cheek muscles may lack the coordination for chewing and speaking. The following exercises improve the control of these muscles as well as those used for "jaw grading," which is the amount of mouth openness needed for the production of the different vowels and consonants. (Only children with oral-motor problems will need these exercises.)

LICKING LIPS: Put sticky, appetizing food such as chocolate sauce or peanut butter on the outside edges of your mouth and your child's mouth. While you both look in the mirror, challenge your child to see who can lick off the food first without using hands. Watch to see if your child can lift her tongue up toward her nose, or to the side, or down to her chin. This game is very beneficial for prespeech skills and waking up the mouth. (If your child cannot move her tongue in the correct direction, in spite of repeated attempts, it is one sign that she could have oral apraxia).

SHAPE AND SIZE: For easier biting and chewing, cut bagels and sandwiches into finger-wide strips and chop meat into small cubes. Cut raw vegetables into french-fry shapes. Chewing long strips of food promotes sideways movement of the tongue to the molars instead of immature front-of-mouth munching.

THICK AND THIN: Instead of using silverware, have your child suck favorite soft foods through a straw. Experiment with pudding, Jell-O, yogurt (most kids like Yoplait cotton candy or bubble gum flavors), applesauce, superthick shakes, or even mashed potatoes. To make the task more difficult, try various types of silly straws and thin drink straws used to stir coffee. Kids think it's entertaining, and drinking food through a straw helps tongue retraction and strengthens the oral and cheek muscles.

PRETZELS AND GUMMY BEARS: Put a pretzel stick in one side of your youngster's mouth, and then the other side, telling him to "Bite, bite, bite." You can also do this exercise with fruit chew candies, which are a bit harder. Pretend that a gummy bear is going for a walk across your child's face, until Mr. Bear sees a cave that he wants to explore—the youngster's mouth. Most children laugh with delight when Mr. Bear enters the cave. Place the gummy bear in the side of your child's mouth and have him bite down on it.

CHASING CHEERIOS: Hold a Cheerio in one hand and say "ma." Then hold a second Cheerio in the other hand and again say "ma." Next, place the two Cheerios together while saying "mama." If the child follows your lead and does this, he or she gets the ultimate reward—eating the Cheerios. The same technique can be used with increasing difficulty; for example, after "mama" comes "mommy." Placing the Cheerios separately and then bringing them together is a visual clue to the breaking of words into syllables. To emphasize the message you can add an auditory clue—clapping your hands or tapping your foot while saying the sounds.

PUPPY DOG GROWLS: Purchase varied widths of clear plastic tubing (the hardware store will have it). Place the tubing inside one corner of your child's mouth and tell her to pretend she's a puppy and to clamp down hard. Silently count to three and then "try" to pull the tubing from the puppy's mouth while she has to growl really loud. After counting to ten (again in your head), switch to the other side. This activity strengthens biting and chewing ability.

BUILDING BREATH SUPPORT FOR SPEAKING

As kids we were all told to stand up straight. There's something to be said for good posture and its effect on the rib cage and diaphragm. Children who have low muscle tone in the trunk and weak abdominal muscles may not have the postural stability to produce speech. Kids also need to build up enough pressure in the oral cavity to produce the puff of air necessary to make the *p* (*puh*) sound. Here are some exercises that help develop breath support and control for children with low muscle tone.

TOOT ECHOES: Using a blow toy that makes a sound, perform a pattern of long and short toots on the horn; for example, one short and one long toot. Have your child follow your example. If he is not able to imitate three toots of the horn, he does not have the breath control for a three-word sentence. This is a great exercise to increase breath support. You can find inexpensive horns as well as other oral-motor toys such as whistles and straws at your local party store and/or toy store.

BUBBLE POPPERS: Teach your child to blow the air out of bubble blowers using a slow and controlled breath. Take turns to see who can make more bubbles, or the biggest bubbles. After each turn, say "pop" as you each try to catch all of the bubbles. Make sure that when your child is blowing bubbles she is sitting up straight with her head erect and in line with her body. Bubble blowing helps build up the intraoral pressure necessary to help make the *puh* and *buh* sounds.

BUBBLE VOLCANO: Using the same plastic tubing that you used in "Puppy Dog Growls" and a plastic cylinder filled with safe bubble liquid and water, have your child blow and blow until the bubble volcano explodes over the sides. If he or she has trouble making the volcano erupt, don't hesitate to join in.

THE MIRROR GAME: Try to get your child to imitate facial expressions looking in the mirror. To help improve upper body strength while doing this, put the mirror on the floor, or lie in front of a full-length mirror. The two of you lie on your bellies with your elbows supporting your upper body and head while you make the funny faces. Upper body strength is important for breath control, which is the basis for all speech.

PLAYTIME ALL THE TIME

Children with communication challenges respond to therapy only if you can grab their interest. Children learn through play. They love toys and they love someone to play with. Mom and dad can deliver both of these elements. To us, playtime is simply joyful experiences in which parent and child play together and in which the activities have value as therapy. Sue Schwartz and Joan E. Heller Miller, authors of *The New Language of Toys: Teaching Communication Skills to Children with Special Needs,* put it very well: "While you are playing with your child you can help him increase his language skills. And you can have fun together at the same time. We know your child can benefit from these times with mom and dad. We also know this play/work time is dramatically more important for children with delays in their language development. They will need the extra effort that their parents can give them to help develop their language skills."

Children with speech problems are no different from other kids; they like to hide things, to nurture things, and to be surprised. It's all part of learning. Use these universal techniques to stimulate the production of sounds and words. There's no need to wait until a speech disorder has been formally diagnosed. And don't feel obligated to fill every moment of every day with structured play. As Schwartz and Miller say, "There are times when children should play alone because that is when they build independence and develop imagination."

Playtime helps any child develop both emotionally and physically. Through play, children improve motor coordination, acquire the ability to interact with others, develop feelings of self-confidence, and master the skills required for each toy. Language and play skills develop simultaneously and playtime activities can stimulate language. Here are some ideas to help you stimulate language and get the most out of the time you get to play with your child. These are good for all late talkers.

INTRODUCING NEW TOYS: Choose toys that can be used to achieve different goals, are developmentally appropriate, and are cognitively demanding. Use a brand-new toy for a limited time, concentrating on just one activity.

KNOW WHEN TO START AND WHEN TO STOP: A good time for "play therapy" is after your child has had a nap, when he is refreshed and more likely to fully participate. Be conscious of your child's level of interest. If he's becoming tired, inattentive, or cranky, there's no point in pushing him to continue. At the beginning, assess how long you can keep his interest—it might be as little as five to ten minutes at a time. But you can have several of these short sessions every day. As your child's ability to pay attention increases, lengthen and increase the number of play sessions.

LET HER INITIATE: Your role is that of a supporting partner, so sit on the floor near your child and wait for an invitation to participate. Eyeball-to-eyeball, she'll get language cues from your facial expressions. Don't intrude and don't take over. Follow her lead. If she's interested in animals, open up the whole world of jungles and farms. If she just doesn't want to know about trains and planes, don't push them on her.

FLEXITIME: Don't limit playtime to structured sessions with toys. Opportunities present themselves all day long whether you're shopping, making cookies, folding clothes, or driving in the car.

ORGANIZING PLAY: Keep a basket of toys in every room. Have a play mat to help define the play area and keep distractions to a minimum. Don't have the TV or radio blaring in the background.

CYCLING TOYS: Don't have all of your child's toys available all of the time. Put some out of sight and bring them out on a rainy day. Cycling toys in this way prevents burnout.

TALKING TEDDY: All kinds of regular toys can be appropriate for non-verbal children. For instance, many electronic toys can talk and can be used for communication. Squeezing the teddy's paw could empower a child to tell mommy "I love you" through the teddy's voice.

SOUND PRACTICE

Sound play is a normal stage in language development. Cooing and babbling repetitive syllables such as *bababa* or *dadada* are precursors of first words. Here are ways to help stimulate more sounds from any late-talking child.

REPEAT. REPEAT. REPEAT. Repetition is important for all children, and especially those with a speech disorder. A baby must hear a word hundreds of times—maybe even thousands—before he or she can produce it. Be sure to give your child a chance to absorb what you say by slightly pausing between sentences. It may become tiresome for you, but repetition is not boring for the child and can enhance the learning opportunity.

SOUNDS OF PLEASURE: Sometimes late talkers are not able to make even the basic sounds that reveal pleasure or excitement. Think of the screams and shrieks you make on a roller coaster ride, or the noise you emit in anticipation of eating ice cream. If your child does not make those sounds, use any opportunity you can to try and initiate a copycat response. Point to rides at the amusement park and say, "Oooooh," or point at food, rub your stomach and say, "Mmmmm." If your child is able to make such sounds, add another syllable, turning *oooooh* into *oooooh-weee*, for instance.

BLOWING UP NAPKINS: At the dinner table, hold a paper napkin in front of your face so that your child can't see you. Keep it close to your mouth while saying the *p* sound, and the napkin will blow up to reveal your face. Then start laughing as if it is the funniest thing you've ever done, and get someone else to do it. Don't demand that your child have a go, but you'll probably find that he wants to follow suit, thereby learning how to say "puh." Once he masters the *p* sound, move on to other sounds.

FUNNY SOUNDS: Employ a funny or odd tone of voice and encourage your child to copy you. Have him or her imitate the sounds of mechanical objects such as the doorbell, the ringing of the phone, or the *vroom* of a car engine. Talk like a cartoon character such as Donald Duck, or like a monster, or like a little old lady.

PURPOSEFUL PLAY: A playground can be a perfect classroom in which to prompt your child to talk. Push your child on the swings or the merry-go-round. Then stop and require him to try to say a specific word before proceeding. Hold your child's hands while he jumps on a minitrampoline, reciting the ABCs or counting one to ten with him.

MARCH TO THE BEAT: While singing simple songs, use instruments to add a beat. Depending upon your child's ability, encourage him or her to fill in words or sing aloud. By marching together you promote oral-breathing coordination. For the same purpose, make use of jump ropes and simple hopscotch.

PUPPET PLAY: Puppets are perfect for stimulating imaginative play and speech sounds. You don't have to invest in expensive puppets. Simply place a gaggle of favorite stuffed animals behind the couch and have your child sit on the other side. Put on a show and afterward breezily ask, "Okay, who wants to put on a puppet show next? Raise your hand." Don't give the impression that the puppeteer is expected to talk, but you'll probably find that your child hums and makes some sounds as he or she moves the animals around.

ANIMAL PLAY: Your child may love to pretend he's a puppy or kitten, or even an elephant, cow, or bear. The way that the animal moves, sounds, and eats are all amusing activities to imitate. You can do this during a trip to the zoo and at home. Animal sounds such as *baa, moo, meow, woof,* and *neigh* have an ideal variety of vowel sounds. As an example, using monkey sounds *eee eee, ah ah,* and *ooh ooh, ah ah* (with corresponding arm action) can be a lot of fun. To create the *eee* sound, make sure your teeth are together; open your lips for a big smile and then make the sound. To make the *ah* sound, just open your mouth all the way. You can use a tongue depressor and pretend you're at the doctor's office. For the *ooh* sound, make a fish face. Place your fingers on the sides of your mouth—and then your child's—and squeeze until the lips become rounded to look like a fish face.

NOW HEAR THIS: Letting a child hear the sound of his or her own voice always encourages more sounds. Good toys for this exercise range from inexpensive plastic echo sound mikes to tape recorders, and even higher priced karaoke machines that can be hooked up to your television.

Using Melody and Rhythm

We have already discussed the role of melody and rhythm as a therapeutic technique for helping children sequence syllables in words. Did we also say that pairing singing and movement was fun? You bet! All late talkers will benefit from these.

SING ALONG: Music, singing, and dancing help children express themselves. Start with basic songs. Sing "Old MacDonald" and see if your child will do the *EIEIO* part.

SSSSSSNAKE SONG: Here's an excellent way to practice the *s* sound. Pretend that your tongue is a snake and that your teeth are the cage. Sing the following song to the tune of "London Bridge" (and insert the name of your child). And do it with a smile, so he's not scared of the "snake."

Ssssssnake crawled up Tanner's leg
Tanner's arm SSSS

Tanner's head SSSS
Ssssssnake crawled up Tanner's leg
And back, in the cage
SSSSSSSSSS.

Teach him that he needs to keep his tongue behind his teeth (the snake behind the cage) in order to make the *s* sound. After learning this song, any time that your child sticks his tongue out while trying to say an *s* sound, tell him to "keep the snake in the cage," and he'll know what you mean.

TIME TO SING: Music tapes featuring well-known songs played at a slower tempo make it easier for children with speech disorders to join in. One highly rated, award-winning CD, *Time to Sing,* was developed after the experiences of Bob Muir, artistic administrator for the Pittsburgh Symphony Orchestra, and Dr. Mary Sturm, an emergency physician at the University of Pittsburgh Medical Center. Bob had noticed his two-year-old son, Colin, trying to sing along while watching Barney, the purple TV dinosaur, croon "I love you." But the words just wouldn't come out. "He started to try to sing and immediately stopped, and I saw those tears rolling down his cheeks. He wasn't making any sound," says Bob. "You can imagine how heartbreaking that was." Mary Sturm felt the same emotion when her five-year-old son, Joshua, was struggling to sing with his preschool class.

Both boys have apraxia, and when Bob and Mary shared their stories at an apraxia support group, it was the catalyst for a remarkable collaboration. The result: a seventy-one-minute, twenty-six-song CD suitable for children with speech disorders. The lyrics and melodies have been slowed to a tempo the kids' voices can follow. The CD can be ordered from www.pittsburghsymphony.org/time2sing or www.center4creative play.org/sing.

Other good music titles include *Animal Soundtracks, Exploring Language Through Song and Play!, Listening and Following Directions Series, Marvelous Mouth Music, Nursery Rhyme Soundtracks, Singing Sounds Cassette, Soundtracks Sound Stories,* and *Tunes that Teach.*

NURSERY RHYMES: Children develop the ability to detect rhyme before they can produce it, and rhyme is important because children learn that changing a sound changes a word. Rhyming is also a significant preliteracy skill. Reading rhyming books like Dr. Seuss's *The Cat in the Hat* helps to sequence syllables, a skill that apraxics have to work hard to acquire. Point out words that rhyme and words that don't rhyme. Play games around the dinner table where one person says a word, and then everyone else has to say a word that rhymes with it by changing the first letter.

TOP TEN TOYS

What are the best toys to encourage your child in his efforts to talk? Here are our favorites for children age three to seven.

- Bubbles and whistles: Great fun! Excellent tools for strengthening muscles of lips and cheeks. They help coordinate the breath stream needed for speech.
- Therapy ball: A large (three feet in diameter) ball can help stimulate your child to verbalize sounds or count, while doing the gross-motor strengthening activities of bouncing, kicking, and pushing.
- My Talking Pooh Plush: With the simple push of a button, your child enables Pooh to say various greetings. Talking toys like this relieve some communication frustrations for a child still learning to talk.
- Little People Animal Sounds Farm: Children love to imitate animal sounds. Put the horse in his stable and hear him neigh. Or listen to the sheep in the grass answer "Baa." Encourages imaginative play and speech when asked, "Where do you think the horse wants to go now?"
- Barnyard Bingo: Friendly animals teach kids matching skills and colors as they try to be the first to call "Bingo."

- Toots the Train: Voice-activated interactive train encourages speech and articulation of commands. For older children, Nintendo's Hey You, Pikachu may be more appropriate.
- Tape recorder: Strictly speaking the tape recorder is not a toy, but it's a powerful way to play back a child's sounds to encourage him or her to repeat them. A low-tech alternative is the plastic echo microphone. Sing or speak into the echo microphone and hear your voice come back to you, amplified.
- Puppets: Any stuffed animal can double as a puppet to encourage imagination and speech. There's a specific—but expensive—puppet designed for speech therapy that has a movable tongue to show the required positioning of the tongue for different sounds. This is available from www.imagepuppets.on.ca/speech.html.
- Books: There's no better way to teach language and repetition than daily reading. There are books for every concept (counting, colors, prepositions, opposites, to name a few) as well as for sound development (animal sounds, for instance). There are even talking books and books about disabilities.
- Electronics: VTech makes computer-oriented interactive toys. The child pushes a button to spark words and rhymes. There are many excellent computer software packages for preschoolers.

Everyday Activities

Who said you had to plan anything special or spend a lot of money on high-tech toys? Creating "speech moments" throughout the day is a natural way to help all late-talking children learn to speak without pressure or stress. Try some of these activities that keep it simple.

GOING SHOPPING: You can pick up items at unusual places to encourage speech. At the office supply store, you'll find a school section with flash cards, stickers for encouragement, and educational wall posters. At craft stores, there are "sensory" toys like clay and finger paints, which can help a child learn how to express emotions and feelings in a nonverbal way. And at trophy stores you can purchase ribbons or trophies to honor your child's accomplishments.

REPETITION AND ROUTINE: In general, parents can help by using low-pressure verbal activities. These include songs (especially repetitive songs, like "Old MacDonald," and finger plays), poems, verbal routines (pat-a-cake, "Willoughby Wallaby Woo"), repetitive books (such as some of Mercer Mayer's books and *Little Bear*), and daily routines (prayers, social greetings, or saluting the flag). Verbalize repetitive activities. For example, when setting the table say, "Plate, plate, plate, plate; fork, fork, fork, fork."

KEEP ON TALKING: Use self-talk and parallel talk—providing a running commentary on all of the events of the day. The more you talk to and with your child, the more you improve her overall development. Your child may not be talking, but she is almost certainly alert to everything that is going on around her, absorbing and learning from it. Make a point of conducting a play-by-play narrative of all of your mundane chores. In doing so, you are teaching your child the nuances of language.

EXPAND VOCABULARY: It's easy to help your child expand vocabulary. For instance, if he or she says, "Nice doggie," you could say, "Yes, he's a big brown dog. Look at his shiny coat."

ECHO AND CORRECT: Your child says, "Her frew dat ball." Don't say, "That's not how you say it." Simply repeat it correctly: "You saw Anne. She threw that ball."

EGO BUILDING

Making your child feel good about himself or herself by praising all attempts to verbalize is one of the most worthwhile of parenting endeavors. Here are ideas.

THE TELEPHONE TRICK: This is a little trick to boost your child's self-esteem. After he has accomplished something special and you've already praised him, phone Grandma, Aunt Mary, or a neighbor and brag about his accomplishment. Before hanging up, say something like, "Yes, thank you, we're very proud of him." Here's the trick: There doesn't have to be anyone on the other end of the line. This is particularly beneficial if you call someone who made a thoughtless criticism of your child's speech in his presence.

DON'T PRESSURE—PRAISE: Never pressure your child to perform. Late talkers do not react positively when put on the spot and told to "Tell Daddy." Be sure, however, to recognize and praise every little achievement. Children love to be told "well done," reinforced with a big hug. Be enthusiastic as you play with her. If she sees that you're having a good time, she's more likely to stay involved. Fifteen-year-old Khalid Mustafa says that it was the support and understanding of his parents that gave him the will to do better: "Even though I had problems with learning, my parents never talked as if I had a disability. When I was afraid to try, my dad would tell me to go for it, anyway. He would say, 'If things don't work out, you will feel good you tried your best.' They believed in me, so I believed in me."

ENCOURAGING LANGUAGE DEVELOPMENT

Here are some proven techniques to boost your child's acquisition of language.

PARENTESE: We address babies in a high-pitched, singsongy voice that we would never dream of using with fellow adults. We do it automatically. And it actually fosters language development by attracting the baby's attention and resembling the pitch of the sounds he or she makes.

ECHOING: Repeating to your baby the sounds that he has made encourages him to say them again and builds communication. It lets him know that he's getting your attention. And he also learns the pattern of turn taking.

RECASTING: When a toddler mixes up words in a sentence and gets them in the wrong order, repeat the sentence back but with the correct phrasing. (Don't say, "No that's wrong." Just do it right.) Another use of recasting is to turn a statement into a sentence. If your child says, "Get teddy," you could rephrase it to, "Would you like me to get teddy for you?"

EXPANDING: Restate a comment your child makes but expand it into a longer sentence. For example, if she says, "My doll," you could stretch it to, "This is your Barbie doll with lovely blond hair."

LABELING: This is something most parents do without thinking. Whenever your child shows interest in something (and even when he doesn't!), you can name things with which he comes into contact—the house, car, bus, table, flower, etc.

READING: Read to your child from birth! It's a critical part of language development. Give hard board books to infants and toddlers so they can look at them when they choose.

The role of the parent is important. By diligently applying the techniques suggested in this chapter you increase your child's prospect of acquiring effective language skills. As Kenn Apel and Julie Masterson, authors of *Beyond Baby Talk*, express it: "In our experiences, children whose parents have learned as much as they can about language development and have been actively involved in the evaluation and interventions . . . are the children who have made some of the best progress in their language skills."

The ideas in this chapter deliver a wealth of ways you can constructively help your children find his or her voice. They are based on longstanding methods and require patience and perseverance—sometimes for seemingly marginal improvement. But there's a recent development that could make a huge difference for many late talkers. It's principally a parent-led initiative that is turning conventional wisdom on its head and falls into the "could it be too good to be true?" category. It is the use of nutritional supplements to help kids speak. From personal observation we feel it has such merit that we have devoted the next chapter to this subject.

8. Alternative Strategies: Nutritional Intervention

Dramatic breakthroughs in speech have been reported by parents of late-talking children.—B. JACQUELINE STORDY, Ph.D., coauthor, *The LCP Solution*

"This morning I cried while listening to him through his baby monitor. For an hour I heard him 'talk' to his toys, argue with his baby brother, and laugh at some books. And all I did was give him some stinky fish oil." Delighted mother Paulette Schmid E-mailed this message to the list at childrensapraxianet@yahoogroups.com just nine days after beginning to give her two-and-a-half-year-old son Dylan an omega-3 fatty acid supplement. Paulette went on to say, "I actually just found myself ready to say 'Sssshhh' to him because he is babbling incessantly into a toy phone. I had to remind myself that this babbling had been almost three years in the making. What a busy little chatterbox he has turned into. He even yells at me. So what if I can't understand half the words? I am hearing his voice, and that's all that matters at this point."

Paulette's comments are similar to those we have repeatedly heard. Often, results have been so extreme that parents have remarked on their child's sudden "explosion of words."

- Jennifer Traub, talking about three-year-old Madelyn-Grace: "To our delight, after about three weeks our daughter began to spontaneously say words. Her speech therapist is amazed."

- Janet Thompson, mother of thirty-three-month-old, Adam: "His vocabulary has exploded. He went from just a very few words to about thirty-five words in less than three weeks."
- Lori Sables, mother of four-year-old Nicholas: "I knew straightaway we were on the right path. It gave me an incredible sense of relief and joy."
- Michelle Lindower, mother of six-year-nine-month-old Zachariah: "We have no hesitation in calling the pills our miracle pills, and my son, our miracle baby."

These are strong, emotional words from parents excited by what they regard as remarkable breakthroughs after months, and even years, of frustration. It is only natural for them to feel exultant and to talk in superlatives. But could the key to unlocking a child's voice be this simple? Could swallowing one fish oil capsule a day be a remarkable "magic bullet" that enables speechless children to talk? It's easy for skeptics to scoff at such a notion, as it may conjure old memories of cod liver oil touted as an elixir for a variety of human ills. But there is such an overwhelming number of success stories that it would be an immense disservice if we failed to raise awareness of this intriguing potential benefit.

Time and again parents have been thrilled by their child's newfound ability to make sounds and say words, often after just a few weeks of supplementation. One SLP even estimated that the improvements seen in three months of supplementation are similar to those that take nine to twelve months of speech therapy. Such reports are not intended to diminish the value of intensive speech therapy, or to suggest that therapy is not needed. But in the vast majority of cases, the only change in a child's routine was the introduction of the nutritional supplement.

Before going any farther, however, let's add a cautionary note. So far, no clinical trials have investigated the benefits of nutritional supplementation for children with speech impairments and it's important that late-talking children receive appropriate therapy, especially if a serious speech disorder is suspected. Nevertheless, the wealth of anecdotal reports (and preliminary research) deserves serious consideration. For reasons that will become apparent in this chapter, we strongly recommend that you raise the issue with your pediatrician and consider supplementing your child's diet with omega-3 fatty acids.

So exactly what is this supplement? Why should it work? And what is the evidence to substantiate such seemingly unbelievable claims? Fish oil supplements contain varying balances of omega-3 long-chain polyunsaturated fatty acids (LCPs), most notably docosahexaenoic acid (DHA) and eicosapentaenoic acid (EPA), as well as the omega-6 fatty acids arachidonic acid (ARA) and gamma-linolenic acid (GLA). These fatty acids are a vital part of the brain's intricate network of 100 billion cells, and they facilitate signaling between brain cells. DHA and EPA are converted in the body from the short-chain essential fatty acid (EFA) alpha-linolenic acid (ALA), and it is possible that children with neurologically based learning disorders do not have enough in their bodies. (Yes, it's a confusing alphabet soup of fatty acids.)

Most infants get all of the LCPs they need exactly when they need them the most—during the early critical phases of brain development. They receive them through the mother's umbilical cord while they are still in the womb and subsequently from being breast-fed. But children with speech and learning disorders may not get enough LCPs, either because their mothers do not have enough, or because of a defect in the conversion process (from the short-chain EFAs). Without sufficient LCPs, there may be a breakdown in the transmission of messages from the brain to the muscles in the larynx, mouth, tongue, and jaw, which have to work together to produce speech.

Why LCPs may help stimulate speech in late-talking children is not really understood. One key theory centers on the fact that LCPs and proteins are the major constituents in the formation of myelin, the insulation that covers nerve fibers. Myelin increases the speed and efficiency of the transmission of signals throughout the entire nervous system. A delay in the formation of myelin (possibly caused by a lack of LCPs) may affect the ability of infants and toddlers to speak, as well as perform gross- and fine-motor acts like crawling and walking and stacking a tower of blocks.

Spanish researcher Manuela Martinez, M.D., whose work has been supported by the U.S. National Institutes of Health, has demonstrated in both animal and human studies a connection between the presence of DHA and effective myelination. In addition, it has been shown that a deficiency of DHA is associated with visual and neurological damage. Children with speech disorders could be deficient in LCPs; therefore, by adding LCP supplements to their diet, myelination and motor planning of speech could be improved. That's the scientific theory, but many parents who pioneered the use of LCP supplementation don't really care why it works—they're just glad that it does.

IN THE BEGINNING

It all began when parents of late talkers heard about the omega-3 research with children who had the motor coordination disorder dyspraxia, and children with dyslexia and ADHD. The positive results prompted them to try fatty acid supplementation with their own children. Internationally, parents have experimented with different LCP products, but they have principally used fish oil capsules marketed as Efalex and ProEFA. When they saw significant improvements, they began to spread the word through Internet lists, and an enthusiastic group of LCP advocates developed.

"INSTANT" SUCCESS

Many parents have been amazed at how quickly the supplements seem to work. Michele Lindower was delighted to hear her son, Zachariah, say "lemonade" on the second day of being given a 3,000-mg omega-3 capsule. "I was quite taken aback and did a double-take. He just laughed because he knew I was shocked," says Michele. A visit to an ice cream stand was their most memorable breakthrough. Michele, as usual, stood ready to repeat his request for "a small chocolate with chocolate sprinkles." But the counter clerk began making the cone without her help. Says Michele, "For the first time, I wasn't needed to interpret what Zach had said. It was a major milestone."

Kathleen Gottshall's identical twin sons, Brendan and Logan, both have apraxia, and she began to supplement them when they were almost three years old. After eight days she reported, "They are both saying words that they never even attempted before." Suddenly, she says, they were using two- and three-word "sentences" such as "I sorry Mommy" and "I jump?" Added Kathleen, "I definitely don't think it's a coincidence since they had been working with SLPs for almost eight months without this kind of progress."

Nicholas Sables, diagnosed with apraxia at the age of four, had no clear words. After three months of private therapy and no progress, his mother, Lori Sables, tried LCP supplementation and after three days reported, "There's an incredible change in his speech and behavior. It seems too much of a coincidence that therapy and preschool were of no help until the DHA." Tests at the end of the school year, when Nicholas was still only four, indicated that his expressive speech was nearly age appropriate. In every other category he scored at the six-year-five-month level.

AFTER SEVERAL WEEKS

Other parents have not seen such "instant" results but have been equally excited by significant progress in a matter of weeks. Attorney Carolyn Allegro IL Grande wanted clear and convincing evidence, so after starting her three-year-old daughter Alexis on a fatty acid supplement she recorded progress by keeping a log of "word events." Her most rewarding entry was the day before Mother's Day, when Alexis kept saying, "Ahhh, ma ma." Said Carolyn, "It's so wonderful, and the most amazing thing is that she hasn't been getting any therapy."

Another mother, Laura Gray, E-mailed her experience of three weeks: "Keenan has had a speech explosion. Before supplementation, he had never said more than one word at a time. Now he puts two and three words together and he's getting the final consonant. *Ee* has become *eat*, *mo* has become *more*, and *ha* is *hat*. Before supplementation, I was told that with lots of therapy he would speak by the time he was seven. Now I'll be surprised if he is still in therapy on his fourth birthday."

Jennifer Traub gives her three-year-old daughter Madelyn-Grace a fish oil supplement by squeezing the contents of the capsule into her apple juice every day. Says Jennifer, "After about three weeks our daughter began to spontaneously say words. Many of them weren't accurate, but almost all were intelligible." After two months, says Jennifer, "Madelyn-Grace's speech therapist told me that she has 'no explanation' for our little girl's vast improvement. She says she's never seen anything like it." And Lindsay Wheaton, after four months of supplementing her son, Quinn, reported, "There has been a huge jump in his speech production and overall behavior." Quinn went from stringing a maximum of three words together to speaking full sentences. All of a sudden, he could hit the *kw* sound and for the first time say his own name correctly—"Quinn" instead of "Finn."

BEST BEHAVIOR

For many parents, the joy at their child's dramatic improvement in speech has been matched by their joy at improvement in behavior. Typical is Karen Rothweiler's story about two-year-old Justin. His frustration at his lack of speech, she says, had led to a variety of behavioral issues. "The whole family felt like we were walking on eggshells trying not to do anything that would set him off. I was mentally drained by the end of each day." Within just a few weeks of giving Efalex to him, they noticed a big change in his personality. "Instead of grunting at me and freaking out when I couldn't figure out what he wanted, he would take me by the hand and lead me to what he wanted," says Karen. "He was much more agreeable and pleasant to be around."

Impressed by reports of greater speech improvements with the ProEFA supplement, they decided to give it a try. Just after Justin's third birthday, when he still could not say a single word and had been taking ProEFA for a month, the Rothweilers took him and his older brother, Brandon, to the Empire State Building. On the eighty-sixth-floor observation deck, as they posed for a picture, Karen told the boys to say "cheese," and for the first time in his young life, a smiling Justin said, "Eeeezzzz." He uttered the same sounds several times throughout the day and didn't stop there. Adds Karen, "He went from absolutely nothing to five words within four days. Now, after six months, he is talking full time, all day long, every day, with consistency."

INDEPENDENT CONFIRMATION

In many instances, teachers and therapists, unaware that a child was being given LCPs, have independently commented on dramatic improvements. Tammy Ingram kept her three-year-old son Kyle's SLP in the dark to see if she would independently remark on a difference. After about three and a half weeks, she says the therapist suddenly noticed a huge increase in Kyle's vocabulary. Four months into supplementation, Kyle's vocabulary had grown from just three-word approximations to more than one hundred words, and he was putting two- and three-word sentences together. Adds Tammy, "It has gone from hopeless to hopeful in such a short time."

After getting the pediatrician's approval ("he said there was nothing harmful in it"), Barbara Shamah did not tell the therapists, wanting to see if they would notice a difference in her just-turned-two daughter, Allison. And they certainly did. After eleven days, Barbara reported, "Allison has been much more mellow. There have been very few meltdowns. This morning, she sat for forty-five minutes with her special ed speech teacher and did not get up once. She usually cannot sit in one place for more than ten minutes. She even approximated the word 'rectangle' when working with the shape sorter. She had never tried a three-syllable word before."

SENSORY INTEGRATION

Fatty acid supplementation has also alleviated problems associated with apraxia, including sensory integration disorder and motor coordination disorder. It dramatically improved four-year-old John's sensory integration issues. Says his mother, Amy Heidenrich, "He hated haircuts, hats, dirty hands, new situations, and new people. We briefly tried medication but couldn't go through with it. The doctor recommended fatty acids, and after eight months of supplementation John's a different child. Now he tolerates haircuts, wears baseball hats like Daddy, plays in the mud, and has no problems at all in new situations, although he is still a little shy."

OLDER CHILDREN

Most accounts have come from parents of youngsters, but LCPs work for older children as well. Eleven days after beginning supplementation, Diane De Groat's ten-year-old son Jacob, out of the blue, said, "Me make you soup for you, Mommy." Says Diane, "It was the longest sentence my little boy had said in all his life, and he said 'mommy,' not 'mama.' I just sat there crying with tears of joy." That night, he surprised her again, saying, "Me love you, Mommy." And a few days later, talking about a chess tournament, he even said, "Mom, I am playing chest for championship."

HALLEY'S DIARY

Liz Miller decided to supplement her daughter's diet, Halley, and closely monitor the outcome by keeping a diary. She posted it on a Web site that she created and went on to display the on-line journals of other parents and their kids. They provide inspiring day-by-day accounts of "life with LCPs." To read the diaries, go to http://kidstalk back. tripod.com/kidstalkback. In Halley's case, at age three, she was getting five speech sessions a week, two from the county therapist and three through the early intervention program. Both therapists reported behavior issues—she was withdrawn and unwilling to cooperate. In spite of all of the therapy, by the age of four Halley could say only sixty-five words and put a handful of two-word sentences together.

Then Liz started to give Halley the ProEFA supplement. The very next day, she says, there were new words. After one month, Halley was saying more than 150 words, using three-word sentences and occasionally even four-word sentences. After a little over two months, Halley had attained 200 words.

THE RESEARCH

The dozens of reports praising LCP supplementation were so astounding that we decided to seek scientific validation. In July 2001, in collaboration with the CHERAB Foundation and Robert Katz, Ph.D., of the Consortium for Fatty Acids, Omega-3 Research Institute, we organized the first major conference on this subject.

At the conference, a panel of experts from leading universities and the National Institutes of Health reviewed reports of supplementation on thirty-three children. This included an analysis of anecdotal case reports from nineteen speech-language pathologists, and separate reports from a developmental pediatrician (coauthor Agin) and SLP Lori Roth. Seventeen of the nineteen children, age twenty-seven to ninety-seven months, who were monitored by the group of SLPs, showed varying degrees of improvement in speech. One child who also had autism was rated as having made moderate improvement in speech and better than moderate improvements in behavior and attention. In general, the children whose speech got better also showed improvements in attention, behavior, social skills, and eye contact.

Ten children examined by the developmental pediatrician ranged in age from thirty-two to ninety-six months. Most had been using supplements for at least three months and were receiving speech therapy at least three times a week. Most showed moderate to significant improvement in speech and attention and, to a lesser degree, in facial expression and eye contact. Two children on the autistic spectrum displayed significant improvement in speech and eye contact.

Speech-language pathologist Roth reported that each of her four clients—just two weeks into supplementation—demonstrated better attention, sustained eye contact, and calmer behavior. Subsequently, they showed enhanced verbal ability. One child, essentially nonverbal at the beginning, progressed to two-word utterances within two months.

By the end of three months, all four children exhibited modest to significant changes in language ability—the kind of changes, says Roth, that would characteristically occur after nine to twelve months of intensive speech therapy.

Overall, in conjunction with speech therapy, LCP supplementation produced a marked shift in the children's ability to talk. Within just a few weeks there were decreases in gesturing, grunting, and single sounds and increases in the use of single words, multiple words, and sentences.

The expert panel that reviewed these reports unanimously agreed that they justified a comprehensive clinical trial "to convincingly validate this new potential therapeutic intervention" for apraxia. The panel also recommended further exploration of the apparent presence of apraxia in some children on the autistic spectrum, and a possible association with other disorders and syndromes, such as hypotonia, sensory integration disorder, dysarthria, attention deficit hyperactivity disorder, Kabuki syndrome, and cerebral palsy.

The case for LCP supplementation in autistic children was bolstered by other research published around the same time. French researchers who compared fifteen autistic children with a control group of eighteen mentally retarded children reported that the autistic kids had "significantly lower levels" of omega-3 fatty acids, especially DHA, in their blood. The study's authors felt that these results could lead to dietary treatment for autism in association with the drugs currently being used.

A few months later, Scottish researcher Dr. Gordon Bell presented evidence of fatty acid deficiency in autistic children. Dr. Bell, whose seven-year-old son has autism, asked parents of fifty-five autistic children and fifty-five youngsters without the condition to look for indicators of fatty acid deficiency. These included rough and dry skin, dull hair, dandruff, soft or brittle nails, and what appear to be goose bumps on the upper arms and legs. Dr. Bell discovered that 65 percent of the autistic kids showed signs of deficiency, compared to just 12 percent of the nonautistic children. He later validated these findings by performing blood tests in a large group.

Subsequently, Dr. Bell supplemented the children's diets with fish oil capsules and commented, "We see improvements in some of the behaviors and characteristics of autism. Parents report that their children are more attentive, their concentration improves, and their sleep patterns stabilize." Dr. Bell believes there is a connection between changes in the Western diet and the huge rise in autism. In 1948, the average Briton ate 10 ounces of oily fish a week. Fifty years later this amount had dropped by half, to 5 ounces. Over the same period, doctors believe that there has been a tenfold increase in autism.

EARLIER RESEARCH

All of this interest in apraxia and autism follows earlier work in which a small number of clinical trials indicated that children with the learning disorders dyspraxia, dyslexia, and ADHD had a deficiency in these LCPs and that supplementation could improve attention, behavior, motor coordination, and even reading ability. The pioneering dyspraxia research was carried out by leading British researcher B. Jacqueline Stordy, Ph.D., in a study of fifteen children, age five to twelve. Over a four-month period, these children, who did not have *verbal* dyspraxia but had motor coordination problems, were given the Efalex supplement. Statistically significant improvements were noted in motor skills, ability to pay attention, level of hyperactivity, and behavior. The children were also significantly less anxious.

As word about Dr. Stordy's study spread, some parents wondered if it would benefit their apraxic children and so began using supplements. Initially, many used the Efalex product and, in general, reported considerable success. At times, some experimented with other fish oil supplements with varying results. Many have since claimed excellent progress with ProEFA, which contains a higher EPA-to-DHA ratio.

WHAT NOW?

Should you immediately give omega-3 fatty acids to *your* child? Anecdotal reports have been dramatic and strongly suggest that LCP supplementation—combined with speech therapy—could become the treatment of choice in disorders such as apraxia. These accounts need to be validated by solid clinical trials. But while the potential benefits are overwhelming, a possible downside is almost nonexistent. One exception is children allergic to fish or those who experience some nausea and, in rare situations, diarrhea. The gastro-intestinal symptoms may be alleviated by lowering the dosage. It's also recommended that you avoid supplements using the liver of the fish, as an excess of oil from this source can cause vitamin A and D toxicity.

Omega-3s are known to be important for early cognitive and visual development. In one study, infants supplemented with both DHA and ARA scored seven points higher on a test of mental development at the age of eighteen months. In the United States, the Food and Drug Administration recently acknowledged the benefits by approving the addition of DHA and ARA to infant formulas, years behind Japan and many European countries. But while fish has had a reputation as a healthy "brain food" long before the recent research, it's always advisable to consult with your pediatrician before giving any supplement to your child.

Which supplement should you use? Dr. Stordy expresses it well by saying that current supplementation is "a blunt tool," and that much more research is needed. It appears, however, that a combination of DHA, EPA, and GLA works best. The children with ADHD, dyslexia, and dyspraxia responded well to daily fish oil supplementation with 480 mg of DHA, a lesser, not-revealed amount of EPA, and 96 mg of GLA. This was the Efalex product. By and large, children with apraxia and autism have reportedly done better with a higher EPA-to-DHA ratio. They mostly received 148 mg of EPA, 99 mg of DHA, and 180 mg of borage oil containing 40 mg of GLA, per day (ProEFA).

We are all unique individuals and there's not a single "magic bullet" that will help everyone. It's too early to make claims about long-term benefits but, at the very least, it's obvious that fish oil supplementation seems to jump-start many children's ability to speak. Until clinical studies are conducted, we're still at the trial-and-error stage and will endeavor to keep readers informed of developments through the Web site, www.apraxia.cc, and the listserv, childrensapraxianet@yahoogroups.com.

RECOMMENDED LCP PRODUCTS

Coromega

European Reference Botanical Laboratories produces Coromega, a palatable form of fish oil in a creamy, orange-flavored, puddinglike emulsion. It can be squeezed out of the packet directly into the mouth or onto a spoon. It can also be added to juice or yogurts and blended.

INGREDIENTS AND NUTRIENT CLAIMS: Omega-3 fatty acids EPA and DHA from fish oil, vitamin C, vitamin E, folic acid, and stevia leaf extract. Each packet contains 230 mg of DHA, 350 mg of EPA, 45 mg of vitamin C, 7 IU of vitamin E, 100 mcg of folic acid, and 5 mg of stevia leaf extract.

AVAILABILITY: Retailers are listed on Coromega's Web site, or you can order directly from the company.

MANUFACTURER:
European Reference Botanical Laboratories, Inc.
P.O. Box 131135
Carlsbad, CA 92013-1135
Phone: 760-599-6088
Fax: 760-599-6089
Web: www.coromega.com

Efalex

A fish oil supplement rich in DHA, Efalex is the product that was used in clinical trials with ADHD, dyslexia, and dyspraxia in the United States and the United Kingdom. This is particularly good for young children.

INGREDIENTS AND NUTRIENT CLAIMS: High DHA fish oil, evening primrose oil, vitamin E, and thyme oil; capsule shell: gelatin and glycerin. Each capsule contains 60 mg of DHA, 12 mg of GLA, 5.25 mg of ARA, 1 mg of thyme oil, and 7.5 IU of vitamin E.

AVAILABILITY: Efalex can usually be found at GNC stores throughout the country.

MANUFACTURER:
Nutricia USA Inc.
2685 Ulmerton Road, Suite 201
Clearwater, FL 33762
Phone: 877-458-6400
Web: www.nutricia.com

ProEFA (Ultimate Omega Complete Omega)

The Nordic Naturals company says that this formula is an excellent source of omega-3 fatty acids in their naturally existing ratios. Advanced lipid antioxidants have been added for freshness, and natural lemon oil for taste.

INGREDIENTS AND NUTRIENT CLAIMS: Purified deep-sea fish oil, lecithin, ascorbyl palmitate, vitamin E, natural lemon flavor. Each 1,000-mg capsule contains 148 mg of EPA, 99 mg of DHA, 41 mg of other omega-3, 180 mg of borage oil, 40 mg of GLA, and 9 IU of vitamin E (mixed tocopherols).

AVAILABILITY: This product is part of the company's professional line and can be ordered from its Web site.

MANUFACTURER:
Nordic Naturals
3040 Valencia Avenue, Suite 2
Aptos, CA 95003
Phone: 831-662-2852
E-mail: admin@nordicnaturals.com
Web: www.nordicnaturals.com

GETTING LCPS FROM FOOD

In general, most parents prefer to use one of the above fish oil supplements, and the clinical trials that have been conducted with children who have ADHD, dyslexia, or dyspraxia have also used supplements. You can, of course, obtain the all-important omega-3 LCPs DHA and EPA from food sources. The richest providers are cold-water fatty fish such as mackerel, salmon, rainbow trout, and tuna. But you would have to consume a diet of fish, fish, and more fish, day after day, which is unrealistic for a small child. Using fish oil capsules is more convenient and takes the guesswork out of the nutritional content.

There is no research as yet to show the optimum dose of omega-3s and whether continued use is necessary for continued benefits. Most parents continue to give supplements to their children, and it is highly unlikely that a child could overdose on these long-chain fatty acids. These are the "good" fats—not the "bad" saturated fats found in fast food. Adults are advised not to take warfarin and high doses of aspirin in conjunction with omega-3 supplementation, but for children this is not usually an issue as these drugs are not often prescribed for them. Caution should be exhibited, however, in giving large amounts of omega-3s to children with cardiac problems and Kawasaki's disease and who are on anticoagulation or aspirin therapy. There is a wealth of evidence that everyone should consume these fatty acids, as there are considerable health benefits for adults as well as children. Studies now suggest that omega-3 fatty acids help fight heart disease, arthritis, depression, neurological disorders, and some cancers.

GETTING STARTED

After talking with your doctor, it's easy to try omega-3 fatty acid supplementation. All you have to do is obtain the product and give it to your child every day. You'll probably see results, and perhaps as quickly as some of the children featured in this chapter. The improvement in your child's condition should go a long way toward alleviating both his or her and your frustration. Best of all, it may begin to unlock his or her voice so that, as one mother put it, "You can find out what's going on inside that beautiful head."

The inability to communicate effectively has wide-ranging negative impact on the emotional well-being of kids with communication challenges. Omega-3 fatty acids certainly have a part to play, but there are many other strategies that parents can employ that can make a huge difference, and this is a subject that we cover in the next chapter.

9. Coping with Your Child's Frustrations

I am like a broken toy. Nobody wants to play with a broken toy.
—Eleven-year-old boy with a language disorder

Imagine being held hostage. You desperately want to shout for help, but your mouth is sealed shut with duct tape. Day after day your mind feverishly works overtime as you plan what you need to say. The words are in your head, but you're physically incapable of talking. You cannot communicate your needs.

This is what it can be like for a child with a serious speech disorder. He knows what he wants to say. The words have formed in his brain. But for some reason they just won't come out of his mouth, no matter how hard he tries. In fact, the harder he tries, the more scrambled the words may become. Worse still, he may emit nothing more than grunting noises that bring curious looks from strangers.

For toddlers the frustration can be overwhelming. Some may lash out and become aggressive; others may withdraw and cease participating in the world around them. Some may have explosive temper tantrums ranging the whole gamut of crying, screaming, kicking, hitting, and breath-holding; others may remain quiet, isolated, and immobile. Frustrations can also be expressed through clinging, bed-wetting, or changes in appetite. At a young age, the late talker's tantrums or withdrawal are the only ways that she is able to tell her parent what she does or does not want, that she is in pain, or that she is hungry. Parents have shared typical stories with us.

- Karen Rothweiler, mother of a three-year-old diagnosed with severe apraxia: "My son's middle name is 'frustration.' He just went to bed with a goose egg on his head from repeatedly banging his head against the wall when I couldn't figure out what he wanted."
- Tammy, mother of apraxic five-year-old Erik: "He really is a sweet little guy, but it's so frustrating for him when he has a whole paragraph inside and can get only one or two words out to describe what he's feeling. The temper tantrums are just awful."
- And there's Nicky, mother of late talker Chloe, age two years and four months: "My daughter can get so frustrated when I don't know what she wants. She just cries and cries. I don't spank, and time-outs don't seem to work. Sometimes, she laughs at me when I try to discipline her. I think I'm going to blow up!"

Mothers like Karen, Tammy, and Nicky struggle to cope with these challenges every day. The frustrations are so intensely felt and vented by most late talkers that they can completely exhaust and infuriate the best-intentioned of parents. Just what can you do to alleviate your child's frustration? How can you ease the torment that he feels? One basic approach with a very young child is to make him feel that his experience is normal and that everyone "learns to talk." Reassure him by saying something along these lines: "I remember when I was your age and learning that sound. You're doing better than I did." You can say, "Just remember what you want to tell me so that you can tell me later when you've learned to talk." Of course, your child is not really going to recollect what was so seemingly important, but you will have soothed the frustration of the moment.

Frustration requires empathy. Offer a comforting "It's okay." Sit down with your child at eye level and caringly tell her, "Mommy and

Daddy are here for you. We love you and are going to help you learn to talk." If your child is calm, explain why it's better to use pointing, sign language, or pictures as ways to communicate so that she doesn't resort to displays of anger. Ask if she can show you what she needs or use another word to describe what she wants, or ask her questions that require only yes or no answers. Try to translate what she means by observing her actions and surroundings. For example, one mother's four-year-old apraxic son said, "Pada tat?" over and over at a neighbor's house, growing ever more irritated as he continued to draw blank stares from everyone. When his mother noticed that he was standing near the neighbor's cat, she queried, "Oh, you want to pet the cat?" and his face lit up as he nodded in agreement.

It can be particularly hard on your child if you have to keep asking him to repeat something. Parents of late talkers often find themselves in guessing games trying to determine what their child is trying to say. Failed deciphering attempts often lead to the child having a screaming fit. There are various ways to avoid this. The simplest is to remember what he said and keep repeating it in your own head until you figure it out. Alternatively, tape-record his words so you can replay what he said. Use a microcassette recorder or, better still, a digital recorder. There's a breaking point that most parents have to discover the hard way—the number of times they can incorrectly guess what their child said before he becomes frustrated and tearful. They learn that it's best to divert the child's attention before reaching that point.

The pediatrician told Nicole Carnell that her son, Justin, was a per-fectly normal toddler. But he was two years old and not talking, and Nicole was concerned. Justin had always been a quiet baby. He had never babbled. He would grunt and point at what he wanted but never tried to say a word. The pediatrician's advice: Don't give him anything until he asks for it by name. "I spent endless hours sitting in front of the refrigerator not getting Justin his juice, waiting for him to say 'juice.' He never said it, and we would both end up crying. It was torture," remembers Nicole. "It looked as though he was trying to say some-thing but couldn't figure out how to move his mouth to make the cor-rect sounds come out. He would get very frustrated and stop trying. He started becoming very angry. He had a lot of tantrums and a very upset and worried mother. I didn't know it at the time, but he was obviously frustrated and angry because he wanted to communicate but didn't know how."

Says Scott Bilker, father of Brandon, "One of our difficulties if we continue to ask him to repeat words is that he starts to cry. He'll become frustrated, not answer any more questions, and simply walk away." Scott originally used a regular microcassette recorder but now finds a digital recorder much more convenient. Says Scott, "I believe that when he says the word, in his mind he may 'hear' it clearly, but when I play it back he can hear with his own ears that it's not quite right. Once he knows that I have the recording, he relaxes, realizing that he won't be asked to continually repeat the words."

Typical two-year-olds can be a handful—the so-called "terrible twos"—never mind a child who can't readily make his or her needs known. The challenge for late talkers is that they do not have the capacity to negotiate. Says Stacey Abenstein, mother of four-year-old Evan, who in addition to apraxia has sensory integration issues, "When you say no to something, they cannot even tell you why they wanted the something in the first place. And for all you know, you could be saying no to the wrong something, causing them even more frustration."

At the age of twenty-six months, says his mother, when Evan's frustration was growing alarmingly, he was kicked out of preschool. "There were too many children in the class, the teachers paid no attention to Evan, and the frustration level grew out of control at an unbelievable rate. He wanted so badly to socialize that he would approach the other children by hitting them on the head." The "terrible twos" were more than just terrible for Stacey and Ted. "It was a very tough year. There were times that I felt like a shut-in, never leaving the house in fear that Evan would become frustrated and hit other kids," says Stacey. Pointing out that the year between the second and third birthdays is a huge year developmentally, she advises, "Try defusing some of the frustration with new responsibilities such as setting the table, cleaning up, or wiping up a spill. Maybe you can let your child toss a salad." Giving children some control over little things fulfills their need for independence and relieves some of the communication aggravations.

Your child may not be able to talk, but there's almost certainly something she excels at. Be sure to point this out to her when she becomes upset with her struggle to speak—and praise her for it. One mother, for instance, told us, "My daughter with apraxia could go across the monkey bars and she learned to swim at a younger age than her twin sister. I would boost her confidence by making sure she was aware of her special talents." Dr. Mel Levine, professor of pediatrics at the University of North Carolina, emphasizes that boosting self-esteem is even more important in the early years of schooling because children with communication disorders often "suffer humiliation in the highly verbal ambience of school." Says Dr. Levine, "They must have opportunities . . . to shine in the areas in which they are more richly endowed. Artistic abilities, mechanical skills, and athletic strengths need to be put on display. All those who interact with such students need to make sure their self-esteem, motivation, and ambition are not thwarted at an early age because of the inordinate but transient stress on language proficiency that occurs during the formative years of schooling."

PUT IT IN WRITING

As it is so difficult for your late-talking child to communicate, it's up to all of the adults in her life to keep in touch with each other and let each other know about the part of her day that they have shared. One of the best ways of keeping everyone in the loop is keeping a "communication book." It's the child's diary, except that there may be half a dozen different contributors. For instance, the highlight of your child's evening may have been a party at which she was given a new toy. But her delight easily turns to frustration the next morning when she cannot share this event with her teacher. By writing the details in her communication book, you provide the teacher with the information needed to open a dialogue with her.

Record other activities in the book: new words your child produced, an explanation of why he has been happy or sad. Correspondingly, the schoolteacher could write a brief message explaining why he has that stamp of a puppy on his hand, or providing the words of a song they've been learning. Your child's baby-sitter or day care provider can write down what he had for lunch, or what games he played. Perhaps there is sensitive information that they don't want to discuss in front of him and prefer to put in writing. If you have a private therapist as well as a school-based therapist, this is a way for them to pool their knowledge, coordinate what words they are working on, what strategies they are employing, and what progress your child has made. The net result is that everyone who cares for your child, and who cares about your child, can have a more informed conversation with him. They will be able to prompt him because of their inside knowledge. It will make him feel more comfortable and relieve his frustration.

Inside the communication book you can also keep a "dictionary" to translate your child's language or actions. As he increases his vocabulary, add each new word to his own personal dictionary.

LISA'S LIST

Here is a list of things that Lisa wrote in Tanner's communication book when he was three years old.

Sound	Translation
Ju pee	Juice please (he'd also sign for drink)
Die die die	Either tight or side
High high high	He wants a lot or it's very big (both hands up in air)
Tee tee tee tee	Little bit, tiny
Ma ma Mommy or da da Daddy	Where is Mommy or Daddy?
Bobo	His brother, Dakota
Doo Doo	His Aunt Julie
Doo doo doodie	I want a cookie
Eeee	Hungry (he'd also sign for eat)
Doe	Go

Me, me, me? No?	Can I?
Tee tee tee tee me?	Is it okay for me to have a tiny bit?
Bow	He can say "ball," but sometimes it comes out like this
Na na know	I don't know
Eah	Egg
Tay	Okay
Die die die die	Can I go outside?
Di di dis	Look at this

THE INVISIBLE MAN

No matter how hard you try, there are going to be times when your child is so totally frustrated that there's a major meltdown. Here's one creative strategy that can work wonders in calming a crying child, but for reasons that will become obvious you have to use it in private. Here's what you do. In plain view of your child—let's call him Brian—you talk to an imaginary, invisible Brian who's standing right in front of you. You talk in an animated, enthusiastic way to the invisible Brian and give him hugs and kisses. You tell the invisible Brian how glad you are that he calmed down and stopped crying, because the two of you can now go and do some fun stuff. You'll probably find that the real Brian stops crying so he can listen to you. You may even get a smile or a laugh!

SOFT TALKER

When those crying fits occur in public—and that's often the way it happens—ignore the onlookers and just talk reassuringly to your child in a very soft voice. If she wants to find out what you're saying, she'll have to quiet down.

CIRCLE OF FRIENDS

It pays to have an open discussion about your child's speech problem. Get neighborhood friends or young classmates into a group and discuss your child's challenges. Explain how difficult it is for him not to be able to communicate as well as they do and emphasize how hurtful it is when he is teased. This openness should lead to better relationships all round.

MOVIE MAGIC

There are some excellent motivational movies that you can watch with your child, depicting situations to which he or she can relate. *Paulie,* for instance, is about a little girl who has severe stuttering. Her grandfather gets her a parrot, one that can understand human language and helps her find her voice. There's *Annabelle's Wish* about a calf called Annabelle, born on Christmas Eve and given as a present to a seven-year-old boy called Billy, who can't talk. Santa gives Annabelle and the other farm animals the gift of speech for a day. It's a story where dreams come true. In *Trumpet of the Swan,* based on E. B. White's book of the same name, Louie is a trumpeter swan with no voice. In order to woo his lady love he makes friends with a young boy, learns to speak, read, and write, and returns to his flock. Louie is ridiculed when no other swans can understand him. Of course, there's a happy ending! And don't forget *ET,* one of the most popular movies of all time, in which the lovable little alien learns how to talk and says the famous line, "ET phone home."

AND BOOKS, TOO

Here are good books to illustrate dealing with disabilities and overcoming adversity.

A Friend for Growl Bear by Margot Austin, David McPhail
(illustrator)

Ben Has Something to Say: A Story About Stuttering by Laurie Lears, Karen Ritz (illustrator)

Don't Stop the Music by Robert Persken

Extraordinary Friends (Let's Talk About It) by Fred Rogers, Jim Judkis (photographer)

Friends Everywhere by Donna Jo Napoli, Lauren Klementz-Harte

Friends at School by Rochelle Bunnett, Matt Brown (photographer)

Helen Keller: Facing Her Challenges, Challenging the World (Another Great Achiever) by Janet Benge, Geoff Benge, Kennon James (illustrator)

I Wish I Could Fly Like a Bird! by Katherine Denison, Tanya Weinberger (illustrator), Richard L. Walley (editor)

Leo the Late Bloomer by Robert Krauss

Many Ways to Learn: Young People's Guide to Learning Disabilities by Judith M. Stern, Uzi Ben-Ami, Michael Chesworth (illustrator)

Mary Marony Hides Out by Suzy Kline, Blanche Sims (illustrator)

Moses Goes to a Concert by Isaac Millman

Moses Goes to School by Isaac Millman

My Brother, Matthew by Mary Thompson

Oliver's High Five by Beverly Swerdlow Brown, Margot J. Ott (illustrator)

Puppies for Sale by Dan Clark, Jerry Dillingham (illustrator)

Rosey: The Imperfect Angel by Sandra L. Peckinpah, Trisha Moore (illustrator)

Someone Special, Just Like You by Tricia Brown, Fran Ortiz

Special People, Special Ways by Arlene Maguire, Sheila Bailey

Succeeding with LD: 20 True Stories About Real People with LD by Jill Lauren

The Boy Who Ate Words by Thierry Dedieu, Julie Harris (translator), Lory Frankel (translator)

The Lion Who Couldn't Roar by John Powers, Alan Colavecchio (illustrator)

Views from Our Shoes: Growing Up with a Brother or Sister with Special Needs by Donald J. Meyer (editor), Cary Pillo (illustrator)

What's Wrong with Timmy? by Maria Shriver, Sandra Speidel (illustrator)

SEPARATION FRUSTRATIONS

It's normal for any child to go through separation frustrations during the first days of preschool or day care. For a child who is nonverbal or just learning to talk, it's even harder because the child is dependent on his caregivers to understand and translate for him. Jeanne, mom of three-year-old Anthony, dashed off this E-mail to us as soon as she arrived home one day: "I just dropped my son off at his preschool. He kept telling me he wanted me to stay with him, so I told him I would walk him to his classroom and show him around, but his teacher would let me walk him only to the end of the hall. Anthony was crying and holding on to my hand so tight. I didn't say anything because I would have started crying, and I didn't want to cry in front of my son. Of course, I feel terrible because I feel like I lied to him. Anyway, I am still crying and hoping he is doing good."

Another mom—with the passage of time and the benefit of more accommodating teachers—was able to put the first-day fears into perspective. Laura Giedl wrote: "I dreaded that first day of school. The teachers had no problem with me going into the classroom with him for the first few minutes to walk him around and point out toys and things. I also didn't want to leave him there for the whole three hours as I thought this would be too much for him. But I was very surprised. He made it. Yes, Jamie took about two weeks to stop crying, and leaving him staring after me, crying, was the hardest thing I ever had to do. I cried all the way home, but they do survive it and he learned to like school."

Most schools don't allow parents to go with their crying preschool child into the classroom, but the National Association for the Education of Young Children takes a different stance. In a newsletter, they reported that early childhood educators suggest staying in the new situation with your child for the first few days, for decreasing amounts of time, until he or she accepts the new environment: "Your child will feel more comfortable with you there for part of the time, especially if he exhibits stranger anxiety, has little experience in being cared for by others, or has had a previous traumatic separation experience."

PLAN AHEAD

Most preschoolers or kindergarteners don't know anyone else, and the first few weeks are often awkward as they try to get used to your absence and make friends. But there are numerous things you can do to prepare your child for that first nerve-racking day. For instance, you can pave the way months in advance by having a close friend or relative baby-sit your child. This will get him or her used to the fact that when you leave you always come back.

Explain to your child exactly what she can expect to happen. Perhaps the facility will give you both a guided tour so that it will not be a totally new experience on her first day. Purchase books or toys to role-play what a day at school might be like. If she has a friend who will be attending the same school, ask that they be placed in the same class. Ask the teacher to give you names of other children who will be in the same class and arrange play dates so they and your child can get to know each other. If this is not possible, once school starts, explain your concerns, and the teacher should match your child up with another child during in-school play and projects. Give your child pictures of you that she can look at during the day, or let her take one of her "treasures" such as her blanket, her teddy, or a favorite book—familiar objects that should raise her comfort level.

If you drive your child to and from school, get him there on time and pick him up on time so he doesn't feel separate or alone. You can teach him what time you will be collecting him—or what time the bus will bring him home—by illustrating it on a piece of paper, which he can fold up and put in his pocket. Draw a circle with the big hand and the little hand, with or without all of the numbers, to show the time that school is over. You can also buy "time timer" clocks, enabling youngsters to judge how much time is left without having to know how to tell the time. The clocks have large numbers and a red disk that diminishes in size to show how much time has elapsed. They are approximately $25 to $30 from www.timetimer.com. Explain time concepts to a young child through association. For example, "I will pick you up when it is time for lunch" or "I will pick you up from school right after your teacher sings the good-bye song." Giving a young child something tangible to think about provides a feeling of security.

If your departure triggers a bout of tears, acknowledge your child's concerns; don't make light of them. Explain that you felt exactly the same when your mommy had to leave you and that it worked out fine. And put up a brave front yourself. Leaving your child may be just as traumatic for you as it is for her, but don't show it. Most children are exquisitely sensitive to their parents' feelings. Sensing your anxiety can increase your child's anxiety. If you need to cry, wait until you leave. Perhaps most important of all, never leave your child without saying good-bye. In an effort to avoid the tears it can be very tempting to sneak away when your child isn't watching, or tell her that you will be right back when she won't be seeing you for hours. By giving in to this temptation, you only diminish her trust in you. Not knowing your whereabouts confuses and worries her. Make a point of gently telling her that you are leaving, and make it clear when she will see you again. Emphasize that Mommy (and Daddy) always comes back.

FRUSTRATIONS FROM TEASING OR BULLYING

As they grow older, children with communication challenges face a whole new set of frustrations, including teasing to bullying. While teasing can be painful, bullying is far more severe and may require the intervention of school personnel or even law enforcement. What can you do to help prevent your child from being bullied? First of all, encourage him to make friends. Bullies tend to pick on loners, so help him establish friendships while young. Depending on your child's age, call parents of other children and set up play dates or sleepovers. Get your child involved with the scouts or similar organizations. Provide your child with a strong and loving home environment. You can teach healthy-relationship and anger management by how you handle conflicts. Encourage independence in your child to raise his confidence. Guide him toward activities in which he can excel, such as sports, arts, computers, and dance. Everyone has some kind of talent, so help your child find his. Contact the school if bullying continues.

Khalid Mustafa, who's now fifteen, says that for him the teasing was worst in third, fourth, and fifth grades. "People thought of me as slow and it bothered me. Many times I felt alone at school. I had problems with learning to read and spell. I knew I wasn't stupid, but it did make me feel different from the others. Luckily, I was told by my tutor that in spite of my disabilities I was a gifted student, and many times children like me often have hidden talents and very high IQs. I remember knowing the answers to many things and I would try to say them, but my words just came out sounding weird." Khalid's mother, Cindy, has a lot of experience with these issues as Khalid's seven-year-old brother Jadd also has apraxia. At the beginning of each school year she and her husband arrange a conference with the teachers. They let them know their sons' communication levels, express their concerns about teasing and bullying, and ask what positive conflict intervention is offered in the classroom. Their sons' speech therapists play key roles in developing positive solutions. On top of this, the Mustafas initiate drama and role-playing activities at home. Says Cindy, "This is a great strategy that can also be implemented in the classroom. My husband and I use this intervention to offer concrete examples of alternative methods of interaction with unpleasant people."

GETTING OLDER, GETTING WISER

As children get older they begin to adjust their dialogue, making accommodations for words they have difficulty saying. Khalid is a good example. He has learned to substitute words he can pronounce for words that he can't. Before he was able to correctly say *hospital*, he would use *med center*. As he had a hard time saying *uary* at the end of *February*, he would announce that the Super Bowl would be held in the second month of the year. The *House of Representatives* was abbreviated to *House of Reps*. When he talks he's often thinking ahead, preparing words to use in the conversation. To buy time, he sometimes asks the people speaking to repeat or rephrase what they have said. Other times, he simply uses facial gestures to communicate his meaning. Smart thinking!

For children without a voice, life can be immensely challenging, but the suggestions in this chapter should go a long way toward easing their frustrations. The children, of course, aren't the only ones whose lives are turned upside down. Parents face their own set of challenges and frustrations dealing with the hand they've been dealt. That's why we devote the next chapter to helping you cope with the special frustrations you will inevitably encounter. Take heart knowing that there are many parents of late talkers willing to share their experiences with you. We hope their stories will help you—if nothing else, you'll see you're not alone.

10. Coping with Your Own Frustrations and Fears

If I feel alone and frustrated, imagine how our apraxic children must feel.
—BARBARA THOMPSON, mother of three-year-old Susan

What's the most frustrating time for parents of a late talker? Is it waiting for those first words to come while everyone constantly asks, "Has he started talking yet?" Is it when your child is two and still can't say "mommy," while your friends' children of the same age are having conversations? Is it when your child, at the age of three, says "mommy" for the first time, and no one appreciates why you're so ecstatic? Is the biggest frustration of all when he's four years old and you're studying special education law into the small hours, and meanwhile your friends' biggest concern is if they let their child eat too much fast food? Or perhaps the frustration turns to fear when your daughter is age five and lost in a shopping mall, unable to tell anyone her name, let alone her address.

Who can appreciate the annoyance of dealing with well-meaning people and their constant reassurance that she'll "talk when she's ready"? Worse still, consider handling strangers who rudely and publicly ask, "What's wrong with her?" Or is the biggest frustration when your child wants to play with other children but they tease and reject her because they can't understand her? Robyn Williams, mother of three-and-a-half-year-old Jacob, provides a poignant example of the latter frustration. Jacob, she says, would always insist on playing the role of the monster. He would raise both arms and turn his hands into claws. He would make scary noises and chase the other kids so that he could play—without having to talk. "It was so frustrating, and it used to drive me crazy," says Robyn. "The other kids thought it was funny and would play along but, unfortunately, if he didn't become the monster, he would get left out. Eventually, I made him stop doing it because I wanted him to be included without having to be the monster."

Forging relationships with new playmates was also a big problem for Jacob. Robyn gratefully remembers the attitude of a caring mother who intervened at a McDonald's Play Place one day. Jacob had made overtures to play with three little boys, but they had rebuffed his efforts. The mother of one of the boys, who had noticed what was happening, went over and asked Jacob if they were being nice to him. He shook his head. She asked him if he wanted to play with them, and he nodded. Says Robyn, "She asked me his name and called the boys over. She told them, 'This is Jacob and he would like to play with you guys today, so you need to play with him.' He played with them for an hour and had the time of his life. Less than five minutes of this mom's time made the day for my son. If only all moms could be so considerate."

For Diane De Groat the main frustration is that her ten-year-old son, also named Jacob, is constantly tormented and bullied at school. Other kids call him "Mute Boy." Says Diane, "He's in a classified classroom, but it's the children in the other classes that are making life miserable for him. He's in the fifth grade and coming home 99 percent of the time in tears. My older boys are getting into trouble because when someone messes with their brother, they step in." Diane begged the school to explain his condition to the other children and stop the teasing, only to be told, "It's the age. Jacob needs to ignore it." Says a distraught Diane, "Can you believe this? I cry myself to sleep at night knowing that the next day he's going to be picked on again. Teasing isn't an age thing! It's cruel and heartless."

Another mother, Carol Holt, whose six-year-old son Micah has global apraxia, a motor-planning disorder, expresses frustration at those people who misguidedly counsel that there's nothing to worry about and that she should just give it time. "Sometimes, it makes me feel somewhat insane. I know what I know and I know what I see, but the people around me act as if they can't see what I'm talking about." The result, she says, is to question herself: "Am I paranoid? Am I trying to baby my youngest? Am I somehow sick and wanting my child to get interventions he doesn't really need so he gets special attention? Am I overprotective?" The answers? Says Carol, "When I reach deep down I know beyond a shadow of a doubt that the answers are a resounding no. It's a constant challenge to face the comments, beliefs, and philosophies of society while trying to raise a child you know needs extra help."

For other parents, the biggest frustration comes when comparing the late-talking child with his siblings and friends. It really hit home for Bridget Kirk at her twenty-month-old daughter Kaeli's play group. Wrote Bridget, "She is one of the older kids, and it is very difficult for me to hear how far behind she is. I know I shouldn't compare, but all of the kids said at least half a dozen intelligible words and Kaeli didn't say but one. This is my first child. I couldn't wait until she started talking and now I sometimes worry if I'll ever hear her talk. More than anything, I just want her to be 'normal.'"

For Pam Campbell, mother of four-year-old Corey, diagnosed with apraxia, the unfortunate comparison hits even closer to home; she also has two-year-old twins who, in stark contrast to Corey, are communicating at or above their age level. Says Pam, "I see the look in Corey's eyes when he hears one of his siblings easily say a new word. Each word for him is so difficult, and as a parent it's so hard to see your child struggle. He understands so much more than he can actually communicate and he is very frustrated with that."

Most parents, like Robyn, Diane, Carol, Bridget, and Pam, are prepared for the predictable challenges of parenting. But having a child who is a late talker creates an uncertainty that causes parents to second-guess not only themselves but also many of the people they trust the most—parents, friends, pediatricians, and other professionals. Bridget Kirk put it this way: "Since the day Kaeli was born I've been talking to her just like all of the books tell you to do. I've always talked about things and labeled everything we come in contact with. I don't think I've done one thing differently than people with kids that talk. In fact, I feel like I've tried harder than many of them."

Parents worry because their child is a late talker and then worry that they're worrying too much. You worry about all of the hard choices that you need to make. You're afraid of making mistakes and you're afraid of venturing into the unknown with greater demands on your parenting skills than you'd ever imagined. Your natural instinct, when you have a child who can't vocalize her needs and who can't be understood by strangers, is to protect her by keeping her with you at all times. So do you quit your job to stay at home, but then not have enough money to cover the evaluations and therapy that she really needs? Perhaps worst of all is the impact on your marriage. Agonizing over a child's inability to talk can put pressure on the most solid of relationships.

Through the huge amount of E-mail we receive we have seen the whirlwind of emotions that parents endure when it dawns on them that their child is not just a late talker but has a severe speech disorder. "I had so many different emotions flowing through me," says Nicole Carnell. "I was elated to finally have a diagnosis and to know what was wrong. I was angry because Justin was a textbook verbal dyspraxic child and I felt that the doctors should have pointed me in the right direction earlier. I was scared because I had no idea what this disorder was all about. I was sad because I didn't want my child to have a disorder. I also felt very lucky to have such a special child in my life." Cindy Mustafa remembers "feeling so horribly alone since there seemed to be nobody else who was going through the same thing as my husband and I. I would go through waves of emotion, from denial to fear, and rage, and then sadness. My pain was for Khalid and what I feared he would face with the challenges before him. I did not want my son to feel different, pitied, or excluded throughout life."

Parents roller-coaster through the "grief and mourning model"—typically denial, anger, fear, guilt, depression, and acceptance—accompanied by constant pain. Most parents go through all of these stages. Some may get stuck in one stage for a while; some may quickly lurch from one to the next. Unfortunately, mother and father can often experience different and conflicting stages at the same time. While one is locked in denial, for example, the other may be sunk in deep depression. You may also find that several of these stages merge together and are endured at the same time. Even though the following pattern appears to be the most common, note that it can vary.

DENIAL

After the speech-language pathologist or doctor announces that your child has a speech disorder, the first reaction of most parents is stunned disbelief. Maybe you suspected there was a genuine problem, but its confirmation leaves you saying, "I don't believe this is happening to us." Typically, one parent remains in this stage while the other progresses. More often than not, the father has the harder time accepting the diagnosis, possibly because men seem to find it more difficult to acknowledge that their child has a problem.

One mother (we'll call her Margot) bluntly put it this way: "Even my husband doesn't get it. I don't think he wants to admit it. His family and friends all say that we shouldn't worry, that our daughter will grow out of it. I have so many emotions running fierce and I am just trying to sort them out." Nancy, mother of two-year-old June, faced the same dilemma: "My husband has been in some sort of denial for more than a year, but I went ahead and called for an evaluation anyway. He came home soon after the evaluators had left and found me sitting in the middle of the dining room floor holding June and sobbing my heart out." June was sixteen months old and had tested at a nine-to-eleven-month level. Says Nancy, "Between tears, I told my husband all about it, and his response was awful. He said that these people didn't know what they were talking about, that they were just in it for the money, and I should have told them to get out of my house! He will still not admit that the therapy sessions are necessary, but he tolerates them because he knows that I would never have it any other way. He believes that June will eventually just start talking and that she will catch up before it's time to go to school."

ANGER

Once the initial shock has begun to wear off, parents become angry that their lives have been turned upside down. They demand, "Why my child?" "Why me?" "What did I do to deserve this?" In their bitterness and rage they may lash out at the doctor or therapist who broke the news to them. They may turn on each other or other members of the family. They may feel that the stress is simply too much to bear.

Holly White posed a typical angry and anguished question to us: "Why did no one ever tell me about this before?" Holly had just come to the realization that her daughter, Samantha, diagnosed as "mildly mentally handicapped," probably had apraxia. Five-year-old Samantha, says Holly, had been evaluated by highly recommended health professionals including ten speech therapists and four ear, nose, and throat specialists. But Holly felt that Samantha was not being properly diagnosed and kept searching for an answer. She found it on the CHERAB Web site. Says Holly, "I read through the characteristics of a child with oral and verbal apraxia. My jaw dropped a little at each one. You had described my little Samantha to a *T.* I sat there crying with relief and anger. I just can't understand why none of the professionals were able to identify her apraxia. Every time I had to fill out a case history it read exactly like the Web site's characteristics page."

Deborah Letterman, mother of ten-year-old Tara, is also upset with and exasperated by the quality of advice she received. "I am so tired of experts telling me about my daughter. I am so tired of relatives, and others, telling all wonderful, caring, intelligent mothers that they don't know their own kids. It's ludicrous. For Tara's entire life the experts have been telling me that she was profoundly retarded. It turns out that she knows a heck of a lot. She just couldn't get it across to us."

FEAR

Anger often gives way to fear when you realize that you're facing years of challenges you never expected. You're hit by the reality that you're going to have to learn skills that the parenting books didn't mention. You begin to hear about the battles that other parents have had to wage with insurance companies and the education system. You're full of doubt and uncertainty, and you feel confused, anxious, and helpless. You wonder if your child will ever lead a normal life, and you ask yourself, "How on earth am I going to cope?" The fear is palpable—fear of the unknown and fear of your ability to handle it.

A typical E-mail from a parent at this stage was sent to us by a mother of four, Renee Sparkman. Her youngest child, a girl, had been diagnosed at two years and three months with severe apraxia and hypotonia. Early intervention had approved only twice-a-week therapy, and Renee was getting ready for a follow-up meeting with them. Her E-mail was a flood of interwoven questions: "The problem? I am terrified. My daughter will be with people who don't know about or understand how to treat apraxia. I need some quick help and support for this meeting. I have spent hours on the Internet and seem to be going in circles. What should I ask for? Should I ask for therapy three times a week for right now? What do I present to them to show how important it is, that the more intervention she gets now, the less likely it is she will need it for years to come? Should she be having occupational therapy (motor planning)? I am also desperate to see what kind of essential fatty acids I can start her on to see if it helps. Should I take her to be evaluated somewhere else? I guess I come to you, confused, upset, hopeful, and desperate."

Allison, mother of three-and-a-half-year-old Joshua, diagnosed with oral-motor apraxia just before his second birthday, revealed similar fears in her first E-mail to the list: "I'm so worried about him feeling different once he starts school. He gets frustrated with communication, of course, but I don't think he realizes it's not the same for other kids." She added, "I wonder what he has trapped in his beautiful head and what kind of person this will make him grow up to be. Will he be introverted and keep his thoughts and feelings to himself because that's how he started? Will he ever be 'normal'? I've never met another apraxia parent and it's great to be able to express these thoughts to people who will understand and not think I'm a worrywart or a fruitcake."

Tricia Lewis, whose two-year-old daughter Madison was believed to have apraxia, became fearful as soon as she began to research the disorder. She wrote, "Honestly, I am scared to death! I thought we would be in therapy a few months and she would be talking, but it looks like we are in this for years. I have to admit, it breaks my heart that I don't have a 'perfect' child." Tricia went on, "Don't get me wrong. I love my baby with all my heart and am so thankful to have her, no matter if she never talks. She tries so hard to say the words—they just don't come out right. She is very intelligent in all other areas and is a wonderful child. I am just so sad about the struggles that she will have to face."

GUILT

Parents frequently blame themselves for their child's condition. They wonder what they did wrong or what they could have done differently. They may feel that they are being punished for something and that their child is suffering as a result. Perhaps it was that glass of wine during pregnancy, or the cord around the neck in the delivery room. Parents reminisce about the time when they thought their child was developing "normally" and wish they could go back to that time. They feel guilty that their child may never achieve the dreams they had held for him or her.

Says Gretchen Weggenmann, mother of six-year-old Kevin, "The first three years were hell and I really try to forget them. I used to cry myself to sleep and wonder what I did to get a child who not only has apraxia but is very high-strung and difficult. I really believe that God gave him to me so that I could learn patience." And Michelle Pollard, mother of three-year-old William, put it this way: "Originally, when I realized that I couldn't help Willy learn to speak just by speaking to him—like most parents do with their kids—I felt this overwhelming sense of guilt, loss, and inadequacy. It was just totally horrible. Now I am way past the grieving stage."

DEPRESSION

At times parents become horribly depressed as they struggle to cope with their child's handicap. They constantly worry about their child's development and what the future has in store for him. The stress can be overwhelming. Wrote Mary, mother of a two-and-a-half-year-old boy, "I know in my head that things could be worse, but in my heart I can't help but feel gut-wrenching sorrow. Sometimes when my son is sleeping at night, I lie down next to him, hold him, and cry. When I first found out, I cried for seven days straight, day and night. I didn't think I'd ever stop. It is still extremely traumatic for me. Not knowing what the future holds for him sometimes makes it difficult to have a positive outlook. I am, however, trying to take one day at a time. The happiness I feel every time he even attempts to say a word, whether it sounds right or wrong, makes it a little easier, because at least he's making some progress. I have a beautiful, very affectionate, and loving little boy, and I am trying to stay positive, which isn't very easy some days."

Another mother's raw, honest message: "I feel completely overwhelmed. When my son was first diagnosed, I took it very hard. I have lived my whole life to be a mom. I guess I always expected I would have perfect children, and having a child with a special need has been devastating. Every day is such a struggle. The temper tantrums have worn me down. I am so thankful for my children and I love them more than anything in the world, but this just doesn't get any easier, does it?"

Gayle, mother of two-year-old Barry, diagnosed with apraxia and sensory integration disorder, dramatically expressed the same rise and fall in emotions: "It really is a roller coaster. Some days I feel that Barry is trying so hard and I'm so happy and proud of his efforts. Other days, I think, 'You have got to be kidding. Why are you getting excited about him making a few sounds when most kids his age are talking?' And I cry because it seems so unfair. What I still find hard is when you tell someone his diagnosis and they look at you with pity eyes as if he were retarded. I want to shout from the rooftops that he is smarter than the average child. He just can't express himself."

ACCEPTANCE

The most difficult stage to achieve is final acceptance of your child's condition. It's the time when you shrug off the negativity and discard the wishful thinking about what might have been. Instead, you accept the cards that you have been dealt and concentrate on implementing the most sensible course of action to help your child's progress. It can take considerable time to reach this point. There will be days when you face the future with extreme confidence and days when you relapse. As a loving parent it may continue to be difficult to accept your child's "differences" totally, but it is now part of your family's day-to-day life. You are comfortable with what needs to be done and have established the necessary goals. Above all, you feel blessed to have been given the child that you have.

Says Michelle Pollard, who had once been told that her son William would probably never talk and that speech therapy was pointless, "I love Willy regardless of his problems. I have always kept in mind that even if he doesn't speak I will give him the opportunity to achieve to his greatest potential. I believe that even if there is the slightest glimmer of hope it is worth pursuing. I do not give up easily." And she accepts where they are at, saying, "I guess we have faced the typical struggles of parents of an apraxic child and now it is part of our everyday life."

Says Stacey Abenstein, "Evan will probably need to be in speech therapy for many years to come, but at least now I can see that he will improve and be able to function like a normal child someday. I still agonize over every decision I make for Evan. I work very hard to ensure that I set him up to succeed. And the thanks I get? How about my adorable, funny, intelligent, happy son saying, "I wu you, Mommy!"

Nicole Carnell tells an inspiring story of the day her two-and-a-half-year-old son Justin was diagnosed and how she later came to terms with it. The diagnosis was made at the world-renowned Duke Medical Center. Says Nicole, "I went into the office believing that they were going to tell me he was just a late talker and that there was really nothing wrong. I was blindsided. All I heard were the terms 'verbal dyspraxia,' 'apraxia of speech,' 'neurological disorder.' I remember asking if other issues would come up and if he was ever going to talk." The response, says Nicole, was "maybe, maybe not." There was no way to know for sure. She left the office with Justin and cried and cried, and just kept walking down hospital corridors until she realized she was lost.

A boy, about nine years old, scooted up to them in his wheelchair and told her it was okay to cry and that he would lead them to the elevators. Says Nicole, "It was apparent he had recently had brain surgery as he was bald and had a horrific scar on his head. He could barely move his arms or hands, but he had the most remarkable smile. My son didn't flinch. He just followed right behind the boy's wheelchair. As we walked along we could see—through open doors—children in therapy sessions. They were all severely disabled, but they all had smiles on their faces. The mothers standing behind their wheelchairs were smiling and laughing as well. It made me realize how lucky I was. Things could have been so much more difficult. I felt like I had been given a gift, a glimpse into the world of these mothers and children who do have really severe situations to deal with every day. I know how big their hearts and spirits are."

Nevertheless, says Nicole, she was still devastated about Justin's condition and cried many more nights before finally reaching acceptance. "We all have it rough and we all sometimes scream, 'It's not fair!' But we all come to the conclusion that we are the lucky ones, as we enjoy our family and our children. My little boy is growing up. I once wanted to shelter him from the world, but now we are experiencing the wonders of life together. I now know that my son is going to be okay. He has to work harder and be stronger and more determined than most children. But he is also more loving, more giving, and more understanding than most children. I will be okay, too. Justin has taught me how to believe and to have faith. Justin Carnell is a true blessing."

FIGHTING THE FRUSTRATIONS

Now that you know what to expect, thanks to the openness of Nicole and all of the other mothers, what can you do to overcome the inevitable frustrations of raising a child with a serious speech disorder?

FIND THE BEST BABY-SITTERS: Find people you can trust to give you a break and baby-sit your child. Do you have sympathetic friends and relatives who can help? Ask for recommendations from your pediatrician, neighbors, people you know at your church or temple, or other children's parents. There might be a baby-sitting co-op club in your area where members occasionally watch each other's kids free of charge. Check out www.babysittingcoop.com.

JOIN A SUPPORT GROUP: There is strength in numbers. Band together with other parents in your community and hold regular meetings. If you can't find enough parents locally, check out Internet listservs where compassionate and intelligent advice may come from a kindred soul who may be a thousand miles but just the click of a mouse away.

FIND A "BIG BROTHER" OR "SISTER": Look for someone who's already been through the same experience and has had a successful outcome, someone who can be a mentor to you, delivering pointers and hope. You can do this in person and through the Internet.

FIND A STRENGTH IN YOUR CHILD: Instead of focusing only on the speech challenge, find an activity or interest that your child enjoys and at which he excels. Perhaps he puts puzzles together quickly. If so, buy lots of puzzles for him and take part in the activity. Perhaps she would like an art class or cooking class. Whatever the pursuit, focus on the positive and praise your child for his or her accomplishments.

BECOME AN INFORMED ACTIVIST: Get educated and take an active role in your child's therapy. The more informed you are, the less frustrating it will be. Don't assume that a medical or speech professional is automatically an expert on each of the wide array of communication disorders. Therapists and medical doctors learn about so many different disorders that they may not know a lot about your child's specific condition. As a parent, with the research you can do on the Internet and with the input of support groups, you can find strategies to share with your child's pediatrician or therapists. If you don't have your own computer or Internet access, use computers at your local library and sign up for free E-mail access through companies such as Yahoo and Hotmail.

LEARN THE LINGO: You'll encounter medical terminology and a slew of abbreviations that you've never heard before. Make it your business to master this exotic vocabulary. Don't be embarrassed to stop someone in midsentence and ask him or her to explain unfamiliar words. (See Appendix E for the most common initials/abbreviations.)

START EXERCISING: By exercising you release endorphins into your system, which make you feel happy. Parents tend to take frustrations out on themselves. An exercise regimen is something to keep you in shape, both physically and mentally. The sense of accomplishment can be extremely rewarding and motivating.

SLEEP TIGHT: Get a good night's sleep. Don't underestimate the importance of a refreshing eight hours of sleep. Research shows that sleeping not only rejuvenates our bodies but also helps our brains process information more efficiently.

EAT RIGHT: "You are what you eat" is not a trite slogan—it's for real. Enjoying good nutrition will build up your body's immune system. You need to be healthy to handle your daily burden. If you're giving your child LCP supplements, consider taking them yourself!

TREAT YOURSELF: Pamper yourself in small or large ways: Luxuriate in a bubble bath, go for a massage, spend a night out with friends, take day trips, or go on vacation.

APPRECIATE YOUR PARTNER: Any challenges with your children can put enormous stress on a marriage, as we tend to take out our frustrations on those closest to us. Couples may ignore each other or fight, which only makes the situation worse. Be aware of this danger and find time to have fun together. Schedule date nights. Try to communicate openly with each other about your concerns and fears. We all confront challenges in different ways, and each spouse needs to understand the other's perspective.

APPRECIATE YOURSELF: Know that it's okay sometimes to feel annoyed, discouraged, angry, worried, or unenthusiastic about your child's struggle with speech. Don't let these "down" times overwhelm you. You know that most of the time you do the very best that you can for your child, and that's important.

MOVIE MAGIC: In Chapter 9 we discussed watching motivational movies such as *Paulie, Annabelle's Wish, Trumpet of the Swan*, and *ET* to be as motivating when your child is frustrated. These movies can be equally therapeutic for parents!

LAUGHTER: Laughter is the best medicine. Research has shown that a sense of humor can defuse anxiety, relax muscles, and make you feel good. Find ways to have fun either with your child or with other adults. Maybe go to a comedy club or watch old Marx Brothers movies, *I Love Lucy* reruns, or whatever is your particular brand of comedy.

SEEK COUNSELING: At times the pressure might seem more than you can stand. That's totally understandable. But if there are times when it all seems too much, don't hesitate to get professional help. Sometimes an expert listener is the best remedy.

DEALING WITH RUDE PEOPLE

It's amazing how insensitive people can be. Often a child's inability to speak makes people believe that he must be mentally retarded. People will ask questions in front of your child, such as "Why does he talk funny?" or "What's wrong with him?" Or they may glare or make remarks about the child's unruly behavior. Some parents can be thick-skinned and simply ignore offensive people. As one father told us, "I've got a child that my wife and I fight for on a daily basis against demons, known and unknown. I don't have the time to dwell on having hurt feelings. I've got too much to do for him, and every second in the fight is critical." Other parents have come up with creative responses that take the sting out of embarrassing encounters.

One mother's simple answer, which usually silences the person questioning a child's speech problem, is, "He's learning to talk and he's doing great." Then she turns to her child and says, "Aren't you, son?" Some mothers carry "business cards" with a brief description of their child's condition and hand them out when people ask rude questions or glare at a temper tantrum. One mother told us about her oldest son's version, which he gives out when people react badly to his brother's behavior. It says, "Please show your kindness and do not stare. He is just a boy trying to fight his illness."

Humor is another way to defuse the situation. Terri White, who's son Andrew had no understandable speech as a toddler, came up with a unique answer to the "What's wrong with him" question. She would usually say something like, "Oh, sorry about that. He's learning his fifth language. I think it's Swahili this week." Then she'd listen to her son a little longer, nod her head, and add, "Yes. He's commenting on the aerodynamic styling of the ceiling fan, and how its functionality in this setting seems appropriate." Says Terri, "Deflecting it like that made it easier for me to deal with the rude questioners."

Even professionals can be insensitive. Diane De Groat remembers a class trip with her ten-year-old son Jacob and his nine-year-old brother Joshua. Jacob's teacher loudly said to her, "Joshua is very bright. Doesn't it upset you that Jacob doesn't talk as well as Joshua?" Diane looked the offending teacher in the eye and responded, "Jacob is very smart, too, and he wouldn't be Jacob any other way." Says Diane, "Jacob reached up and gave me the biggest hug. I had him removed from her class the next day." Michelle Pollard feels the same: "I wish others knew that Willy is fully capable of understanding them. People talk in front of him as if he wasn't there."

Beyond the inevitable frustrations of parents, perhaps even worse are the fears. The strongest parental urge of all is to protect one's child, and the parents of a nonverbal child have worries that others don't. For instance, they worry about leaving him in day care, preschool, or with baby-sitters with whom he can't communicate, and they worry about his inability to speak if he gets lost.

THE FEAR OF STARTING SCHOOL

As discussed earlier, one of the most stressful situations for any child can be the initial days of day care or preschool. It can be equally stressful for the parent, perhaps even more so. Leaving any child in the care of strangers for the first time is usually cause for concern, and it's especially so with nonverbal toddlers. How will they communicate their needs? How will they cope? How will they get along with the other kids?

First of all, late-talking children need to go to school. They benefit from being in the classroom, participating with other youngsters in play, and taking part in learning opportunities that are difficult to simulate at home. In addition to teaching the basics, preschool helps them develop socialization skills. It's quite normal for *any* child to feel some separation anxiety, exhibited by crying and clinging. And it's equally normal for you to feel a range of emotions: excitement mixed with fear about your child dealing with tough situations without you, relief that you finally have some time for yourself, and maybe some guilt about wanting that time.

THE FEAR OF GETTING LOST

What about when you are with your nonverbal child at the park, at the shopping mall, or on vacation far from home? What if she gets lost? How is she going to tell people who she is and where she's from? Work out some kind of identification system. The simplest way is to take a business card or an index card. Write on it something like, "I am still learning to talk, but I understand you. Please call my mom and dad for me. They are here with me and I lost them. My mom's cell phone number is [XXX-XXXX]. Thanks." Place the card in a plastic ziplock bag and put it inside one of her socks. Tell her that if she gets lost she should find a policeman, uniformed security guard, a mommy with kids, or, if in a store, a salesclerk, show him or her the card, and have that person call you.

One mother's creative and inexpensive approach was to go to her local pet store where they have an automatic tag maker and a variety of tags. She chose a small gold circle about two inches in diameter with enough room for three lines of type. The tag comes with a little O ring that would normally be attached to a pet's collar. This mother attached it to her son's shoelace, near the toes. In those three lines you can write

LEARNING TO TALK
Able to understand
Phone: 123-456-7890

The police and other authorities suggest that you don't add your child's name because it is better not to give his or her name to strangers who might have evil intent. "Learning to talk" offers a more positive presentation of the child's speech challenge and is typically more accurate than saying "nonverbal." The expression "Able to understand" should prevent people from talking in front of the child as if he isn't there, or mistakenly believing him to be deaf or mentally retarded. There are other, more "sophisticated" methods, including scopes (miniature microscopes that can hold valuable information) and bracelets. For more details, see the Resources section at the end of the book. Whatever your frustrations, whatever your fears, you're not the first to experience them. You are not alone. Fortunately, other pioneering parents have banded together to help each other—and to help you.

A HELPING HAND

Self-help and support groups make a dramatic difference, enabling you to share your experiences with other parents and become informed advocates. Such groups have been around for many years and the common bond and the pooling of knowledge clearly benefit the participants. But the explosive growth of the Internet has taken self-help into an entirely new dimension. The Internet has empowered parents, enabling them to access research and information about medical conditions in a way that was unimaginable just a few years ago.

In some circumstances, parents have found that their passionate focus on a *specific* condition has made them as knowledgeable as—sometimes possibly more knowledgeable than—a health professional who invariably has to handle a wide variety of medical complaints. The Internet, however, can be a double-edged sword. As it is accessible to everyone, information may be posted—even on seemingly reputable Web sites—that can be wildly inaccurate or even downright dangerous. Always check and double-check from where you are obtaining information. Is it from a well-established organization? Is it from someone with professional credentials you can verify? Is the data based on scientific research or just someone's opinion? Make sure that the Web site is overseen by a health professional such as an M.D. or a speech-language pathologist.

Beyond providing information, the Internet enables parents to connect with each other across the country and across the world. No longer are you limited to the support of others in your own community. No longer are you limited by geographical boundaries. Through Web sites, listservs, E-zines, and chat rooms, you can find a sympathetic ear for moral support and for hard, practical advice, twenty-four hours a day, seven days a week. Who better to provide wise counsel than another parent who has already experienced a situation that you are nervously encountering? As one mother put it, "Navigating the terrain in the world of the developmentally challenged can feel like wandering around in the dark with blinders and no flashlight. Any helping hand is a welcome and comforting sight."

The Internet is particularly helpful in linking people together who are enduring problems that are not widely known or are just beginning to gather attention, as well as people who live in rural areas or who find traveling difficult. Time and time again, we have heard parents who had been concerned that their child was more than just a late talker express immense relief at finding other parents in the same dilemma. Just the knowledge that they are not alone gives strength and hope. Typically, in a week of postings on the childrensapraxianet@yahoogroups.com list you'll find some newcomers glad to have discovered an explanation for their child's condition. You'll also find more experienced parents offering useful information on everything from speech therapy to the benefits of fatty acid supplementation to encounters with the insurance companies and school system. Some will be sharing joyful moments of progress in their child's journey toward speech; others will be taking advantage of sympathetic ears to let off steam. To give you a sense of what parents feel about the benefits of support groups and the Internet, here are some examples taken from the list.

- "I feel like crying and doing a cheerleading dance at the same time. Thank you for supplying all this information. Finally, I have an explanation," wrote the mother of a four-year-old boy.
- "I am so relieved to finally find a support group of people who know what my son and I have been going through," wrote Janice, introducing herself as a new member.
- "Without places like this to vent, without people listening who might have had like experiences, the alienation and isolation is one dark pit," wrote another mom.
- "This site was an angel from above that happened on my computer one day. As a result, I have learned so much and been able to help my son so much more," commented Robyn Williams, mother of Jacob.
- And another mother, after an E-mail expressing her fears and frustrations, wrote, "Sorry . . . just had to vent a little. I have nobody else to talk to who would even begin to understand."

The Internet connection is a dynamite tool. In fact, in a New Mexico State University survey, a staggering 82 percent of parents said that they obtained the "most helpful information" about apraxia from the Internet. You can use E-mail to arrange everything from individual get-togethers with other parents and their children to group meetings involving expert speakers. The CHERAB Foundation has a growing number of associated groups throughout the country and welcomes parents who want to step forward and initiate groups in their own areas. It's not difficult. A support group can have two members or two hundred members. You could meet for a weekly coffee klatch at some-one's home or at a coffee shop. You could simply organize play dates with other parents and their kids. Or you could organize professional monthly meetings at a hospital or community center with specialist presenters, such as doctors, SLPs, and special needs attorneys. One mother tells how beneficial the support group meeting was in opening her husband's eyes. She says that he was in denial until he attended an apraxia meeting where an attorney was discussing IEPs. "My husband saw this was not just a bunch of moms sitting around complaining about their kids. He heard concerned parents talk about what is involved with getting our children the appropriate education. It made a difference," she says.

Support groups can make a difference. And *you* can make a difference. Your child can have a bright future, especially if you follow the advice we've given you. But we've covered a lot of ground and, therefore, summarize it for you in the final chapter.

11. Putting It All Together

He needs a mom who is capable of working to get him better
services, better understanding, and a better life as a whole.
—GRETCHEN WEGGENMANN, mother of six-year-old Kevin

Khalid Mustafa is fifteen years old, stands six feet four inches tall, and weighs 195 pounds. His size and prowess on the basketball court led friends and teammates to call him "the Gladiator." His mother, Cindy, feels that he deserves the nickname for an entirely different reason. Khalid valiantly fought to get the better of his apraxia and won victory after victory. "I love the nickname," says Cindy. "It fits him very well. I've always imagined him suited for battle and, thanks to great strength of character, overcoming the adversities of his life." Says Khalid, a champion in sport and academic contests and a shining example of what can be achieved through determination and perseverance, "My message to all of the kids who have apraxia is, 'Don't give up! Things have their way of looking up. Try to be the best at what you can do.'"

As a baby, Khalid didn't babble very much. During preschool years, Cindy and her husband, Moses, thought of him as their "captivating, beautiful little boy who was just quiet most of the time." To try and open his voice, Khalid began speech therapy when he was four years old, but it was not until four years later, after little progress, that he was diagnosed as apraxic thanks to the efforts of one caring SLP. Once he started getting the right kind of intensive therapy, Khalid showed steady improvement. Today, says his mom, he's "a very well-adjusted, confident, popular teenager." It would, says Cindy, take a skilled ear to know that Khalid has apraxia. His speech has improved so dramatically that he has the confidence to take part in class and competitive presentations. He's socially outgoing and has lots of friends. Academically, he's an A and B student and works hard to keep his grades up. In both 2000 and 2001, he qualified for his state's National History Day competition, in which he not only had to write scripts but also play all of the characters. To end his seventh-grade year, he won a schoolwide outstanding leadership award for excellence in teamwork, and that year, in spite of the fact that he has limb apraxia, also excelled in sport, making his school's basketball team.

Lisa's son, Tanner, is now six years old, and his parents no longer worry about his future. His speech is still not perfect, of course. At times you can see that he concentrates and works hard to say simple things that most of us take for granted. Today, though, he's able to order his own dinner, ask instructions, tell jokes, or say just about anything to any stranger and be understood almost all of the time. He no longer requires his parents or brother to be his translator. Now he can explain the bad dream that upset him instead of leaving his parents puzzled about the nighttime crying episode. He can tell anyone how it was his brother and not he who spilled the juice all over the floor, or how he got a scratch on his face riding the new bike he got for his birthday, or how he was going to marry Tiffany or Brittany (two little girls in his preschool), but since Mike likes Brittany he'll marry "just Tiffany." These are the simple things that most parents take for granted but that are so precious to parents like Lisa and Glenn. Sometimes Lisa ends up laughing, wondering how she could ever have understood a complicated sentence that the new talkative Tanner produces. For instance, after seeing the recent theatrical rerelease of *ET,* Tanner stated, "ET's spaceship landed at Todd's house in the woods and first ET went to Todd's house and then ET came to our house and now ET in our basement to hide so I'm stared to go downstair by myself. So you go wit me, Mommy?"

Tanner is ready to enter kindergarten. The professionals who have worked with him believe he's ready to be mainstreamed. He's very social and easily blends into a crowd of other children. He has a few more years of therapy ahead of him and Lisa fully anticipates he'll do as well as eight-year-old Dakota (also a late talker) who now excels in school. As Lisa says, "It's a good feeling to look back and know we did all we could to help, and because of that, both of our boys are okay today and will be okay tomorrow, too!"

Tanner is six years old. Khalid is fifteen. But what about older kids and adults? Twenty-three-year-old Rachel Horowitz is a teacher's assistant in a day-care center who has triumphed over her language impairment. At the age of two she had few words and was largely unintelligible. Years of intensive speech therapy followed, and it was not until she was in high school and the disorder was beginning to become better known that apraxia was diagnosed. Rachel was so tormented and teased that, she says, she was afraid to speak. Says her mother, Susan, "It hasn't been easy for us, and many tears have been shed over the years. There were never any support groups when she was growing up. It was hard to always feel alone. I dealt with the issues by learning all that I could about language and learning disabilities, eventually becoming a special education teacher." Her advice: "Be an advocate for your child and teach her to be an advocate for herself. And never give up. Although your child may not learn things quickly, as long as she is learning there is hope." That's certainly true in Rachel's case. Rachel still has difficulty pronouncing many multisyllabic words and is sometimes difficult to understand. But she works hard and has an extremely positive attitude. After graduating from high school, she attended college and, majoring in early childhood education, received her associate's degree. She intends to continue her education so that she "can help children like me from going through what I went through."

WHAT'S THE OUTCOME?

Khalid, Tanner, and Rachel have made great strides forward since those early dark days when the ability to talk seemed so elusive. Are they typical? What does the future have in store for children like them diagnosed with apraxia? Will they ever become effective communicators? Will they ever attain intelligible speech? As you have discovered, it's a complicated subject and there is no simple answer. Much depends on the severity of the disorder and the association of neurologic soft signs. Children with milder problems can see them resolved relatively quickly—possibly in six months to two years—although some may have a residual articulation defect like a lisp or distortion of the *r* sound. Those children who have more than one disorder—for example, apraxia combined with dysarthria—have a steeper road to travel. Most will learn to talk at some point, even though it may take years. Those who have severe apraxia may become adults who have functional verbal communication but still do not sound "normal." Some will ultimately need high-tech communication devices. Each individual's motivation and cognitive abilities also influence how successful therapy will be.

Children who are just late talkers or those with mild delays may find their voice after just months of therapy—and sometimes without any therapy at all. Others may need as much as two years of therapy. But treating children with severe disorders such as apraxia requires a long-term commitment. Experts project that anywhere from two to twelve years of treatment will be necessary. According to the American Speech-Language-Hearing Association, "One of the most important things for the family to remember is that treatment takes time, commitment, and a supportive environment that helps the child feel successful with communication. Without this, the disorder can persist into adulthood with years of speech-related anxiety and frustration." Families of children with apraxia face a difficult course. There are not enough speech pathologists who have acquired the special training needed to work with these children. There may be regressions, and it may feel as if your child is learning to speak one word at a time. What can you do to give your child the best opportunity?

You now have something that most parents of children with serious speech disorders have not had before: a wealth of knowledge, advice, support, motivation, and hope all in the palm of your hand. Let's close by furnishing you with a recommended plan of action for you and your late talker.

1. GET TESTED

Have your child evaluated as soon as you have serious concerns about his or her delay in speech. Use the clinical clues in Chapter 1 as your wake-up call to initiate a consultation and use the predictors and risk factors in Chapter 2 as further evidence that a speech disorder might exist. If your child is under three years of age, run, don't walk to early intervention services.

2. FOLLOW YOUR INSTINCTS

Don't settle for a doctor's reassuring words that your child is probably "just a late talker" and "let's wait and see." A six-month wait in the life of a toddler is a disproportionately long time in his or her life, developmentally. A parent's gut feel often proves to be right. If the professional you consult does not give your child's speech delay the consideration it deserves, find another professional. Early identification of a possible speech disorder can make a tremendous difference in your child's life.

3. GET THE RIGHT THERAPY

Children with apraxia need one-on-one therapy at least three times a week with an experienced SLP who understands the seriousness and complexity of this speech disorder. Group therapy is not sufficient. In particular, these kids need the touch- and gestural-cueing methods that we outlined in Chapter 5 and they need to receive it consistently all year round. No summer breaks. Check if your child also needs physical therapy and/or occupational therapy.

4. INVOLVE THE WHOLE FAMILY

Everyone in the household needs to get on board to help the late-talking child. It can be an uphill climb. If feasible, for a child with a severe impairment of speech or language, daily practice, multiple times, is highly desirable. Some children—those with apraxia, for instance—have a tendency to regress because it is a motor planning disorder and requires repetition to train the neural pathways. So the family needs to make a commitment to keep intensive home therapy in place until there is significant improvement.

5. GET TOUGH

Obtaining the right kind of frequent, intensive therapy from the system doesn't always come easily. Be prepared to do battle with both the school system and your insurance carrier. They may not be familiar with apraxia and the treatment that your child truly needs, and they may also put their fiscal concerns ahead of your child's best interests. By arming yourself with the information in this book, you should have enough ammunition to win the day.

6. FIND SUPPORT

Join a support group like the CHERAB Foundation. You'll find the helping hand that you need to embrace the challenge of raising a child with a speech disorder. You'll get morale-boosting support and good advice from other parents who have already lived through the experience. If you can meet in person, so much the better. If not, you'll find the Internet list a wonderful forum in which to share concerns and ideas—and vent when you need to.

7. USE THOSE LCPs

Try LCP supplementation after discussing it with your pediatrician. If he or she is not familiar with some of the literature, share the data in Chapter 8 and suggest that he or she read *The LCP Solution* by Jacqueline B. Stordy and Malcolm J. Nicholl. Omega-3 fatty acids are safe, and the side effects are hard nails and shiny hair! Taking it daily is like having a fish meal concentrated in a gel cap. The anecdotal reports have been dramatic. The speech of so many children has been jump-started that supplementation—combined with therapy—could well become the treatment of choice. We do not make this statement lightly. Skeptics will quite rightly point out that there have been no clinical trials. On the other hand, how can anyone argue against supplementing a child's diet in this way for a few months and measuring the results? We have seen a child respond so well and so quickly that parents and professionals begin to question whether a child really did have a serious speech disorder.

8. STAY VIGILANT

Remember the research we presented about the association between speech and language disorders and later reading and academic problems? Even if your child becomes a functional communicator, there is still a risk of language-based learning difficulties. It's a problem that can dog him into adulthood, creating social and career challenges. Therefore, it's important to keep advocating on behalf of your child. Make sure he receives special services to handle the possibility of specific language impairment or reading disability. Even if he begins to talk, pay attention to his reading and writing skill development in case he needs extra help. According to neuroscientist Dr. Paula Tallal, there is growing evidence of considerable overlap between oral language deficits and subsequent learning disabilities, including dyslexia.

9. PROTECT SELF-ESTEEM

Support your child and praise her for all of her efforts. She doesn't have to get As in school to be a success. Discover the pursuits in which your child excels so she can develop a sense of pride in her achievements. Tell her you love her no matter what. Feeling good about oneself is the best antidote for depression and low self-esteem. Seek counseling for your child (or yourself) if you are concerned about mood or behavior.

IN CONCLUSION

That's our advice in a nutshell. Whether your child is "just a late talker" or requires years of speech therapy, you should now have acquired a mountain of useful information. Our goal has been to speak on behalf of those who can't speak for themselves. As the Ontario Association for Families of Children with Communication Disorders so aptly says, late talkers are an "invisible and voiceless minority who cannot always understand or speak for themselves, yet deserve to be treated as equitably as those with more obvious disabilities." It is our hope that this book will go a long way toward giving these kids and their families the voice that they deserve. Late talkers have not been able to speak for themselves; it is up to parents, speech pathologists, and doctors like us to speak for them.

Resources

Government Agencies

National Institute on Deafness and Other Communication Disorders (NIDCD)
NIDCD Information Clearinghouse
1 Communication Avenue
Bethesda, MD 20892-3456
Phone: 800-241-1044
E-mail: nidcdinfo@nidcd.nih.gov
Web: www.nidcd.nih.gov/health/health.htm

A national information and referral center that provides information on disabilities and disability-related issues for families, educators, and other professionals. Has information specialists available to answer questions. Excellent Web site.

Office of Special Education Programs (OSEP)
Office of Special Education and Rehabilitative Services
U.S. Department of Education
Mary E. Switzer Building
330 C Street, SW
Washington, DC 20202
Phone: 202-205-5507
Web: www.ed.gov/offices/OSERS/OSEP

OSEP is dedicated to improving results for infants, toddlers, children, and youth with disabilities, age birth through twenty-one, by providing leadership and financial support to assist states and local districts. The Web site has infor-

mation about the implementation of the Individuals with Disabilities Education
Act as well as studies and research.

IDEA Information

National Early Childhood Technical Assistance System (NECTAS)
137 East Franklin Street, Suite 500
Chapel Hill, NC 27514-3628
Phone: 919-962-2001
Fax: 919-966-7463
E-mail: nectas@unc.edu
Web: www.nectas.unc.edu

Funded by the U.S. Department of Education's Office of Special Education
Programs, NECTAS is a consortium project of six organizations coordinated
by the Frank Potter Graham Child Development Center at the University of
North Carolina at Chapel Hill. Its excellent Web site provides a wealth of information about IDEA. Its extensive database includes a listing of state coordina-
tors for early intervention.

Legal Help

Sussan and Greenwald
407 Main Street
Spotswood, NJ 08884
Phone: 732-251-8585
E-mail: info@special-ed-law.com
Web: www.special-ed-law.com

Attorney Theodore Sussan was drawn to special education because of his disabled son. His partner, Staci Greenwald, was a special education teacher before
attending law school and has a degree in speech pathology. Their Web site has
information for parents and professionals for this quickly changing area of law.

Wrightslaw and The Special Ed Advocate
PO Box 1008
Deltaville, VA 23043
Phone: 804-776-7008
E-mail: webmaster@wrightslaw.com
Web: www.wrightslaw.com

Attorney Pete Wright and his wife, Pam, a psychotherapist, have put together
an extremely comprehensive Web site with a free newsletter. Pete Wright represents children with special needs and has successfully argued before the United
States Supreme Court.

On-Line Resources

www.apraxia.cc
   A support group for apraxia.

www.communicationdisorders.com
   An excellent "library" of resources with numerous links compiled by Judith Maginnis Kuster, certified SLP and associate professor in the Department of Communication Disorders and Rehabilitation Services at Minnesota State University.

www.debtsmart.com/talk
   Scott and Larissa Bilker's innovative "talking page" enables parents to compare voices of children with apraxia.

www.dec-sped.org/eilinks.html
   This site provides a large selection of useful links covering all aspects of early intervention.

www.ldonline.org
   LD OnLine, a leading Web site for parents and professionals, provides information and resources about learning and learning disabilities.

www.lib.utah.edu/ResGuides/comdis.html
   The University of Utah's Communication Disorders Research Guide has extensive information and links to other sites.

www.speechteach.co.uk
   This site contains a wealth of information, resources, and personal advice from a parent, for parents and professionals supporting children with speech difficulties.

www.speechtx.com
   This speech therapy activity site has a variety of printable activities, products, and ideas for people of different ages.

www.speechville.com
   Speechville is a resource for families, educators, and medical professionals, containing information about communication delays and disorders in children. Cofounded by coauthor Lisa Geng.

www.tayloredmktg.com/dyspraxia
This is an excellent general information site put together by parents of a child with apraxia.

WEB LISTS
http://clubs.yahoo.com/clubs/speechdelays
"A club where parents can come together to talk about our children's speech delay."

http://kidstalkback.tripod.com/kidstalkback
On-line journals of parents and their kids.

http://groups.yahoo.com/group/IEP_guide
Special education support group with free IEP guide. Parents and others share their experiences and offer advice.

http://groups.yahoo.com/group/Latetalkers
"To discuss developmental speech delays caused by apraxia, phonological disorders, autistic spectrum disorders, learning disabilities, or other causes."

http://groups.yahoo.com/group/NaturalLateTalkers
"For those with children who are late talkers and have some or many characteristics of children in Thomas Sowell's books."

Parent Support Groups

CASANA: Childhood Apraxia of Speech Association of North America
123 Eisele Road
Cheswick, PA 15024
Phone: 412-767-6589
Fax: 412-767-0534
E-mail: helpdesk@apraxia.org
Web: www.apraxia.org and www.apraxia-kids.org
CASANA is a nonprofit organization established to provide information and support to families and professionals concerned with apraxia and associated disorders.

CHERAB: Communication Help, Education, Research, Apraxia Base
Foundation

P.O. Box 8524
Port St. Lucie, FL 34952-8524
Phone: 772-335-5135
E-mail: help@cherab.org
Web: www.apraxia.cc and www.cherab.org
Internet list: http://clubs.yahoo.com/clubs/childrensapraxianet
CHERAB is the nonprofit organization founded by coauthor Lisa Geng. The site contains a wealth of information covering all aspects of apraxia and related speech disorders.

Expressive Communication Help Organization (ECHO)
P.O. Box 2439
Station 8
Richmond Hill, Ontario, L4E 1A5
Canada
Phone: 905-780-1489
E-mail: rjacobson@home.com
Web: www.apraxiaontario.homestead.com
Internet list: http://clubs.yahoo.com/clubs/apraxiacanadiansupportecho
Founded by Rhonda Jacobson Cherry, this is Canada's first nonprofit support group for parents, family, and friends of children with oral-motor speech disorders.

Personal Identification Systems

Kid Scope: A nickel-sized pendant/miniature microscope. Phone: 800-840-1311; Web: www.escopes.com/kidsid.html

Lauren's Hope: Fashionable gold and silver bracelets combining multicolored crystals and beads. Phone: 800-360-8680; Web: www.laurenshope.com

Medic Alert: A long-established emergency ID with children's sports band version. Phone: 800-825-3785 or 209-668-3333; Web: www.medicalert.org/emblemssports.asp

Road ID: Personal ID medals in stainless-steel wrist and ankle bands, as a necklace, and as a shoe attachment. Phone: 800-345-6336 or 859-341-1102; Web: www.roadid.com

Professional Organizations

American Occupational Therapy Association (AOTA)
4720 Montgomery Lane
PO Box 31220
Bethesda, MD 20824-1220
Phone: 301-652-2682 or 800-377-8555
Fax: 301-652-7711
Web: www.aota.org

   AOTA is a nationally recognized association of more than 50,000 occupational therapists. It advances the quality, availability, use, and support of occupational therapy through standard setting, advocacy, education, and research.

American Physical Therapy Association (APTA)
1111 North Fairfax Street
Alexandria, VA 22314-1486
Phone: 703-684-APTA (2782), 800-999-2782, or 703-683-6748
Fax: 703-684-7343
E-mail: research-dept@apta.org
Web: www.apta.org

   APTA represents physical therapists. Its mission is to further the profession's role in the prevention, diagnosis, and treatment of movement dysfunctions.

American Speech-Language-Hearing Association (ASHA)
10801 Rockville Pike
Rockville, MD 20852
Phone: 301-897-5700 or 800-638-8255
E-mail: actioncenter@asha.org
Web: www.asha.org

   ASHA is a professional organization of speech-language pathologists (SLPs) and audiologists. It also provides information about communication disorders and refers parents to local qualified professionals.

National Association for the Education of Young Children (NAEYC)
1509 Sixteenth Street, NW
Washington, DC 20036
Phone: 800-424-2460
E-mail: naeyc@naeyc.org
Web: www.naeyc.org

   Founded in 1926, NAEYC is the nation's largest and most influential organization of early childhood professionals that helps improve the quality of programs for children from birth through third grade. It has more than 100,000 members nationwide.

Support Organizations

Girls and Boys Town
13603 Flanagan Boulevard
Omaha, NE 68010
Phone hot line: 800-448-3000
E-mail: Hotline@boystown.org
Web: www.girlsandboystown.org
    This is an around-the-clock hot line where stressed-out parents can talk to highly trained, sympathetic counselors who give "right now" answers.

Easter Seals
230 West Monroe Street, Suite 1800
Chicago, IL 60606
Phone: 312-726-6200 or 312-726-4258
800-221-6827 (for information about services for children and youth)
E-mail: info@easter-seals.org
Web: www.easter-seals.org
    For more than eighty years, Easter Seals has been helping children with disabilities in communities nationwide.

ERIC Clearinghouse on Disabilities and Gifted Education
1110 North Glebe Road
Arlington, VA 22201-5704
Phone: 800-328-0272
E-mail: ericec@cec.sped.org
Web: ericec.org
    ERIC gathers and disseminates the professional literature, information, and resources on the education and development of individuals of all ages who have disabilities and/or who are gifted.

Learning Disabilities Association of America (LDA)
4156 Library Road
Pittsburgh, PA 15234
Phone: 412-341-1515, 412-341-8077, or 888-300-6710
E-mail: ldanatl@usaor.net
Web: www.ldanatl.org

LDA advances the education and general welfare of children with normal or potentially normal intelligence who have various kinds of disabilities.

National Information Center for Children and Youth with Disabilities
   (NICHCY)
PO Box 1492
Washington, DC 20013-1492
Phone: 800-695-0285 or 202-884-8200
E-mail: nichcy@aed.org
Web: www.nichcy.org
   NICHCY is a national information and referral center that provides information on disabilities and disability-related issues for families, educators, and other professionals. Its special focus is children and youth from birth through the age of twenty-two.

Schwab Learning
1650 South Amphlett Boulevard, Suite 300
San Mateo, CA 94402
Phone: 650-655-2410 or 800-230-0988
E-mail: webmaster@schwablearning.org
Web: www.schwablearning.org
   SchwabLearning.org is a parent's guide to learning differences and how to help their kids cope and be successful in learning and life.

Scottish Rite Foundation
1733 Sixteenth Street, NW
Washington, DC 20009-3199
Phone: 202-232-3579
E-mail: ritecare@srmason-sj.org
Web: www.srmason-sj.org/web/cld.htm
   The Scottish Rite Foundation began helping children with speech disorders in the early 1950s. There are now nearly 150 Scottish Rite clinics and centers throughout the United States. A complete directory can be found on the Web site. All services are available regardless of race, creed, or the family's inability to pay.

Zero to Three
National Center for Infants, Toddlers and Families
2000 M Street, NW, Suite 200

Washington, DC 20036

Phone: 202-638-1144

Web: www.zerotothree.org

Zero to Three is a leading resource on the first three years of life. It is a national nonprofit organization whose aim is to strengthen and support families, practitioners, and communities to promote the healthy development of babies and toddlers.

Therapy and Support Tools

American Sign Language Browser

Communication Technology Lab

Michigan State University

East Lansing, MI

Phone: 517-353-5497

E-mail: webmaster@commtechlab.msu.edu

Web: www.commtechlab.msu.edu/sites/aslweb/browser.htm

You can click on a word to both read and see an animated description of the sign for that word.

ASL Access

4217 Adrienne Drive

Alexandria, VA 22309

E-mail: webmaster@aslaccess.org

Web: www.aslaccess.org/sources.htm

ASL Access provides a comprehensive list of resources for American Sign Language.

Fast ForWord/Brain Connection

Scientific Learning

300 Frank H. Ogawa Plaza, Suite 500

Oakland, CA 94612-2040

Phone: 888-665-9707

E-mail: info@scilearn.com

Web: www.scientificlearning.com

www.brainconnection.com

The Fast ForWord family of programs helps develop critical thinking, listening, and reading skills. Brain Connection provides information about brain development, specifically how the brain learns language and reading.

Innovative Therapists International
3420 North Dodge Boulevard, Suite G
Tucson, AZ 85716
Phone: 888-529-2879
E-mail: oroitioffice@ultrasw.com
Web: www.oromotorsp.com
   Sara Rosenfeld-Johnson founded Innovative Therapists International as a
speakers' bureau and source for oral-motor therapy tools.

Kaufman Speech Method
5793 West Maple Road, Suite 150
West Bloomfield, MI 48322
Phone: 248-737-3430
E-mail: KCCinfo@kidspeech.com
Web: www.kidspeech.com
   The Kaufman Method gives children a way to attempt enunciation of diffi-
cult words using word approximations and refining and reinforcing these
attempts toward whole target words and phrases.

Lindamood-Bell
416 Higuera Street
San Luis Obispo, CA 93401
Phone: 805-541-3836 or 800-233-1819
Fax: 805-541-8756
Web: www.lblp.com
   Lindamood-Bell is an organization dedicated to enhancing human learning
and developing the sensory cognitive processes that underlie reading, spelling,
language comprehension, math, and visual motor skills.

PECS
Pyramid Educational Consultants
226 West Park Place, Suite 1
Newark, DE 19711
Phone: 888-PECS INC (888-732-7462)
Web: www.pecs.com
www.pyramidproducts.com
   The Picture Exchange Communication System is an augmentative alternative
system that allows children and adults with communication deficits to initiate
communication.

PROMPT Institute
27 Pan de Vida
Santa Fe, NM 87507
Phone: 505-466-7710
E-mail: thepromptins@earthlink.net
Web: www.promptinstitute.com

The nonprofit PROMPT Institute promotes holistic, dynamic, multisensory assessment and interventions for individuals with speech disorders.

Read Right Systems
310 West Birch Street, Suite 2
Shelton, WA 98584
Phone: 360-427-9440
Fax: 360-427-0177
E-mail: info@readright.com
Web: www.readright.com

A commercial program with an innovative approach to the teaching of reading to all age groups.

Sensory Integration International (SII)/The Ayres Clinic
1602 Cabrillo Avenue
Torrance, CA 90501-2817
Phone: 310-787-8805
Fax: 310-787-8130
E-mail: info@sensoryint.com
Web: sensoryint.com

A nonprofit organization founded by a group of occupational therapists based on the pioneering work of Dr. A. Jean Ayres. It provides resources to help educate people with sensory integration and several other dysfunctions.

The Speech Bin, Inc.
1965 Twenty-Fifth Avenue
Vero Beach, FL 32960
Phone: 800-4-SPEECH (800-477-3324)
Fax: 888-FAX 2 BIN (888-329-2246)
E-mail: speechbin.com
Web: www.speechbin.com

Products for both professionals and parents to help people of all ages with speech-language problems.

Super Duper Publications
P.O. Box 24997
Greenville, SC 29616
Phone: 864-288-3426
Fax: 864-288-3380
E-mail: custserv@superduperinc.com
Web: www.superduperinc.com

Publishers of fun, colorful materials for speech-language pathologists, special educators, teachers, parents, and caregivers in educational, home, and health care settings.

Appendix A.

A Week in the Life: Tanner's Therapy

Although there's no "typical" week of therapy for a child with apraxia, we can give you an idea of what it's like by sharing an average week for Lisa and her son, Tanner, when he was three years old. According to neuromedical and speech professionals, Tanner had severe oral and verbal apraxia, hypotonia, and sensory integration dysfunction.

Tanner was essentially nonverbal to the outside world, but could make his needs known through gestures and pointing. He attended a preschool disabled program from 9:00 A.M. to 11:30 A.M. Monday through Friday and, during the course of a week, received five half-hour sessions of one-on-one speech therapy and two half-hour sessions of group occupational therapy. Outside of the preschool services, Tanner also had private speech therapy and private occupational therapy once a week. Here is a typical week of therapy based on records that Lisa kept in his communication book.

Monday

At breakfast Tanner points to pictures of the foods that he wants. He signs for a drink and brings me to the refrigerator to show me what he wants. While I pour, he signs indicating that he wants more. It's time for Tanner's fatty acid therapy, so I use a pin to put a hole into two fish oil gel caps and squeeze the oil onto a spoon. For months—because of its taste—we struggled to hide fish oil in Tanner's food, but I've found a new trick that works. With a big smile I shout, "Who wants to watch Tanner eat his yucky magic fish oil that helps him talk?" Tanner waits until someone is watching. Then I hold his nose and quickly put the spoon of fish oil into his open mouth. While I'm still holding his nose he quickly drinks his orange juice. We clap, and Tanner smiles. Every day it amazes me that this actually works. Before school we quickly do some of the homework from his private speech-language pathologist that we're supposed to do three times a day, every day this week. This is the list:

1. Facial massage—tapping
2. Tongue massage—tapping
3. "Where is the peanut butter?" tongue game
4. "Brushing" his body—therapy for sensory integration
5. Something called "VC" (vowel consonant). I need to put each of the *a, e, i, o,* and *u* vowel sounds in front of the consonants *t* and *n*. Each VC five times each: *at, et, it, ot, ut,* and then *an, en, in, on,* and *un* five times. Use fingers to count down each time.

The bus comes and takes Tanner to preschool. I follow him and observe his class through a double window. Tanner and five other children are sitting in a circle singing songs about the weather and the days of the week while using gestures. The children are sitting on large, round therapy balls. I'm happy to see the SLP is sitting behind Tanner talking to him and rubbing his cheeks, which is part of his therapy. After singing, the children go to their cubby boxes, and most are helped to put on their bibs. All of the professionals are very animated when they pull out Funny Foam and spray a large amount for each child. I watch a bit of the sensory integration therapy time. It looks fun. After school we go to an amusement park. When Tanner lets us know which rides he wants to go on by pointing and saying, "Why why why'd?" I slowly model for him the correct way to ask.

I say	Tanner repeats
I	I
want	wa
to	to
go	doe
on	ah
that	da
ride	rie

"Good talking, Tanner!" I praise him. Before the end of the day, we do all of the homework assigned by his private SLP.

Tuesday

Tanner wakes up, put his hands over his eyes, and then pulls his hands away yelling, "Poopie!" He does this a few times. I ask if he's saying "peekaboo," and he nods his head. I write this in Tanner's communication book that goes back and forth from school to home and to all of the therapists. If he tries this at school today they'll know he's not saying he wants to go to the potty. Tanner gets breakfast and his fish oil. When Tanner reads his favorite Bambi book, I take one of my hands, turn it over and say, "Bam." Then I turn my other hand over and say, "Bee." This is a new motor planning strategy that Tanner's private SLP taught us to help him visually break down longer words. When I do this, Tanner can say "Bambi," so I try this for peekaboo . . . and it works. Well, almost. It comes out, "pee . . . a . . . bah." Still, it's way better than "poopie." I write this in the book, too. Tanner now holds his eyes just for a second, imitates me, and turns his hands one at a time as he says "peeabah." He is still practicing when his bus comes, so he does it for the bus driver, who laughs.

Tanner comes home with a note from the speech therapist saying that he had an excellent day. Instead of using the hand turning, they did something similar using blocks to break down the syllables in a word. For example, they would take one block and say the *h* sound and the second block and say, "AT." They would then push them together to say, "H-AT." This is a great way for me to take his VC speech homework to the next step! (I'm getting good at the SLP lingo!) Working on Tanner's oral-motor therapy with my "peanut butter homework" he clearly says, "Oh tay!" Since repetition is good, I make a funny game out of it, laughing hard whenever he says "Oh tay," so he keeps saying it over and over. In between, Tanner keeps trying to move his tongue toward the peanut butter, but his tongue still goes down if the peanut butter is on top of his lip. He can't lift his tongue off the floor of his mouth.

Wednesday

This morning Tanner keeps saying, "Bo bo bo." I think he's trying to say "ball," but he's not. Every time I guess wrong, he gets angrier. I ask him to show me what he's saying, and he starts crying. I write this in his communication book to let his teachers at preschool know what's happened. Then, as usual, I give him his fish oil with breakfast.

After school we go to a party. Tanner points to a plate of cookies and says, "Do do doodie," pointing to the cookies. A few of the children start to laugh. Luckily, Tanner doesn't appear to notice. I phone his private SLP to ask her about this. She says that until he learns to say the *k* sound, to "give Tanner a better approximation," the letter *t* is a better "bridge" than the letter *d*, and "tootie" sounds more like "cookie" than does "doodie." When I work on Tanner's homework I work this in too, and he asks for a "tootie." Much better!

I take Tanner to private occupational therapy. The therapist gets him to lie on his belly on something that looks like a skateboard with a rug on it. He has to roll around with his head and feet raised, knocking down cardboard-box walls. She says this improves his truncal strength, which will help with breath control. She then takes various colored plastic objects and "hides" them in play dough. Tanner has to try to find all of the objects, put each one into the matching colored cup, and attempt to say the color of the object. I like to watch the therapy sessions. It helps me know what I can do at home to help.

Thursday

In the morning we work on our therapy homework and then have breakfast and fish oil. I write everything in his communication book. I go to Tanner's school to observe, and as always I let the teacher know that I'm there. She comes out to tell me that they don't believe in using approximations and would I please use only correct word models with Tanner. She says to get him to say "cookie" and not settle for "tootie." So now I'm getting conflicting advice from the experts! I watch Tanner having fun painting and see that the SLP is saying the names of the colors very slowly and clearly, but I can't hear if Tanner is attempting to repeat them. Later the private speech therapist plays games with Tanner to get him to do his sounds. Each time he does them correctly he gets a reward; sometimes it's food, but today she uses marbles. They work on sounds, and when Tanner gets them right she praises him and he gets to "feed" a marble to Mr. Ball (a tennis ball with a face painted on it). When Mr. Ball eats too many, he spits the marbles out of his mouth and says, "Ahhh," very dramatically. And we all laugh. I've made one of these to use at home. Tanner's speech therapist writes in the communication book why she advised me to give him an approximation for the letter *c* and also explains the hand signals she uses that I've found worked really well for him.

At home Tanner goes to the refrigerator when I'm not looking, takes some jelly, and rubs it into his cheeks doing his facial massage. I think that's my cue to stop writing in his therapy book and start doing his therapy with him!

Friday

Tanner's still trying to work on the VC with the *t* sound, which appears to be a tough one for him. He usually drops the *t* or replaces it with *s* or *f*. So while eating breakfast, I bounce in my seat like I'm dancing, tilt my head to the right, and say in a singsong way, "eeeee." Then I tilt my head to the left and say, "t." Tanner's brother, Dakota, imitates me and we both start laughing. Then Tanner does it, and he says, "ea-t." Okay. It's a bit slower than usual, but he said it. I then say, "Who wants magic fish oil that helps you to talk?" Tanner yells out, "Me!" and raises his hand. This time Dakota does the therapy with Tanner while I watch.

I go to the school again to observe what they're working on so I can carry it through at home. The OT has set up a kind of maze that they need to make their way through and Tanner volunteers to go first. The OT also holds Tanner's hands while he jumps on a small trampoline and she sings the alphabet. I can't hear if he tries to repeat it. They write in his book that they are working on "frequent intonational and rhythmic cueing." I'm still learning all this speech pathology lingo and have an idea it means something about changing the tone of voice or clapping, but I'm not sure. It may have something to do with the trampoline. I have one at home so I hold Tanner's hands and say the alphabet while he jumps up and down. He has hypotonia so he tires quickly, but he really likes this. He does attempt the alphabet, so I plan on including this in our homework. They also commented that he tried to say the word *it* and it came out *is* (as usual), but he self-corrected and said "it." I didn't ask if he was tilting his head when he did that.

Tanner and I shop for more toys to help with therapy, and I find great puzzle cards at the office supply store that break down words into sounds and pictures! They even have the word *hat* with each letter separate. It's almost like they made them for a child with apraxia, even though I know it's more to help with reading.

Saturday

Before breakfast, while Tanner and I are doing his therapy homework, I finally figure out what he meant when he was saying "Bo bo bo" the other day. It means, "Where is brother?" No wonder he cried when I asked him to show me what he wanted. He was actually saying "Ba bo bo." *Ba bo* is what Tanner calls Dakota. *Ba bo* for brother, I guess. After breakfast we drive to Tanner's private SLP, and she says he's actually now doing well with the CV homework for *t* but is still weak with *n*. Our homework is still the CV with *t* and *n* for this week. We then work on the letter *k*. We lay Tanner on a ball on his back and she actually gets him to do the *k* sound twice in that position.

While driving home I teach Tanner how to say a knock-knock joke.

> Tanner: "Na-na." (knock-knock)
> Me: "Who's there?"
> Tanner: "Boo."

> Me: "Boo who?"
> Tanner: "Don-f tie." (don't cry)

I write this down in his communication book so he can tell them the joke at preschool on Monday.

My husband, Glenn, and I take both boys to a fair and then out to eat. At the restaurant we use sugar packets to help Tanner plan his words in the same way they used the blocks at school. We take two or three sugar packets and bring them together to break down the syllables. He's doing great. Tanner is attempting to "parrot" almost everything we say. It's slightly annoying to Dakota, who keeps saying, "Ma, Tanner's copying me again."

Sunday

Tanner wakes up, puts his finger in his ear, and says, "Ow bee." He doesn't appear to be sick, but knowing his high tolerance for pain we figure we ought to take him to the pediatrician. Tanner doesn't eat much, but he still takes his fish oil. We go to the doctor, who says he has an infection in both ears. Tanner's lying on the floor laughing and the pediatrician looks at him puzzled, saying, "Well, it doesn't seem to be bothering him at all." I remind her that this is the same child who doesn't cry when he gets his shots but says "Ow" if you pat his head or tickle him. Tanner is put on antibiotics for the next ten days. Even though it doesn't seem like Tanner's feeling any pain from the ear infection, we decide that today's a "no therapy" day.

Appendix B.

Excerpt from a Neurodevelopmental Examination

The following is the "assessment and recommendations" section excerpted from a comprehensive neurodevelopmental evaluation of a child with apraxia, requesting "appropriate" services from the school system.

Assessment:

Matthew is an almost-three-year-old boy who has a history of being a quiet, serious-looking baby with oral-buccal hypotonia and significant feeding problems, which is consistent with a diagnosis of severe oral apraxia. He continued to have difficulties with nonspeech movements, including puckering his lips, licking his lips, and blowing bubbles, until recently. In addition, Matthew has a history of being a "late talker" with a speech pattern that includes groping behaviors, vowel distortions, omissions of syllables, dropped endings, inconsistency in speech productions, and difficulty imitating speech sounds other than the bilabial sounds: /p/, /b/, /m/ and /t/, /d/, /n/, /f/, /sh/, and /ch/. He has generic words that he uses for a number of other words, because of his difficulty in coordinating the movements of the oral musculature.

Matthew has signs of a verbal apraxia, which is a neurologic speech disorder affecting the motor planning and sequencing of speech sounds, which becomes even more difficult to understand with the increasing length and complexity of the sentence. His speech is so severely unintelligible to the unfamiliar listener that, out of context, it would be almost impossible to understand what he is saying. Even in context, his speech is just a series of approximations, and his grammar and syntax are also disordered. His cognitive skills and receptive language, however, are within normal limits. Associated with Matthew's verbal apraxia is an expressive language impairment, with deficits in grammar and syntax as well as a limited lexicon (vocabulary) for age. Research has shown that early speech and language problems are correlated with later reading and academic problems in school-aged children. Matthew also has a coordination difficulty and sensory motor integration deficits. He trips and falls and has poor spatial awareness, running into things. His dyspraxic symptoms carry over to the motor planning involved in gross-motor activities and overall coordination, e.g., riding a tricycle. He is "heavy footed," and fixes his right arm when he runs. He also has issues with sensory motor integration, which involves processing of proprioceptive and vestibular stimuli along with difficulties with balance, equilibrium reactions, and postural stability.

Diagnoses:

1. (#784.69)   Oral/verbal apraxia
2. (#784.6)   Expressive language disorder
3. (#781.3)   Hypotonia, coordination disorder, sensory integration dysfunction

Recommendations:

1. Matthew should be placed in an integrated language-based preschool classroom, with both typically developing children and children who have developmental difficulties, where there is typically a small student-to-teacher ratio. The original recommendation of the CPSE evaluation team, to place Matthew in a classroom with typically developing children, would do him a tremendous disservice; he is already feeling the frustration of not being able to communicate with peers and adults, and not being understood, which has caused him to be reserved and generally noncommunicative with unfamiliar people. The only person who truly understands him the majority of the time is his mother. If Matthew is placed in a class with typically developing children who may make fun of him or not understand him, this could cause self-esteem issues that could last for years to come. He also would not get the extra attention and expertise of a special education teacher who would understand his needs.

2. Matthew will need intensive speech therapy by an experienced speech pathologist knowledgeable about working with children with verbal apraxia and oral hypotonia. He will need individual therapy at least three to four times per week for thirty-minute sessions. Children with verbal apraxia do not benefit from group therapy. Speech pathologists who work with this population use touch-cue techniques like PROMPT. The thera-

pist must be trained in a multisensory approach using auditory, visual, and tactile cues to facilitate speech productions. One of the significant values in correctly diagnosing a child with verbal apraxia is that the diagnosis alternatively changes the direction of the therapeutic management of these children. Traditional methods of speech therapy do not work. Matthew has had a focus on oral-motor therapy, oral sensory training, and touch-cue prompting up until now in early intervention.

3. Matthew will need a twelve-month program [an extended school year (ESY)], as he regresses when he is not in therapy.

4. Matthew will require occupational therapy two to three times per week for forty-five-minute sessions to improve sensory motor integration.

5. It is recommended that Matthew receive physical therapy once to twice weekly for thirty-minute sessions to improve higher-level gross-motor functioning, balance reactions, and postural responses.

6. A trial of essential fatty acid (EFA) supplements is recommended as anecdotal evidence has shown an improvement in apraxic symptoms. *The LCP Solution* by Stordy and Nicholl is recommended reading for background information. I would be happy to offer advice in administration of the supplements as needed.

7. Reevaluation is recommended in six months.

A. Goode, M.D., FAAP

Appendix C.

Letter of Medical Necessity

This is an example of a letter by an insurance company, emphasizing that your child's problem is neurologic and not developmental.

Re: LM
Date of Birth: 3/10/99

Dear Dr. Smith,
   LM, a thirty-three-month-old boy, continues to carry the diagnoses of:

742.9	*Static encephalopathy*
388.40	*Hypoxia at birth*
784.69	*Oral/verbal apraxia*
783.3	*Feeding disorder*
781.3	*Hypotonia, sensory integration dysfunction*
388.40	*Auditory processing disorder*

   He has made some improvement in speech and motor abilities, and has responded well to therapy. He does, however, continue to require intensive treatment in order to overcome these disabilities. They all have a neurologic *basis and are* not developmental. *Intensive treatment by qualified, experienced speech, physical, and occupational therapists is required. Oral/verbal apraxia of speech is a disorder where the brain signals that go to the muscles and structures of the speech mechanism are disrupted. Without therapy, children do not outgrow verbal apraxia. LM also has feeding problems associated with his speech disorder. He requires speech treatment at least four times a week by experienced oral-motor speech therapists who are trained in the PROMPT methodology. He will also need occupational therapy two times a week by an occupational therapist knowledgeable about his sensory integration dysfunction, and physical therapy once weekly to improve muscle coordination. Without these therapies his prognosis is poor.*

I am asking for three months of the therapies requested above followed by a reevaluation to assess progress.

Thank you for your assistance.

Yours truly,
A. Goode, M.D., FAAP

Appendix D.

Guideline for Speech-Language Eligibility Criteria/Matrix for Schools

These are general guidelines for school-based SLPs showing how much therapy is required for children with varying degrees of speech impairment. You should make sure that your SLPs—school-based and private—are aware of these recommendations, especially when your child's IEP is being drawn up. (Mild, moderate, severe, and profound refer to the severity of the child's speech disorder.)

	Mild **1 Service Delivery Unit: minimum of 15–30 minutes per week**	Moderate **2 Service Delivery Units: minimum of 31–60 minutes per week**
Severity of Disorder	Impairment minimally affects the individual's ability to communicate in school learning and/or other social situations as noted by at least one other familiar listener, such as teacher, parent, sibling, peer.	Impairment interferes with the individual's ability to communicate in school learning and/or other social situations as noted by at least one other familiar listener.
Articulation/ Phonology	Intelligible over 80% of the time in connected speech. No more than two speech sound errors outside developmental guidelines. Student may be stimulable for error sounds.	Intelligible 50–80% of the time in connected speech. Substitutions and distortions and some omissions may be present. There is limited stimulability for the error phonemes.

	Mild **1 Service Delivery Unit: minimum of 15–30 minutes per week**	Moderate **2 Service Delivery Units: minimum of 31–60 minutes per week**
Language	The student demonstrates a deficit in receptive, expressive, or pragmatic language as measured by two or more diagnostic procedures/standardized tests. Performance falls from 1 to 1.5 standard deviations below the mean standard score.	The student demonstrates a deficit in receptive, expressive, or pragmatic language as measured by two or more diagnostic procedures/standardized tests. Performance falls from 1.5 to 2.5 standard deviations below the mean standard score.
Fluency	2–4% atypical dysfluencies within a speech sample of at least 100 words. No tension to minimal tension. Rate and/or prosody: minimal interference with communication.	5–8% atypical dysfluencies within a speech sample of at least 100 words. Noticeable tension and/or secondary characteristics are present. Rate and/or prosody: limits communication.
Voice	Voice difference including hoarseness, nasality, denasality, pitch, or intensity inappropriate for the student's age is of minimal concern to parent, teacher, student, or physician. Medical referral may be indicated.	Voice difference is of concern to parent, teacher, student, or physician. Voice is not appropriate for age and sex of the student. Medical referral may be indicated.

	Severe **3 Service Delivery Units: minimum of 61–90 minutes per week**	Profound **5 Service Delivery Units: minimum of 91+ minutes per week**
Severity of Disorder	Impairment limits the individual's ability to communicate appropriately and respond in school learning and/or social situations. Environmental and/or student concern is evident and documented.	Impairment prevents the individual from communicating appropriately in school and/or social situations.
Articulation/ Phonology	Intelligible 20–49% of the time in connected speech. Deviations may range from extensive substitutions and many omissions to extensive omissions. A limited number of phoneme classes are evidenced in a speech-language sample. Consonant sequencing is generally lacking. Augmentative communication systems may be warranted.	Speech is unintelligible without gestures and cues and/or knowledge of the context. Usually there are additional pathological or physiological problems, such as neuromotor deficits or structural deviations. Augmentative communication systems may be warranted.
Language	The student demonstrates a deficit in receptive, expressive, or pragmatic language as measured by two or more diagnostic procedures/ standardized tests (if standardized tests can be administered). Performance is greater than 2.5 standard deviations below the mean standard score. Augmentative communication systems may be warranted.	The student demonstrates a deficit in receptive, expressive, or pragmatic language which prevents appropriate communication in school and/or social situations. Augmentative communication systems may be warranted.

	Severe **3 Service Delivery Units: minimum of 61–90 minutes per week**	Profound **5 Service Delivery Units: minimum of 91+ minutes per week**
Fluency	9–12% atypical dysfluencies within a speech sample of at least 100 words. Excessive tension and/or secondary characteristics are present. Rate and/or prosody: interferes with communication.	More than 12% atypical dysfluencies within a speech sample of at least 100 words. Excessive tension and/or secondary characteristics are present. Rate and/or prosody: prevents communication.
Voice	Voice difference is of concern to parent, teacher, student, or physician. Voice is distinctly abnormal for age and sex of the student. Medical referral is indicated.	Speech is largely unintelligible due to aphonia or severe hypernasality. Extreme effort is apparent in production of speech. Medical referral is indicated.

Source: Illinois State Board of Education. 1993. *Speech-Language Impairment: A Technical Assistance Manual.* Reprinted by permission.

Appendix E.

Abbreviations

AAC augmentative and alternate communication
AAP American Academy of Pediatrics
ACT adapted cueing technique
ADA Americans with Disabilities Act
ADHD attention deficit hyperactivity disorder
AIT Auditory Integration Training
ALA alpha-linolenic acid
AOS apraxia of speech
ARA arachidonic acid
ASD autistic spectrum disorder
ASHA American Speech-Language-Hearing Association
ASQ Ages and Stages Questionnaire
BCH benign congenital hypotonia
CAT computerized axial tomography
CAT/CLAMS Cognitive Adaptive Test/Clinical Linguistic and Auditory Milestone Scale
CELF clinical evaluation of language functions
CPK creatine phosphokinase
CPSE committee on preschool special education
CSE committee of special education
CST Child Study Team
CTONI Comprehensive Test of Nonverbal Intelligence
CV consonant-vowel (and assorted combinations, CVC, CVCV, etc.)
DAS developmental apraxia of speech

DHA docosahexaenoic acid

DOE U.S. Department of Education

DSI or **SID** dysfunction of sensory integration/sensory integration dysfunction

DTRs deep tendon reflexes

DVD developmental verbal dyspraxia

EEG electroencephalogram

EFA essential fatty acid

EI early intervention

EIOD early intervention official designee

ELMS Early Language Milestone Scales

EMG electromyography

EOWPVT Expressive One-Word Picture Vocabulary Test

EPA eicosapentaenoic acid

ESY extended school year

FAPE free and appropriate public education

fMRI functional magnetic resonance imaging

GAPs general all purpose verbs

GFTA Goldman-Fristoe Test of Articulation

GLA gamma-linolenic acid

ICD international classification of diseases

IDEA Individuals with Disabilities Education Act

IEE Independent Educational Evaluation

IEP Individualized Education Program

IFSP Individual Family Service Plan

KABC Kaufman Assessment Battery for Children

KSPT Kaufman Speech Praxis Test for Children

LCP long-chain polyunsaturated fatty acids

LD learning disabled

LLD language-based learning disability

MDE multidisciplinary evaluation

MIT melodic intonation therapy

MR mentally retarded

MRI magnetic resonance imaging

NDT neurodevelopmental treatment

NECTAS National Early Childhood Technical Assistance System

NIDCD National Institute on Deafness and Other Communication Disorders

OSEP Office of Special Education Programs

OT occupational therapy or occupational therapist

PAT Photo Articulation Test

PDD—NOS pervasive developmental disorder—not otherwise specified

PECS picture exchange communication system

PEDS Parents' Evaluation of Developmental Status

PET positron emission tomography

PLS-3 Preschool Language Scale-3

PM&R physical medicine and rehabilitation

PROMPT Prompts for Restructuring Oral Muscular Phonetic Targets

PT physical therapy or physical therapist

ROWPVT Receptive One-Word Picture Vocabulary Test

SD school district

SI speech impaired or sensory integration

SID or **DSI** sensory integration dysfunction

SLI specific language impairment

SLP speech-language pathologist

SMO supramalleolar orthotics

ST speech therapy

TELD-3 Test of Early Language Development-3

TX treatment or therapy

VMPAC Verbal Motor Production Assessment for Children

Glossary

acquired. Occurring after birth.

American Sign Language (ASL). A manual language with its own syntax and grammar, used primarily by people who are deaf.

aphasia. An impairment due to localized brain injury typically following a stroke in adults that affects understanding, retrieving, and formulating meaningful and sequential elements of language. The term is sometimes used to describe children with a receptive and/or expressive language disorder.

apraxia. Inability to execute a voluntary movement because of a motor planning difficulty in the absence of any paralysis.

apraxia of speech or **verbal apraxia.** A neurological impairment of the ability to program, organize, and execute movements of the speech muscles, unrelated to muscle weakness, slowness, or paralysis.

articulation. Rapid and coordinated movement of the tongue, teeth, lips, and palate to produce speech sounds.

articulation disorder. Inability to correctly produce speech sounds (phonemes) because of imprecise placement, timing, pressure, speed, or flow of movement of the lips, tongue, or throat.

assistive devices. Technical tools and devices such as alphabet boards or text-to-speech conversion software used to aid individuals who have communication disorders.

attention deficit hyperactivity disorder (ADHD). A disorder where a child has difficulty sustaining attention, following directions, and organizing tasks. In addition, some children may have symptoms of hyperactivity and/or impulsivity. ADHD is categorized as combined type with characteristics of both inattention and hyperactive-impulsive behavior; predominantly inattentive type; or predominantly hyperactive-impulsive type.

audiologist. A health care professional who is trained to evaluate hearing loss and to fit and dispense hearing aids and other assistive devices for hearing.

augmentative and alternative communication (AAC). The field of providing individuals with speech and expressive language difficulties with alternative ways of communicating. AAC includes simple picture boards and sign language as well as sophisticated electronic devices or speech synthesizers.

augmentative devices. *See* augmentative and alternative communication.

autism and autistic spectrum disorders. Abnormal functioning in three areas, including social interaction, language used for social communication, and displays of stereotypical and restricted patterns of behavior.

babbling. Single-syllable nonpurposeful consonant-vowel (CV) or vowel-consonant (VC) vocalizations that begin in the second half of the first year.

breath support. Efficient and appropriate use of the breath stream for phonation.

central auditory processing disorder (CAPD). A deficit in efficiently utilizing and interpreting auditory information, although hearing is within the normal range.

central nervous system (CNS). The brain and spinal cord.

cerebral palsy. A motor disorder produced by damage to the brain; it usually occurs prenatally, at the time of birth, or in early infant life.

cerebrum. The upper brain, which is divided into two hemispheres. The outermost layer is called the cortex.

child study team. A team of special educators and therapists, usually including a psychologist, learning consultant, social worker, SLP, PT, and OT, that evaluates children for eligibility for special services.

cognition. Thinking skills that include perception, memory, awareness, reasoning, judgment, intellect, and imagination.

communication. Receiving, sending, processing, and comprehending concepts or verbal, nonverbal, and written symbol systems. Communication is an umbrella term that includes language, speech, and/or hearing abilities.

congenital. Present at birth.

delay. A maturational lag in development. Often, with time, a child will catch up with his or her peers without any specific interventions. Some refer to children like this as "late bloomers." It is not always evident at an early age whether a child has a delay or disorder.

developmental pediatrician. An M.D. who specializes in child development and is able to diagnose and treat developmental disabilities and behavior problems.

disorder. A severe delay with a disruption in the normal sequence of development. A child will not catch up if you adopt a "wait and see" attitude. Neurologic "soft signs" like coordination difficulties, low muscle tone, a history of seizures, or the physical signs of a syndrome (e.g., Down syndrome) may be present.

dominance. The hand you write with, the eye you prefer when you look through a pinhole, and the foot you use when kicking a ball. Most people have right dominance, some have left, and a few have mixed dominance (e.g., right-handed, left-eyed, and left-footed).

due process hearing (impartial hearing). Procedure to resolve disputes between parents and schools; administrative hearing before an impartial hearing officer or administrative law judge.

dysarthria. One of several motor speech disorders that involve impaired articulation, respiration, phonation, or prosody as a result of paralysis, muscle weakness, or poor coordination.

dysfluency. Disruption in the smooth flow or expression of speech.

dyslexia. A disability characterized by difficulty comprehending printed symbols and recognizing words. Children with dyslexia often exhibit delayed language development, listening comprehension problems, and poor phonological awareness.

dyspraxia. A motor coordination disorder, sometimes called "clumsy child syndrome."

early intervention (EI). Birth-to-three programs mandated by federal law in which infants and toddlers with developmental delays are entitled to speech, OT, PT, special education, and other services, often provided in the home.

early intervention official designee (EIOD). The early intervention representative who assists the family in developing an IFSP and follows the child while in EI and through transition to the preschool system.

expressive language. The formation of words into sentences.

fluency. Smoothness of rhythm and rate in speech.

gene. The unit of heredity, composed of a sequence of DNA, that is located in a specific position on a chromosome.

genetic. Inherited and passed on through the generations.

grammar. The rules of a language.

gross-motor skills. Use of large muscle groups, for activities such as running, jumping, and riding a bike.

hypotonia. Low muscle tone, also known as "floppy baby syndrome." It can either be associated with serious neuromuscular disorders or, in its more benign form, with speech disorders such as apraxia.

Individualized Education Program (IEP). An annually updated, federally mandated program for the education of children with special education needs.

Individual Family Service Plan (IFSP). In EI, a plan that is developed by the family, service coordinator, evaluation representative, and EIOD to address the concerns, priorities, and resources of the child and family, and develop functional outcomes for the child.

Individuals with Disabilities Education Act (IDEA). Enacted by Congress in 1986, this is the federal legislation authorizing the Early Intervention Program.

intelligibility. The degree to which a speech-impaired individual can be understood, expressed in percentages. For example, if someone is 75 percent intelligible to the unfamiliar listener, anyone can understand three quarters of his or her speech.

jargon. Strings of unintelligible sounds with adultlike intonation that develop at about eight months of age and exhibit the pitch and intonational pattern of the language to which the child is exposed.

kinesthetic feedback. The perception of muscular movement and tension perceived by the body or in the mouth for speech.

language impairment. A deficit in the comprehension and/or production of spoken or written language.

language sample. A systematic collection and analysis of a person's speech output, used as a part of language assessment.

language. System for communicating ideas and feelings using sounds, words, gestures, and signs.

language disorders. Deficits in verbal communication (expressive language disorder) and/or the ability to use or understand a symbol system for communication (receptive language disorder).

larynx. Valve structure that sits at the opening of the trachea (windpipe) that is the primary organ of voice production, more commonly called the voicebox.

late talker. A child eighteen to twenty months old who has fewer than ten words, or twenty-one to thirty months with fewer than fifty words and no two-word combinations like "mommy car." He or she is age-appropriate (or close to it) in other areas of development including comprehension, play, motor skills, and cognitive (problem-solving) skills.

learning disabilities. Include disorders that affect the ability to understand or use spoken or written language; may manifest in difficulties with listening, thinking, speaking, reading, writing, spelling, and doing mathematical calculations; include minimal brain dysfunction, dyslexia, and developmental aphasia.

least restrictive environment (LRE). An educational setting or program that provides a student with disabilities with the chance to work and learn to the best of his or her ability; it also provides the student as much contact as possible with children without disabilities while meeting all of the child's learning needs and physical requirements.

macrocephaly. A head size that is more than two standard deviations greater than average; is sometimes associated with a brain anomaly, a syndrome, or a familial trait.

magnetic resonance imaging (MRI). A system of visualizing the inside of the body or brain without the use of X rays. The body is placed in a magnetic field and bombarded with radio waves, which enables viewing of various abnormalities.

mainstreaming. Integrating children with speech and language impairments (or other disabilities) into the "least restrictive" educational setting. This often implies placement in a regular school classroom with special educational assistance, when necessary.

mediation. Procedural safeguard to resolve disputes between parents and schools; must be conducted by a qualified and impartial mediator.

microcephaly. A head size that is more than two standard deviations below average; is usually correlated with cognitive deficits.

monotone. Speech without variations in pitch.

motor speech disorders. Group of disorders caused by the inability to accurately produce speech sounds (phonemes) because of muscle weakness or incoordination (dysarthria) or difficulty performing voluntary muscle movements (apraxia).

myelination. Development of a protective myelin sheath or sleeve around nerves that allows for more efficient transmission of nerve impulses.

neurologist. An M.D. who specializes in disorders of the brain and nervous system.

occupational therapy. Includes therapy to improve fine-motor skills.

oral apraxia. A neurological impairment in programming and executing nonspeech movements of the mouth.

oral cavity. The mouth, housing the teeth and tongue.

oral-motor therapy. Exercises and activities that increase muscle strength and control over movements needed for speech.

pervasive developmental disorder (PDD). A disorder characterized by deficits in areas of development that usually include socialization and communication. The child does not meet all the criteria for autism.

phonation. Production of sound when exhaled air passes through the vocal cords.

phoneme. Individual sound; phonemes can be combined to form words, phrases, and sentences.

phonological. The way in which individual speech sounds are combined to form words.

phonological (phonemic) awareness. The ability to segment words into syllables and sounds and identify similarities in sound patterns, as in rhyming.

phonological process. A system of describing children's articulatory patterns that improve with maturity.

pragmatics. The social aspects of communication.

proprioceptive sense. Feedback received from muscles and joints.

pull-out therapy. Removing a child from a classroom so that she or he can participate in a therapy session.

receptive language. Language comprehension.

reflex. An automatic, involuntary physical response, such as a sneeze.

related services. Services that are necessary for child to benefit from special education; includes speech-language pathology and audiology services, psychological services, physical and occupational therapy, recreation, early identification and assessment, counseling, rehabilitation counseling, orientation and mobility services, school health services, social work services, parent counseling, and training.

screening test. An assessment tool used to decide which children may need further testing to assess development.

semantics. The meaning of words, including their connotations.

special education. Specially designed instruction, at no cost to the parents, to meet the unique needs of a child with a disability.

specific language impairment (SLI). Difficulty with language or the organized-symbol system used for communication in the absence of problems such as mental retardation, hearing loss, or emotional disorders.

speech. Spoken language; oral communication.

speech-language pathologist. Health professional trained to evaluate and treat people who have voice, speech, language, or swallowing disorders (including hearing impairment) that affect their ability to communicate.

speech-language pathology services. Include identification and diagnosis of speech or language impairments, speech or language therapy, and counseling and guidance.

speech sample. A systematic collection and analysis of a person's speech, used in language assessment.

stuttering. Frequent repetition of words or parts of words that disrupts the smooth flow of speech.

support group. Individuals with similar problems who meet together to share feelings, information, and ideas.

syndrome. A set of symptoms that appear together to indicate a specific condition.

syntax. How words are arranged in sentences.

tactile. Related to touch or the sense of touch.

tactile defensiveness. Not liking to be touched on certain parts of the body or exposed to certain textures.

treatment plan. Recommendations for addressing a problem, including placement, therapy approaches, counseling suggestions, and referrals.

vestibular input. Processing information about movement, gravity, and balance.

voice. Sound produced by air passing out through the larynx and upper respiratory tract.

voice disorders. Group of problems involving abnormal pitch, loudness, or quality of the sound produced by the larynx (voice box).

Bibliography

Books for Parents

Beyond Baby Talk: From Sounds to Sentences. A Parent's Complete Guide to Language Development, by Kenn Apel, Ph.D., and Julie J. Masterson, Ph.D. Roseville, CA: Prima, 2001.

The Child with Special Needs: Encouraging Intellectual and Emotional Growth, by Stanley I. Greenspan, M.D., and Serena Weider, Ph.D. Cambridge, MA: Perseus Press, 1998.

Childhood Speech, Language & Listening Problems, by Patricia McAleer Hamaguchi. New York: John Wiley & Sons, 1995.

The Complete IEP Guide: How to Advocate for Your Special Ed Child, by Lawrence M. Siegel. Berkeley, CA: Nolo Press, 2000.

Does My Child Have a Speech Problem? by Katherine L. Martin. Chicago: Chicago Review Press, 1997.

Easy Does It for Apraxia & Motor Planning, by Robin M. Strode, MA, CCC-SLP, and Catherine Chamberlain. East Moline, IL: LinguiSystems, 1993. www. linguisystems.com.

Easy Does It for Apraxia—Preschool, by Robin M. Strode, MA, CCC-SLP, and Catherine Chamberlain. East Moline, IL: LinguiSystems, 1994.

Guide to Writing Quality Individualized Education Programs: What's Best for Students with Disabilities? by Gordon S. Gibb and Tina Taylor Dyches. Needham Heights, MA: Allyn & Bacon, 1999.

How Well Does Your IEP Measure Up? by Diane Twachtman-Cullen and Jennifer Twachtman-Reilly. Higganum, CT: Starfish Specialty Press, 2002.

Mouth Madness: Oral Motor Activities for Children, by Catherine Orr. New York: Academic Press, 1998.

Negotiating the Special Education Maze: A Guide for Parents and Teachers, by Winifred Anderson, Stephen Chitwood, and Deidre Hayden. Bethesda, MD: Woodbine House, 1997.

The New Language of Toys: Teaching Communication Skills to Children with Special Needs, by Sue Schwartz and Joan E. Heller Miller. Bethesda, MD: Woodbine House, 1996.

The Out-of-Sync Child: Recognizing and Coping with Sensory Integration Dysfunction, by Carol Stock Kranowitz. New York: Perigee Books, 1998.

A Parent Guide to Verbal Dyspraxia, by Judy Michels Jelm. De Kalb, IL: Janelle Publications, 2002.

Quick and Easy: Ideas and Materials to Help the Nonverbal Child "Talk" at Home, by Carolyn Rouse and Katera Murphy. Solana Beach, CA: Mayer-Johnson. www.mayer-johnson.com.

Sound and Articulation Activities for Children with Speech-Language Problems, by Elizabeth Krepelin. West Nyack, NY: Center for Applied Research in Education, 1996.

Special Kids Need Special Parents: A Resource Guide for Parents of Children with Special Needs, by Judith Loseff Lavin. New York: Berkley Publishing Group, 2001.

Wrightslaw: From Emotions to Advocacy: The Special Education Survival Guide, by Peter W. D. Wright and Pamela Darr Wright. Hartfield, VA: Harbor House Law Press, 2001.

Wrightslaw: Special Education Law, by Peter W. D. Wright and Pamela Darr Wright. Hartfield, VA: Harbor House Law Press, 1999.

You, Your Child, and "Special" Education: A Guide to Making the System Work, by Barbara Coyne Cutler. Baltimore: Paul H. Brookes, 1995.

Professional Resources

Adams, R. D., and M. Victor. *Principles of Neurology*. New York: McGraw-Hill, 1985.

Agin, Marilyn. "Verbal Apraxia and the Role of Essential Fatty Acids: The Perspective of a Developmental Pediatrician." Paper presented at the Research Workshop on Fatty Acids in Neurodevelopmental Disorders, St. Anne's College, Oxford, England, 2001.

———. "Verbal Apraxia: The Perspective of a Developmental Pediatrician." Paper presented at the CHERAB Foundation Workshop on Essential Fatty Acids and Verbal Apraxia: A New Potential Therapeutic Intervention, Morristown, New Jersey, 2001.

Agin, Marilyn, H. Huberman, and K. Lobach. "Developmental Delay in Young Children." *City Health Information* 20, no. 3 (2001): 1–8.

American Board of Pediatrics. "Certification in the Pediatric Subspecialties." 2001. http://www.abp.org.

American Board of Psychiatry and Neurology. "Certification." 2001. http://www.abpn.com.

American Speech-Language-Hearing Association. *Membership and Certification Handbook of the American Speech-Language-Hearing Association.* Rockville, MD: ASHA, 2001.

Apel, K., and J. Masterson. *Beyond Baby Talk.* Roseville, CA: Prima, 2001

Apraxia-Kids. "Characteristics of Children with Apraxia of Speech." 1998. http://www.apraxia-kids.org/definitions/characteristics.html.

———. "What Causes Apraxia." 1999. http://www.apraxia-kids.org/faqs/faq.html.

Aronson, A. E. "Motor Speech Signs of Neurologic Disease." In *Speech Evaluation in Medicine,* edited by J. K. Darby. New York: Grune & Stratton, 1981.

Bates, Betsy. "Clues to Separate Dysarthria from Verbal Apraxia." *Pediatric News* 2000, 34(3): 32.

———. "Hypotonia Often Signals Serious Course in Infants." *Pediatric News* 32 (2000): 1, 8.

Beitchman, J. H., B. Wilson, C. J. Johnson, L. Atkinson, A. Young, E. Adlaf, M. Escobar, and L. Douglas. "Fourteen-Year Follow-up of Speech/Language-Impaired and Control Children: Psychiatric Outcome." *J Am Acad Child Adolesc Psychiatry* 40, no. 1 (2001): 75–82.

Belcher, H. M. "Developmental Screening." In *Developmental Disabilities and Treatment: Neurodevelopmental Diagnosis and Treatment,* edited by A. J. Capute and P. J. Accardo. Baltimore: Paul H. Brookes, 1996.

Biehl, R. F. "Legislative Mandates." In *Developmental Disabilities in Infancy and Childhood,* edited by A. J. Capute and P. J. Accardo. Baltimore: Paul H. Brookes, 1996.

Birch, E. E., S. Garfield, D. Hoffman, R. Uauy, and D. G. Birch. "A Randomized Controlled Trial of Early Dietary Supply of Long-Chain Polyunsaturated Fatty Acids and Mental Development in Term Infants." *Developmental Medicine and Child Neurology* 2000 (2001): 174–81.

Black, B., and N. L. Hazen. "Social Status and Patterns of Communication in Acquainted and Unacquainted Preschool Children." *Developmental Psychology* 26 (1990): 379–87.

Bowen, Caroline. "Questions and Answers About Phonological Disorders, Articulation Disorders, Developmental Dyspraxia, and the Dysarthrias." 1999. http://members.tripod.com/Caroline_Bowen/phonol-and-artic.htm.

Burgess, J. R., L. Stevens, W. Zhang, and L. Peck. "Long-Chain Polyunsaturated Fatty Acids in Children with Attention-Deficit Hyperactivity Disorder." *American Journal of Clinical Nutrition* 71 (2000): 327–30.

Burns, Martha S. "Access to Reading: The Language to Literacy Link." Paper presented at the Learning Disabilities Association Conference, 1999.

Campbell, Thomas F. "Functional Treatment Outcomes in Young Children with Motor Speech Disorders." In *Assessment Procedures for Treatment Planning in Children with Phonologic and Motor Speech Disorders*, edited by Anthony J. Caruso and Edythe A. Strand. New York: Thieme, 1999.

Caplan, David. "Language and the Brain." *The Harvard Mahoney Neuroscience Institute Letter on the Brain* (Fall 1995). www.med.harvard.edu/publications/On_ The_Brain/Volume 4/Number 4/F95 Lang.html

———. "Speech, Sign Language All the Same to Brain. Communication Modes Light up Same Centers." 2002. http://healingwell.subportal.com/health/ Diseases_and_Conditions/Sensory/Hearing_Loss/106129.html.

Capone, G. "Human Brain Development." In *Developmental Disabilities in Infancy and Childhood*, edited by A. J. Capute and P. J. Accardo. Baltimore: Paul H. Brookes, 1996.

Caruso, Anthony J., and Edythe A. Strand. "Motor Speech Disorders in Children: Definitions, Background, and a Theoretical Framework." In *Clinical Management of Motor Speech Disorders in Children*, edited by Anthony J. Caruso and Edythe A. Strand. New York: Thieme, 1999.

Catts, H. W. "The Relationship Between Speech-Language Impairments and Reading Disabilities." *J Speech Hear Res.* 36, no. 5 (1993): 948–58.

———. "Speech Production Deficits in Developmental Dyslexia." *J Speech Hear Res* 54, no. 3 (1989): 422–28.

———. "Speech Production/Phonological Deficits in Reading-Disordered Children." *J of Learning Disabilities* 19 (1986): 504–08.

Chapman, James. "Oils That Are Beneficial for the Heart Can Also Treat Brain Condition: How a Fishy Diet Can Help Autistic Children." *Daily Mail* (London), September 24, 2001.

Cohen, Shannon M., and Teresa Whitt. "Early Recognition and Intervention Is the Key to Recovery for Benign Congenital Hypotonia." 1999. http://www. lightlink.com/vulcan/benign/thekey.htm.

Colquhoun, I., and S. Bunday. "A Lack of Essential Fatty Acids as a Possible Cause of Hyperactivity in Children." *Medical Hypotheses* 7 (1981): 673–79.

Committee on Children with Disabilities of the American Academy of Pediatrics. "Developmental Surveillance and Screening of Infants and Young Children." *Pediatrics* 108, no. 192 (2001): 192–96.

———. "The Pediatrician's Role in Development and Implementation of an Individual Education Plan and/or Individual Family Service Plan." *Pediatrics* 104, no. 1 (1999): 124–27.

———. "The Pediatrician's Role in the Diagnosis and Management of Autistic Spectrum Disorder in Children." *Pediatrics* 107, no. 5 (2001): 1221–26.

———. "Role of the Pediatrician in Family-Centered Early Intervention Services." *Pediatrics* 107, no. 5 (2001): 1155–57.

———. "Screening Infants and Young Children for Developmental Disabilities." *Pediatrics* 93, no. 5 (1994): 863–65.

Corballis, Michael C. "The Gestural Origins of Language." *American Scientist* 87, no. 2 (1999): 138–146.

Cowley, Geoffrey. "The Language Explosion." *Newsweek*, 1997.

Crary, Michael A. *Developmental Motor Speech Disorders*. San Diego: Singular Publishing Group, 1993.

Daniels, M. *Dancing with Words: Signing for Hearing Children's Literacy*. Westport, CT: Bergin and Garvey, 2001.

———. "The Effects of Sign Language on Hearing Children's Language Development." *Communication Education* 43 (1994): 291–98.

———. "Seeing Language: The Effect over Time of Sign Language on Vocabulary Development in Early Childhood Education." *Child Study Journal* 26 (1996): 193–208.

Darley, F., A. E. Aronson, and J. R. Brown. *Motor Speech Disorders*. Philadelphia: W. B. Saunders, 1975.

Degangi, Georgia. *Pediatric Disorders of Regulation in Affect and Behavior: A Therapist's Guide to Assessment and Treatment*. San Diego: Academic Press, 2000.

DeHouwer, Annick. *Two or More Languages in Early Childhood: Some General Points and Practical Recommendations*. Bloomington, IN: ERIC, 1999. http//www.cal.org/ericill/digest/earlychild.html.

Demott, Kathryn. "Differential Diagnosis of Hypotonia, Hypertonia." *Pediatric News* 32 (1998): 33.

Dowden, Patricia A. "Augmentative and Alternative Communication for Children with Motor Speech Disorders." In *Assessment Procedures for Treatment Planning in Children with Phonologic and Motor Speech Disorders*, edited by Anthony J. Caruso and Edythe A. Strand. New York: Thieme, 1999.

Dworkin P. "Developmental Screening: (Still) Expecting the Impossible?" *Pediatrics* 89, no. 8 (1992): 1253–55.

Ellison, Patricia. "The Neurologic Examination of the Newborn and Infant." In *Pediatric Neurology for the Clinician*, edited by Ronald B. David. Norwalk, CT: Appleton and Lange, 1992.

Epstein, Randi Hutter. "Fix Speech Problems Early, Experts Now Urge." *New York Times*, November 30, 1999.

Erasmus, Udo. *Fats That Heal, Fats That Kill*. Burnaby, B. C., Canada: Alive Books, 1993.

Ervin, Margaret. "SLI—What We Know and Why It Matters." 2002. http://professional.asha.org/news/sli.cfm.

Filipek, P. A., P. J. Accardo, and S. Ashwal. "Practice Parameter: Screening and Diagnosis of Autism: Report of the Quality Standards Subcommittee of the American Academy of Neurology and the Child Neurology Society." *Neurology* 55 (2000): 468–79.

Fisher, S. E., F. Vargha-Khadem, K. E. Watkins, A. P. Monaco, and M. E. Pembrey. "Localization of a Gene Implicated in a Severe Speech and Language Disorder." *Nat Genet* 18, no. 2 (1998): 168–70.

Frost, Lori, and Andrew Bondy. *The Picture Exchange Communication System*. Newark, DE: Pyramid Educational Consultants, 2002.

Gertner, B. L., M. L. Rice, and P. A. Hadley. "Influence of Communicative Competence on Peer Preferences in a Preschool Classroom." *Journal of Speech and Hearing Research* 37 (1994): 913–23.

Golden, Frederick. "10 Foods That Pack a Wallop." *Time*, January 21, 2002: 115.

Goodwyn, S. W., L. P. Acredolo, and C. Brown. "Impact of Symbolic Gesturing on Early Language Development." *Journal of Nonverbal Behavior* 24 (2000): 81–103.

Gopnik, A., A. N. Meltzoff, and P. K. Kuhl. *The Scientist in the Crib: Minds, Brains, and How Children Learn*. New York: William Morrow, 1999.

Goshulak, Debra. "Minutes of ECHO Support Group Meeting." Toronto, Ontario, Canada, 2001.

Groenen, P., B. Maassen, T. Crul, and G. Thoonen. "The Specific Relation between Perception and Production Errors for Place of Articulation in Developmental Apraxia of Speech." *J Speech Hear Res.* 39, no. 3 (1996): 468–82.

Guenther, M. M. "Developmental Verbal Dyspraxia." 1999. http://www.pitt.edu/~uc lid/apraxia.htm.

Hafer, J. *Signing for Reading Success*. Washington, D.C.: Gallaudet University Press, 1986.

Hall, Penelope K. "A Letter to the Parent(s) of a Child with Developmental Apraxia of Speech. Part 1: Speech Characteristics of the Disorder." *Language, Speech and Hearing Services in Schools* 31 (2000): 169–72.

Hall, Penelope K., Linda S. Jordan, and Donald A. Robin. *Developmental Apraxia of Speech: Theory and Clinical Practice*. Austin, TX: Pro-Ed, 1993.

Hammer, D. W. "Brief Thoughts on Therapy for Children with Apraxia of Speech." 2001. http://www.apraxia-kids.org/slps/hammer. html.

Hanen Centre. "Parent Frequently Asked Questions." 2001. http://www.hanen. org.

Hayden, Deborah, and Paula Square. *Verbal Motor Production Assessment for Children*. San Antonio, TX: Psychological Corporation, 1999.

Haynes, Sara. "Developmental Apraxia of Speech: Symptoms and Treatment." In *Clinical Management of Neurogenic Communication Disorders*, edited by D. F. Johns. Boston: Little, Brown, 1985.

Hazel, E., A. McBride, and L. S. Siegel. "Learning Disabilities and Adolescent Suicide." *Journal of Learning Disabilities* 30 (1997): 652–59.

Hazen, N. L., and G. Black. "Preschool Peer Communication Skills: The Role of Social Status and Interaction Context." *Child Development* 60 (1989): 867–76.

Helfrich-Miller, Kathleen. "A Clinical Perspective: Melodic Intonation Therapy for Developmental Apraxia." *Clinics in Communication Disorders* 4, no. 3 (1994): 175–82.

Illinois State Board of Education. "Guideline for Speech-Language Eligibility Criteria/Matrix for Schools." Springfield, IL, 1993.

Jaffe, M. B. "Neurologic Impairments of Speech Production: Assessment and Treatment." In *Speech Disorders in Children: Recent Advances*, edited by J. Costello. San Diego: College-Hill Press, 1984.

Jones, Kenneth Lyons. *Smith's Recognizable Patterns of Human Malformation*. 5th ed. Philadelphia: W. B. Saunders, 1997.

Kaminer, R., and E. Jedrysek. "Early Identification of Developmental Disabilities." *Ped Annals* 11 (1982): 427–37.

Kantrowitz, Barbara, and Anne Underwood. "Dyslexia and the New Science of Reading." *Newsweek*, November 22, 1999.

Katz, Robert, and Marilyn Agin. "Outcomes of Essential Fatty Acid Supplementation in Verbal Apraxia: An Analysis of Professional Anecdotal Reports." Paper presented at the Research Workshop on Fatty Acids in Neurodevelopmental Disorders, St. Anne's College, Oxford, England, 2001.

Kaufman, Nancy R. *Kaufman Speech Praxis Test for Children*. Detroit: Wayne State University Press, 1995.

———. *Signs and Symptoms: Apraxia of Speech*. Kaufman Children's Center for Speech, Language and Sensory Disorders, 2002. http://www.kidspeech. com/signs.html.

Kelly, Desmond P., and Janine I. Sally. "Disorders of Speech and Language." In

Developmental-Behavioral Pediatrics, edited by Melvin D. Levine, William B. Carey, and Allen C. Crocker. Philadelphia: W. B. Saunders, 1999.

Kelley, Richard I. "Metabolic Diseases." In *Developmental Disabilities in Infancy and Childhood*, edited by A. J. Capute and P. J. Accardo. Baltimore: Paul H. Brookes, 1996.

Kertesz, A. "Subcortical Lesions and Verbal Apraxia." In *Apraxia of Speech: Physiology, Acoustics, Linguistics, Management*, edited by J. C. Rosenbek, M. R. McNeil, and A. E. Aronson. San Diego: College Hill Press, 1984.

kidshealth.org. "Assistive Technology and Your Child." 2002. http://www. kidshealth.org/parent/system/ill/assistive_tech.html.

Koehler, L., and L. Loyd. "Using Fingerspelling/Manual Signs to Facilitate Reading and Spelling." Paper presented at the Biennial Conference on the International Society for Augmentative and Alternative Communication, Cardiff, Wales, September 1986.

Lai, C. S., S. E. Fisher, J. A. Hurst, E. R. Levy, S. Hodgson, M. Fox, S. Jeremiah, S. Povey, D. C. Jamison, E. D. Green, F. Vargha-Khadem, and A. P. Monaco. "The SPCH1 Region on Human 7q31: Genomic Characterization of the Critical Interval and Localization of Translocations Associated with Speech and Language Disorder." *American Journal of Hum Genet* 67, no. 2 (2000): 278–81.

Lai, C. S., S. E. Fisher, J. A. Hurst, F. Vargha-Khadem, and A. P. Monaco. "A Forkhead-Domain Gene Is Mutated in a Severe Speech and Language Disorder." *Nature* 413, no. 6855 (2001): 519–23.

Levine, M., and M. Reed. "Language." In *Developmental Variation and Learning Disorders*. Cambridge, MA: Educators Publishing Service, 1999.

Lipkin, P. H. "Epidemiology of the Developmental Disabilities." In *Developmental Disabilities in Infancy and Childhood*, 2d ed., edited by A. J. Capute and P. J. Accardo. Baltimore: Paul H. Brookes, 1996.

Lohman, P., R. M. Manning, and R. Dean. "Current Trends in Developmental Apraxia of Speech." Paper presented at the American Speech-Language and Learning Association, New Orleans, 2001.

Love, Russell J. *Childhood Motor Speech Disability*, 2d ed. Needham Heights, MA: Allyn and Bacon, 2000.

Lyon, Reid. "Education Research and Evaluation and Student Achievement: Quality Counts." 2002. www.house.gov/ed_workforce/hearings/106th/ecyf/oeri5400/lyon.htm.

———. "Overview of Reading and Literacy." 1998. www.readbygrade3.com/readbygrade3co/lyon.htm.

Martinez, Manuela. "Peroxisomal Disorders and Their Treatment." 2002. http://www.momtahan.com/mmartinez.

McBride, H. E. A. and L. S. Siegel. "Learning Disabilities and Adolescent Suicide." *Journal of Learning Disabilities* 30 (1997): 652–59.

McCauley, Rebecca J., and Edythe Strand. "Treatment of Children Exhibiting Phonological Disorder with Motor Speech Involvement." In *Clinical Management of Motor Speech Disorders in Children*, edited by Anthony J. Caruso and Edythe A. Strand. New York: Thieme, 1999.

Meisels, S. A., and B. A. Waik. "Who Should Be Served? Identifying Children in Need of Early Intervention." In *Handbook of Early Childhood Intervention*, edited by S. A. Meisels and J. P. Shonkoff. Cambridge: Cambridge University Press, 1990.

Menkes, John H. *Textbook of Child Neurology*. 4th ed. Philadelphia: Lea and Febiger, 1990.

Merzenich, M. M., W. M. Jenkins, S. L. Miller, C. Schreiner, and P. Tallal. "Temporal Processing Deficits of Language—Learning Impaired Children Ameliorated by Training." *Science* 271 (1996): 77–81.

Morgan, Andrew. "Clues to Separate Dysarthria from Verbal Apraxia." *Pediatric News* 34(3): 32.

Morgan, David. "Parents Produce CD for Kids with Speech Disorders." Reuters, April 6, 2001.

Morris, Suzanne E., and Marsha D. Klein. *Pre-Feeding Skills: A Comprehensive Resource for Mealtime Development*, 2d ed. St. Louis: Therapy Skill Builders, 2000.

Moser, H. W., and M. Noetzel. "The Role of DHA in Zellweger Syndrome, a Representative Peroxisomal Biogenesis Disorder." Paper presented at Brain Uptake and Utilization of Fatty Acids: Applications to Peroxisomal Biogenesis Disease Conference, Bethesda, Maryland, 2000.

Mowren, D., P. Wahl, and S. Doolan. "The Effects of Lisping on Audience Evaluation of Male Speakers." *Journal of Speech and Hearing Disorders* 42, no. 2 (1978): 140–48.

Mueller, Elizabeth. "Fact Sheet on Hypotonia." 1997. http://www.lightlink.com/vulcan/benign/factsht.htm.

National Center for Injury Prevention and Control. "Suicide Prevention Fact Sheet." http://www.cdc.gov/ncipc/factsheets/suifacts.htm.

National Institute of Mental Health. "Suicide Facts." 1999. http://www.nimh.nih.gov/research/suifact.htm.

National Institute of Neurological Disorders and Stroke. "International Workshop on Brain Uptake and Utilization of Fatty Acids: Application to Peroxisomal Biogenesis Diseases." 2000. http://www.ninds.nih.gov/news_and_events/bfaworkshop.htm.

New York City Department of Health. "Developmental Delay in Young Children." In *City Health Information*. 2001.

New York State Department of Health, Early Intervention Program. *Early Inter-vention, the Communication Domain.* New York: New York State Association of Counties, 2000.

———. "Clinical Practice Guideline: The Guideline Technical Report, Com-munication Disorders, Assessment and Intervention for Young Children (Age 0–3 Years)." II 3–16, III 13–25, III 85, III 89–95. Albany: New York State Department of Health, 1999.

Nicolosi, L., E. Harryman, and J. Kresheck. *Terminology of Communication Disor-ders.* 4th ed. Baltimore: Williams and Wilkins, 1996.

Nopola-Hemmi, J., B. Mullyluoma, T. Haltia, M. Taipale, V. Ollikainen, T. Ahonen, A. Voutilainen, J. Kere, and E. Widen. "A Dominant Gene for Developmental Dyslexia on Chromosome 3." *J Med Genetics* 38 (2001): 658–64.

Office of Special Education. "Youth with Disabilities in the Juvenile Justice Sys-tem." 2002. Washington, D.C. http://specialed.principals.org/discidea/OSEPdocs/youthinjjsystem.htm.

Olswang, L. B., B. Rodriguez, and G. Timler. "Clinical Focus. Recommending Intervention for Toddlers with Specific Language Learning Difficulties: We May Not Know All the Answers, but We Know a Lot." *American Journal of Speech Language Pathology* 7, no. 1 (1998): 23–32.

Pannbacker, Mary. "Management Strategies for Developmental Apraxia of Speech: A Review of the Literature." *Journal of Communication Disorders* 21 (1988): 363–71.

PBS. *The Secret Life of the Brain.* Episode 2: "The Child's Brain." 2002. http://www.pbs.org/wnet/brain/episode2/index.html.

Pennington, Sara. "How to Get a Toddler of Few Words to Talk." *The Times* (London), July 31, 2001.

Perkins, W. H. *Dysarthria and Apraxia. Current Therapy of Communication Disorders.* New York: Thieme, 1983.

Perrin, E. "The Social Position of the Speech Defective Child." *Journal of Speech and Hearing Disorders* 19 (1954): 250–62.

Place, K. S., and J. A. Becker. "The Influence of Pragmatic Competence on the Likeability of Grade-School Children." *Discourse Processes* 14 (1991): 227–41.

Plante, Elana. "MRI Findings in the Parents and Siblings of Specifically Lan-guage Impaired Boys." *Brain and Language* 41 (1991): 67–80.

Portwood, Madeleine. *Understanding Developmental Dyspraxia: A Textbook for Stu-dents and Professionals.* London: David Fulton, 2000.

Rapin, I. "Neurological Examination." In *Preschool Children with Inadequate Com-munication: Developmental Language Disorder, Autism, Low IQ,* edited by Isabelle Rapin. Cambridge: Cambridge University Press, 1996.

Rapin, Isabelle, and Barbara Wilson. "Children with Developmental Language Disorders: Neurological Aspects and Assessment." In *Developmental Dysphasia*, edited by M. A. Wyke. New York: Academic Press, 1978.

Rescorla, Leslie. "Language and Reading Outcomes to Age 9 in Late-Talking Toddlers." *Journal of Speech and Hearing Research* 45 (2002): 360–71.

Rice, M., M. Sell, and P. Hadley. "Social Interactions of Speech- and Language-Impaired Children." *Journal of Speech and Hearing Research* 34 (1991): 1299–1308.

Rice, M. L. "Don't Talk to Him; He's Weird: A Social Consequences Account of Language and Social Interactions." In *Enhancing Children's Communication: Research Foundations for Intervention*, edited by A. P. Kaiser and D. B. Gray. Baltimore: Paul H. Brookes, 1993.

Rice, M. L., P. A. Hadley, and A. L. Alexander. "Social Biases Toward Children with Speech and Language Impairments: A Correlative Casual Model of Language Limitations." *Applied Psycholinguistics* 14 (1993): 443–72.

Richardson, Alexandra J., Jane Cox, Janet Sargentoni, and Basant K. Puri. "Abnormal Cerebral Phospholipid Metabolism in Dyslexia Indicated by Phosphorus-31 Magnetic Resonance Spectroscopy." *NMR in Biomedicine* 10 (1997): 309–14.

Richardson, Alexandra J., Terese Easton, Anna C. Corrie, C. Clisby, and Jacqueline B. Stordy. "Is Developmental Dyslexia a Fatty Acid Deficiency Syndrome?" Paper presented at the Proceedings of the Nutrition Society, 1998.

Richardson, Alexandra J., Terese Easton, Ann Marie McDaid, Jacqueline A. Hall, Paul Montgomery, Christine Clisby, and Basant K. Puri. "Essential Fatty Acids in Dyslexia: Theory, Evidence and Clinical Trials." In *Phospholipid Spectrum Disorder in Psychiatry*, edited by M. Peet, Glen Lain, and David F. Horrobin. Carnforth, England: Marius Press, 1999.

Richardson, Alexandra J., and Basant K. Puri. "Brain Phospholipid Metabolism in Dyslexia Assessed by Magnetic Resonance Spectroscopy." In *Phospholipid Spectrum Disorder in Psychiatry*, edited by M. Peet, Lain Glen, and David F. Horrobin. Carnforth, England: Marius Press, 1999.

———. "A Randomized Double-Blind, Placebo-Controlled Study on the Effects of Supplementation with Highly Unsaturated Fatty Acids on ADHD-Related Symptoms in Children with Specific Learning Difficulties." *Progress in Neuro-Psychopharmacology and Biological Psychiatry* 26 (2001): 233–39.

Robbins, Jim. "Research Suggests Positive Effects from Living Off the Fat of the Sea." *The New York Times*, April 24, 2001.

Rosenbeck, J., and R. T. Wertz. "A Review of 50 Cases of Developmental Apraxia of Speech." *Language, Speech and Hearing Services in Schools* 3 (1972): 23–33.

Roth, Lori. "Essential Fatty Acid Supplementation in Verbal Apraxia: A Time-

Line of Therapeutic Outcomes in Speech/Communication." Paper presented at the Research Workshop on Fatty Acids in Neurodevelopmental Disorders, St. Anne's College, Oxford, England, 2001.

Sander, E. "When Are Speech Sounds Learned?" *Journal of Speech and Hearing Disorders* 37 (1972): 55–63.

Schmidt, Michael A. *Smart Fats: How Dietary Fats and Oils Affect Mental, Physical and Emotional Intelligence.* Berkeley, CA: Frog, Ltd., 1997.

Shaywitz, S. E. "Dyslexia." *New England J of Medicine* 338 (1998): 307–12.

Shaywitz, S. E., J. M. Fletcher, J. M. Holaham, A. E. Shneider, K. E. Marchione, K. K. Stuebing, D. J. Francis, K. R. Pugh, and B. A. Shaywitz. "Persistence of Dyslexia: The Connecticut Longitudinal Study at Adolescence." *Pediatrics* 104 (1999): 1351–59.

Shaywitz, S. E., B. A. Shaywitz, K. R. Pugh, R. K. Fulbright, R. T. Constable, W. E. Mencl, D. P. Skankweiler, A. M. Liberman, P. Skudlarski, J. M. Fletcher, L. Katz, K. E. Marchione, C. Lacadie, C. Gatenby, and J. C. Gore. "Functional Disruption in the Organization of the Brain for Reading in Dyslexia." *Proc Natl Acad Sci, USA* 95 (1998): 2636–41.

Sheppard, Justine Joan. "Apraxia, Early Identification and Therapeutic Parenting." CHERAB Foundation Meeting, May 7, 2001.

Shonkoff, Jack P., and Deborah A. Phillips, eds. *From Neurons to Neighborhoods: The Science of Early Child Development.* Washington, D.C.: National Academy Press, 2000.

Shriberg, L. D., D. M. Aram, and J. Kwiatkowski. "Developmental Apraxia of Speech." *J of Speech, Language and Hearing Research* 40, no. 2 (1997): 273–337.

Simopoulos, Artemis P., M.D., and J. O. Robinson. *The Omega Diet.* New York: Harper, 1999.

sinetwork.org. "What Is Sensory Integration Dysfunction and How Can It Be Treated?" 2001. http://www.sinetwork.org/whatisdsi.htm.

Soueidan, S. "Neuromuscular Diseases." In *Pediatric Neurology*, edited by Ronald David. Norwalk, CT: Appleton and Lange, 1992.

Sowell, Thomas. *The Einstein Syndrome: Bright Children Who Talk Late.* New York: Basic Books, 2001.

———. *Late Talking Children.* New York: Basic Books, 1997.

Square, Paula A. "Treatment of Developmental Apraxia of Speech: Tactile-Kinesthetic, Rhythmic, and Gestural." In *Clinical Management of Motor Speech Disorders in Children*, edited by Anthony J. Caruso and Edythe A. Strand. New York: Thieme, 1999.

Squires, J., L. Potter, D. Bricker, and S. Lamorey. "Parent-Completed Developmental Questionnaires: Effectiveness with Low and Middle Income Parents." *Early Childhood Research Quarterly* 13, no. 2 (1998): 345–54.

Stephens, Linda. "Sensory Integrative Dysfunction in Young Children." *AAH-BEI News Exchange* 2, no. 1 (winter 1997): 1, 4–7.

Stevens, Laura J., and John R. Burgess. "Essential Fatty Acids in Children with Attention-Deficit/Hyperactivity Disorder." In *Phospholipid Spectrum Disorder in Psychiatry*, edited by M. Peet, Lain Glen, and David F. Horrobin. Carnforth, England: Marius Press, 1999.

Stevens, Laura J., Sydney S. Zentall, Marcey L. Abate, Thomas Kuczek, and John R. Burgess. "Omega-3 Fatty Acids in Boys with Behavior, Learning, and Health Problems." *Physiology & Behavior* 59 (1996): 915–20.

Stevens, Laura J., Sydney S. Zentall, J. L. Deck, Marcey L. Abate, Bruce A. Watkins, Steven R. Lipp, and John R. Burgess. "Essential Fatty Acid Metabolism in Boys with Attention-Deficit Hyperactivity Disorder." *American Journal of Clinical Nutrition* 62, no. 4 (1995): 761–68.

Stoll, Andrew L. *The Omega-3 Connection: The Groundbreaking Anti-Depression Diet and Brain Program.* New York: Free Press, 2001.

Stordy, Jacqueline B. "Benefit of Docosahexaneoic Acid Supplements to Dark Adaptation in Dyslexics." *Lancet* 346 (1995): 385.

———. "Dark Adaptation, Motor Skills, Docosahexaenoic Acid and Dyslexia." *American Journal of Clinical Nutrition* 71 (2000): 323S–26S.

———. "Dyslexia, Attention Deficit Disorder, Dyspraxia—Do Fatty Acids Help?" *Dyslexia Review* 9 (1997): 5–7.

———. "Long-Chain Fatty Acids in the Management of Dyslexia and Dyspraxia." In *Phospholipid Spectrum Disorder in Psychiatry*, edited by M. Peet, Lain Glen, and David F. Horrobin. Carnforth, England: Matius Press, 1999.

Stordy, Jacqueline B., and Malcolm J. Nicholl. *The LCP Solution: The Remarkable Nutritional Treatment for ADHD, Dyslexia and Dyspraxia.* New York: Ballantine, 2000.

Strand, Edythe A. "Treatment of Motor Speech Disorders in Children." *Seminars in Speech and Language* 16, no. 2 (1995): 126–39.

Strand, Edythe A., and Rebecca J. McCauley. "Assessment Procedures for Treatment Planning in Children with Phonologic and Motor Speech Disorders." In *Clinical Management of Motor Speech Disorders in Children*, edited by Anthony J. Caruso and Edythe A. Strand. New York: Thieme, 1999.

Strand, Edythe A., and Amy Skinder. "Treatment of Developmental Apraxia of Speech: Integral Stimulation Methods." In *Clinical Management of Motor Speech Disorders in Children*, edited by Anthony J. Caruso and Edythe A. Strand. New York: Thieme, 1999.

TALK. "The Association Method Symposium." Paper presented at Teaching Apraxic and Language Disordered Kids Conference, West Chester University of Pennsylvania, Downingtown, March 3, 2001.

Tallal, P., S. L. Miller, G. Bedi, G. Byma, X. Wang, S. Nagarajan, C. Schreiner, W. M. Jenkins, and M. M. Merzenich. "Fast-Element Enhanced Speech Improves Language Comprehension in Language-Learning Impaired Children." *Science* 271 (1996): 81–84.

Thompson, B. M., and S. R. Andrews. "The Emerging Field of Sound Training." *IEEE Engineering in Medicine and Biology* (March/April 1999): 89–96.

Thoonen, G., B. Maassen, F. Gabreels, R. Schreuder, and B. deSwart. "Toward a Standardized Assessment Procedure for Developmental Apraxia of Speech." *Eur J Disord Commun* 32, no. 1 (1997): 37–60.

Toppelberg, C. O. "Language Disorders: A 10-Year Research Update Review." *J Am Acad Child Adolesc Psychiatry* 39, no. 2 (2000): 143–52.

U.S. Congress. *Public Law 99-457*. 99th Congress, 1985.

U.S. Department of Education. "The 22nd Annual Report to Congress on the Implementation of the Individuals with Disabilities Education Act." 2000. http://www.ed.gov/offices/OSERS/OSEP/Products/OSEP2000AnlRpt/.

U.S. Department of Health and Human Services. "Substance Abuse and Mental Health Services Administration: Summary of findings from the 2000 National Household Survey on Drug Abuse." Publication no. SMA 01-3549. 2001.

Vancassel, S., G. Durand, C. Barthelemy, B. Lejeune, J. Martineau, D. Guilloteau, C. Andres, and S. Chalon. "Plasma Fatty Acid Levels in Autistic Children." *Prostaglandins, Leukotrienes and Essential Fatty Acids* 65, no. 1 (2001): 1–7.

Vargha-Khadem, F., K. E. Watkins, K. Alcock, P. Fletcher, and R. Passingham. "Praxic and Nonverbal Cognitive Deficits in a Large Family with a Genetically Transmitted Speech and Language Disorder." *Proc Natl Acad Sci USA* 92 (1995): 930–33.

Velleman, Shelly. "Childhood Apraxia of Speech. General Information for Parents." 2002. http://www-unix.oit.umass.edu/~velleman/cas.html.

———. "The Interaction of Phonetics and Phonology in Developmental Verbal Dyspraxia: Two Case Studies." *Clinics in Communication Disorders* 4, no. 1 (1994): 67–78.

Velleman, S., and K. Strand. "Developmental Verbal Dyspraxia." In *Child Phonology: Characteristics, Assessment, and Intervention with Special Populations*, edited by J. E. Bernthal and N. W. Bankson. New York: Thieme, 1994.

Voigt, Robert G., Antolin Llorente, Marcia Berretta, Cynthia Boutte, J. Fraley, Jensen Kennard, L. Craig, and William C. Heird. "Effect of Dietary Docosahexaenoic Acid (DHA) Supplementation Does Not Improve the Symptoms of Attention-Deficit/Hyperactivity Disorder (ADHD)." *Pediatric Research* 45, no. 4 (1999): 17A.

Waltz, Mitzi. *Pervasive Developmental Disorder: Finding a Diagnosis and Getting Help.* Sebastopol, CA: O'Reilly & Associates, 1999.

Watkins, R. V. "Grammatical Challenges for Children with Specific Language Impairment." In *Specific Language Impairments in Children*, edited by R. V. Watkins and M. L. Rice. Baltimore: Paul H. Brookes, 1994.

Weistuch, L., and N. B. Schiff-Myers. "Chromosomal Translocation in a Child with SLI and Apraxia." *J Speech Hear Res.* 39, no. 3 (1996): 668–71.

Wetherby, Amy, Barry Prizant, and Adriana Schuler. "Understanding the Nature of Communication and Language Impairments." In *Autism Spectrum Disorders*, edited by Amy Wetherby and Barry Prizant. Baltimore: Paul H. Brookes, 2000.

Williamson, G. Gordon, and Marie Anzalone. "Sensory Integration: A Key Component of the Evaluation and Treatment of Young Children with Severe Difficulties in Relating and Communicating." *Zero to Three Bulletin* 17:5 (April/May 1997): 29–36.

Wilson, R., J. Teague, and M. Teague. "The Use of Signing and Fingerspelling to Improve Spelling Performance with Hearing Children." *Reading Psychology* 4 (1985): 267–73.

Yoss, K., and F. Darley. "Developmental Apraxia of Speech in Children with Defective Articulation." *J of Speech and Hearing Research* 17 (1974): 399–416.

Index